P9-DZA-851

PUBLIC LIBRARY

MAY   2002

PUBLIC LIBRARY

REF
398
.2
Myt
V. 1

REFERENCE DEPARTMENT

Myths
and
Legends
of the
World

Editor in Chief

John M. Wickersham
Professor of Classics
Ursinus College

Editorial Board

Lillian A. Ackerman
Associate Professor of Anthropology, Adjunct
Washington State University

Douglas M. Cameron
Associate Professor of Spanish
Ursinus College

Françoise Dussart
Associate Professor
University of Connecticut

Joseph Harris
Professor of English and Folklore
Harvard University

Michiko Oda
Professor of Japanese
Tohoku Gakuin University

Thomas J. Sienkewicz
Minnie Billings Capron Professor of Classics
Monmouth College

Gerald P. Verbrugghe
Associate Professor of History
Rutgers University, Camden

Steven F. Walker
Professor of Comparative Literature
Rutgers University

Qiguang Zhao
Chair of the Department of Asian Languages and Literatures
Carleton College

Paul G. Zolbrod
Emeritus Professor of English
Allegheny College

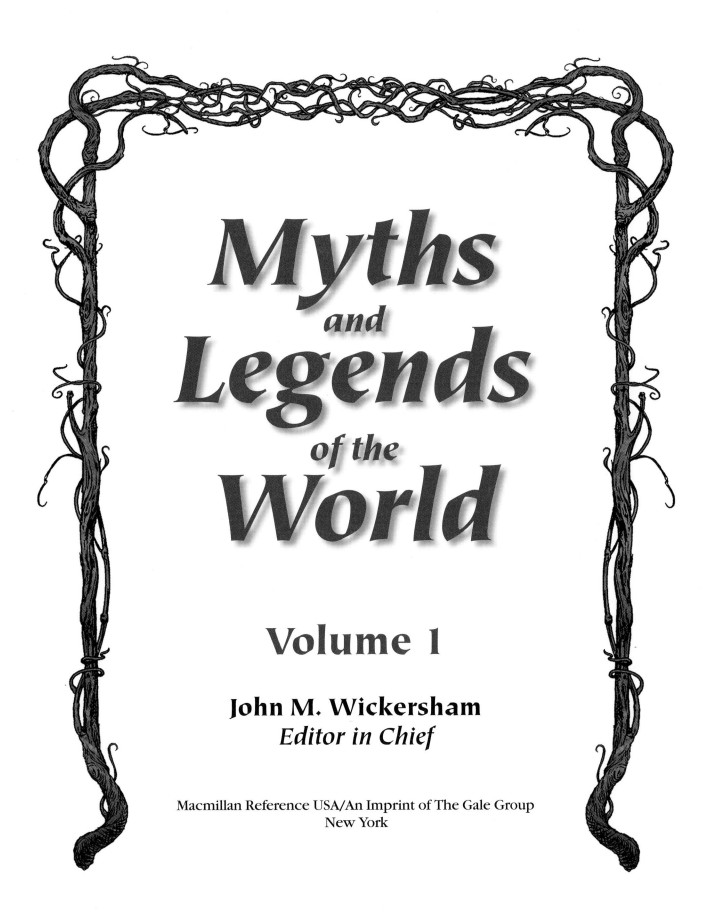

Myths
and
Legends
of the
World

Volume 1

John M. Wickersham
Editor in Chief

Macmillan Reference USA/An Imprint of The Gale Group
New York

WATERLOO PUBLIC LIBRARY

Developed for Macmillan Reference USA by
 Visual Education Corporation, Princeton, NJ.

For Macmillan

Publisher: Elly Dickason

Editor in Chief: Hélène G. Potter

Cover Design: Irina Lubenskaya

For Visual Education

Project Director: Darryl Kestler

Writers: John Haley, Charles Roebuck, Rebecca Stefoff

Editors: Cindy George, Eleanor Hero, Linda Perrin, Charles Roebuck

Copyediting Supervisor: Helen A. Castro

Indexer: Sallie Steele

Production Supervisor: Marcel Chouteau

Photo Research: Susan Buschhorn, Sara Matthews

Interior Design: Maxson Crandall

Electronic Preparation: Fiona Torphy

Electronic Production: Rob Ehlers, Lisa Evans-Skopas, Laura Millan, Isabelle Ulsh

Copyright © 2000 by Macmillan Reference USA

All rights reserved. No part of this book may be reproduced or transmitted in any form or by any means, electronic or mechanical, including photocopying, recording, or by any information storage and retrieval system, without permission in writing from the Publisher.

Macmillan Reference USA
1633 Broadway
New York, NY 10019

Printed in the United States of America
1 2 3 4 5 6 7 8 9 10

Library of Congress Cataloging-in-Publication Data

Myths and legends of the world / John M. Wickersham, editor in chief.
    p. cm.
    Includes bibliographical references and index.
    Contents: v. 1. Abel-Coriolanus — v. 2. Corn-Io — v. 3. Iphigenia-Quetzalcoatl — v. 4. Ra-Zoroastrian mythology.
    ISBN 0-02-865439-0 (set : alk. paper)
    1. Mythology—Juvenile literature. 2. Legends. [1. Mythology—Encyclopedias. 2. Folklore—Encyclopedias.] I. Wickersham, John M. (John Moore), 1943-
BL311 .M97   2000
398.2—dc21   00-030528

Table of Contents

Volume 1

Table of Contents

Volume 2

Volume 3

Table of Contents

Volume 4

List of Maps and Charts

Preface

Throughout history, myths and legends have served a variety of functions. Some cultures have relied on these stories to preserve their history, traditions, and identity. Some have used myths to teach values and beliefs to the members of a community and to explain natural and social phenomena. At the same time, myths have often served as a form of entertainment.

Myths and legends are still so much a part of our lives that we tend to take them for granted. Over the years, they have been incorporated in works of literature, art, and music and even in movies and television programs. Learning about the world's myths and legends—and the messages they often convey—can enrich our understanding of great cultures of the past and how they are woven into the present.

Filled with heroism, conflict, joy, and sorrow, myths explore the human condition or explain the world around us. Passed down from generation to generation, they often feature deities, animals, or supernatural creatures. Legends tend to be concerned with brave or clever individuals who actually existed. However, the facts of their lives and their role in events are usually exaggerated or embellished to create larger-than-life characters who accomplish extraordinary, even impossible, feats.

Myths and Legends of the World is a four-volume reference work that offers middle- and high-school students a comprehensive collection of myths from ancient, medieval, and modern cultures. Cultures from around the world are represented, with large bodies of myths from Africa, the Americas, Asia, Europe, and Oceania. In addition to entries recounting specific legends, overview articles such as African Mythology and Greek Mythology introduce students to the traditions of a particular culture. A distinguished editorial board—scholars in the fields of classics, history, anthropology, and literature—helped compile the entry list and reviewed each article.

Myths and Legends of the World also includes articles on major themes that run through many of these stories—themes as diverse as devils and demons, floods, giants, trees, twins, and the underworld. Many myths deal with fundamental questions such as how the world began, where people came from, and what happens after death. Similar stories from different parts of the world suggest a common set of fears and concerns and a universal desire for understanding.

The entries in *Myths and Legends of the World* are arranged alphabetically. Sidebars highlighting additional information related to the topics appear in the margin, along with definitions of difficult or unfamiliar terms. Names and places that appear frequently in the work are marked with a dagger in the text and identified in a list at the end of each volume. Charts listing the major deities of particular cultures and cross-references at the end of the articles make the material more accessible for students. Colorful maps and illustrations of paintings, sculptures, prints, and mosaics bring distant times and places to life. Volume 4 includes a cultures index listing all the entries related to each culture and a bibliography to guide students who are interested in learning more about the subject.

Our knowledge of the past, our perception of the universe, and our sense of a community's identity go beyond the explanations of historians, scientists, and sociologists. Likewise, the nature of the human soul extends beyond the scope of psychology. The power of myth lies in its ability to shed light on these essential areas of human experience. In the words of Gregory Nagy, "Myth is a society's way of encoding its values in narrative or dramatic form."

John Wickersham and the Editors

Abel

Acastus

Achilles

centaur half-human, half-animal creature with the body of a horse and the head, chest, and arms of a human

epic long poem about legendary or historical heroes, written in a grand style

supernatural related to forces beyond the normal world; magical or miraculous
nymph minor goddess of nature, usually represented as young and beautiful

invulnerable incapable of being hurt
underworld land of the dead

See *Cain and Abel.*

In Greek mythology, Acastus was a king who sailed with the Argonauts, a group of adventurers seeking a famous treasure called the Golden Fleece. Jason, his fellow Argonaut, brought a witch named Medea to Acastus's kingdom of Iolcus. There Medea tricked the king's sisters into murdering their father. Discovering this treachery, Acastus drove Jason and Medea from his kingdom.

Acastus held funeral games in honor of his murdered father. Among the guests was his friend Peleus, another Argonaut. Acastus's wife, Hippolyte (or in some versions Astydameia), fell in love with Peleus but was rejected by him. Hurt and angry, she told Acastus that Peleus had made advances to her. Acastus decided to take his friend hunting and steal his sword, leaving him to be killed by wild **centaurs.** However, Peleus survived. Later he conquered Iolcus and killed both Acastus and his wife. *See also* ARGONAUTS; GOLDEN FLEECE; JASON; MEDEA.

A hero in the war between the Greeks and the Trojans, Achilles was the foremost warrior in Greek mythology. He figures prominently in the *Iliad,* the **epic** by Greek poet Homer that tells the story of the Trojan War†. Achilles possessed strength, bravery, military skills, pride, and honor—all the qualities the ancient Greeks prized as manly virtues. Yet his conduct was also shaped by anger and stubbornness. The tension between Achilles' larger-than-life virtues and his all-too-human weaknesses plays a role in the mood of heroic tragedy found in the *Iliad.*

Achilles' Heel. Like many mythological heroes, Achilles was part human and part **supernatural** being. His parents were Peleus, a king of Thessaly in northern Greece, and a sea **nymph** named Thetis. According to Homer, Thetis raised both Achilles and his closest friend and companion, Patroclus.

Other accounts added various details to Achilles' life. In one story, Thetis, fearful for her son's safety, tried to protect him by rubbing him with ambrosia, the food of the gods, and holding him in a fire to burn away his human weakness. This action horrified Peleus, and Thetis, angry at his distrust, abandoned her husband and child and returned to the sea.

Another version of Achilles' story said that Thetis tried to make her infant son **invulnerable** by dipping him into the river Styx, which flowed through the **underworld.** However, the water did not touch the heel by which she held Achilles, and this spot remained vulnerable. This myth is the source of the term *Achilles' heel,* which refers to a person's one great weakness.

Achilles' strength and athletic superiority emerged early. At age six, he could run fast enough to catch deer and was strong enough to kill lions and wild boars. Some myths say that Achilles

centaur half-human, half-animal creature with the body of a horse and the head, chest, and arms of a human

prophecy foretelling of what is to come; also something that is predicted
seer one who can predict the future

learned to run from the **centaur** Chiron, who also taught him music, medicine, and the skills of warfare. According to some legends, Achilles was destined from birth to suffer one of two fates: a long life without glory or a glorious death in battle at Troy.

The Trojan War. When the Trojan War began, Achilles' parents sent him to the court of King Lycomedes on the island of Skyros, where he was disguised as a girl. They hoped this would keep him from being drawn into the combat and suffering the fate of the **prophecy** that said he would die at Troy. Meanwhile, a **seer** warned the Greeks that they would never defeat the Trojans without the help of Achilles.

The Greeks searched for the boy, and Odysseus†, the most cunning and resourceful of the Greek leaders, learned of Achilles' hiding place. Passing as a traveling merchant, Odysseus displayed ornaments to the women of the royal household at Skyros. Among the ornaments were weapons. When one "girl" admired a shield and spear, Odysseus knew that he had found Achilles.

Odysseus persuaded Achilles to join the Greek forces against Troy, even though Achilles owed no loyalty to them. Some stories say that he agreed to fight to prove his courage. Other versions claim that both Achilles and Odysseus were reluctant to join the war, which was fought over the kidnapping of a beautiful Greek woman named Helen by the Trojan prince Paris. In any case, both Achilles and Odysseus joined the Greek forces led by King Agamemnon, which were camped outside the walls of Troy in Asia Minor†.

In the tenth year of the Trojan War, Achilles and Agamemnon became involved in a fierce dispute. Forced to return a young woman he had taken as a prize of war, Agamemnon demanded the woman Achilles had received as a prize instead. Achilles was furious and withdrew into his tent, refusing to fight.

When Hector, son of the Trojan king and Troy's leading warrior, attacked the Greek forces, Achilles still refused to fight. His friend Patroclus asked if he could borrow Achilles' armor. He thought that the Trojans, seeing the armor of the most feared Greek warrior, would certainly retreat. Achilles reluctantly agreed. However, to his great horror and sorrow, Patroclus was killed in combat by Hector.

Achilles rushed into battle in a furious desire to avenge the death of Patroclus. Three times he chased Hector around the walls of Troy before killing the Trojan prince in one-on-one combat. He then dragged the body behind his chariot, preventing the Trojans from

Guilio Romano painted this fresco called *Thetis Delivering Arms to Achilles* in the early 1500s. Thetis, Achilles' mother, brings him a new suit of armor to wear when he rejoins combat in the Trojan War.

† See **Names and Places** at the end of this volume for further information.

The Achilles Paradox

In the 400s B.C., the Greek philosopher Zeno created a paradox—something that seems contradictory and impossible to explain. It involved a race between a tortoise and Achilles, a famously fast runner. According to Zeno, if the tortoise received a head start and continued to move on, Achilles could never catch up. By the time he reached the tortoise's starting point, the tortoise would have moved on to another point. This situation would occur again and again, with the tortoise always remaining ahead of Achilles.

This so-called Achilles paradox dealt with the problem of a continuum, a limited distance divided into unlimited smaller units. The Greek philosopher Aristotle proposed a solution: Because Achilles never actually stops at the points on the continuum, they do not exist. Thus Achilles would be able to catch the tortoise.

pyre pile of wood on which a dead body is burned in a funeral ceremony

burying it and holding a proper funeral, as the Greeks had done for Patroclus. The gods forced Achilles to surrender the body of Hector to his grieving father, King Priam of Troy.

Achilles in Literature and Art. The *Iliad* ends with Hector's funeral and does not mention what happened to Achilles. Other sources, however, say that Achilles died in the Trojan War, shot through the vulnerable spot in his heel by Hector's brother Paris, who had started the war by kidnapping Helen. In the *Odyssey,* the Greek epic that is a sequel to the *Iliad,* Achilles descends to the underworld, where he meets Odysseus. Other accounts say that Thetis seized her son's body from its funeral **pyre** and carried him away to a new existence on the island of Leuke in the Black Sea.

Several ancient Greek playwrights wrote works that deal with the legacy of Achilles. The tragedy *Ajax* by Sophocles† is about the contest over who should receive the dead warrior's armor. The ghost of Achilles appears as a character in *Hecuba,* a play by Euripides†.

Later writers also focused on Achilles. In *The Divine Comedy,* a long poem by the Italian writer Dante Alighieri in the early 1300s, Achilles is shown living in the Second Circle of Hell, a place reserved for those who died because of love. Dante wrote that Achilles "fought with love at the last"—a reference to the legend that Paris lured Achilles to his death by making him think that he would be meeting a woman he loved. A French opera called *Achille et Polyxène,* written by Jean-Baptiste Lully in 1687, is based on the same myth. More than 50 other operas have been written about Achilles.

English writers such as Geoffrey Chaucer and William Shakespeare mention Achilles in a number of works. The power of Achilles is mentioned in Chaucer's *The Canterbury Tales,* and Shakespeare made the Greek warrior a central character in his long poem *Troilus and Cressida.* The mighty Achilles has also been the subject of many art works, from ancient Greek vases to paintings by the Flemish artist Peter Paul Rubens (1577–1640) and French painter Nicolas Poussin (1594–1665). *See also* AGAMEMNON; AJAX; GREEK MYTHOLOGY; HECTOR; HEROES; ILIAD, THE; ODYSSEY, THE; PARIS; THETIS; TROJAN WAR.

Adad

Adad was the god of weather in the Babylonian and Assyrian cultures of Mesopotamia† in the ancient Near East. Other cultures in the region called the god Ishkur, Rimmon, Addu, Hadad, or Baal-Hadad.

The son of the sky god Anu, Adad was believed to control storms and rain. He was often portrayed as a warrior holding a forked lightning bolt or a club, and his animal was the bull, whose bellowing and roar were like the sound of thunder.

Like the weather itself, Adad had two sides—one beneficial and the other destructive. As the bringer of rain, Adad was hailed as the Lord of Abundance whose gift made the land fertile and nourished

Adam and Eve

crops. People in many arid Mesopotamian lands worshiped him for this reason. As the bringer of drought or fearful storms, however, Adad could strike his enemies with famine, flood, darkness, and death. *See also* ANU; BAAL; SEMITIC MYTHOLOGY.

The mythologies of many cultures include stories of a first couple, a man and woman who were the parents of the entire human race. In the Jewish, Christian, and Islamic religious traditions, these first parents were Adam and Eve.

The Story of Adam and Eve. Genesis, the first book of the Bible, contains two accounts of how Adam and Eve came into being. The first version, which most likely dates from between 600 and 400 B.C., says that God created all living things—including a man and woman "in his own image"—on the sixth day of creation. According to the second version, which is longer and probably several centuries older, God (here named Yahweh) made Adam from dust and breathed "the breath of life" into his nostrils. God then created animals so that Adam would not be alone. However, God saw that Adam needed a human partner, so he put Adam to sleep, took a rib from his side, and created Eve from it.

Adam and Eve lived in a garden called Eden, from which four rivers flowed out into the world. Like other earthly paradises in mythologies of the arid Near East, Eden was a well-watered, fertile place that satisfied all of the needs of Adam and Eve. God imposed only one restriction on life in this paradise: not to eat the fruit of a certain tree—the tree of the knowledge of good and evil.

A sly serpent in the garden persuaded Eve to eat the forbidden fruit, and Adam tasted the fruit as well. The two lost their innocence immediately. Ashamed of their nakedness, they covered themselves with leaves. God saw that they had disobeyed him and drove them from the Garden of Eden.

When Adam and Eve left Eden, human history began. The two worked long and hard to wrest a living from the earth. Eventually, they grew old and died, but not before they had borne children. The first two were their sons, Cain and Abel. According to Jewish, Christian, and Islamic tradition, all the people of the world are descended from the sons and daughters of Adam and Eve.

Christian Interpretations. The Jewish, Christian, and Islamic traditions each have their own versions of the story of Adam and Eve as well as their own interpretations of its meaning. In Christian thought and belief, three important aspects of the story are the serpent, the Fall, and the **doctrine** of original sin.

The serpent was identified with Satan, God's great opponent and the force behind all evil. The importance of the serpent is that, although Adam and Eve were weak and gave in to temptation, they did not sin entirely on their own; Satan encouraged them to do so.

Adam's Rib

The image of God fashioning Eve out of Adam's rib may have originated in an ancient legend from Mesopotamia†. After the god Enki ate eight plants belonging to the goddess Ninhursag, she cursed him so that eight parts of his body became diseased. When he was nearly dead, the gods persuaded Ninhursag to help him, and she created eight healing goddesses. The goddess who cured Enki's rib was Ninti, whose name meant "lady of the rib" or "lady of life." In Hebrew mythology, Adam names the woman created from his rib Hawwah, which means "life." The Mesopotamian story probably influenced the Hebrew one, which became the basis for one biblical version of Eve's creation.

doctrine set of principles or beliefs accepted by a group

† *See **Names and Places** at the end of this volume for further information.*

Islamic tradition includes a tale about Adam and Eve that is similar to the version in the Bible. This Islamic work of the 1800s shows Adam and Eve standing next to the Tree of Knowledge.

epic long poem about legendary or historical heroes, written in a grand style

The Fall refers to the expulsion of Adam and Eve from the Garden of Eden into the world of ordinary, imperfect human life (sometimes called the fallen world). Some people interpret the Fall to mean that in the original state of existence before the beginning of history, people lived in harmony with each other, God, and the natural world.

Closely related to the idea of the Fall is the doctrine of original sin. This idea came from the writings of the apostle St. Paul, whose work appears in the New Testament of the Bible, and of later Christian thinkers whom he influenced. According to this doctrine—which not all branches of Christianity accept—the sin that Adam and Eve committed when they ate the forbidden fruit marks every human being descended from them. As a result, no one is born completely innocent and free from sin.

Art and Literature. During the many centuries when European art dealt mostly with religious ideas, the story of Adam and Eve was a favorite subject. Among the famous images of the couple are the paintings in the Sistine Chapel in Rome by Italian artist Michelangelo. Completed in the early 1500s, they show the creation of Adam and Eve and the Fall. Another well-known painting of Adam and Eve comes from German artist Albrecht Dürer and was done in 1507. Artists of all periods have used fruit and snakes as symbols of temptation and evil.

Aside from the story of creation and the Fall in the book of Genesis, the Bible contains little information about Adam and Eve. Other writings, however, have added details to their story. One such work, the *Life of Adam and Eve,* was presented in the form of a biography. Written sometime between 20 B.C. and A.D. 70 in a biblical style, it provides a lively account of the Fall and the sufferings of Adam and Eve after leaving Eden. The greatest and most famous literary treatment of Adam and Eve is the long **epic** *Paradise Lost,* written by English poet John Milton and published in 1667. It tells the story

> Of man's first disobedience, and the fruit
> Of that forbidden tree whose mortal taste
> Brought death into the world, and all our woe,
> With loss of Eden. . . .

See also CREATION STORIES; EDEN, GARDEN OF; FRUIT IN MYTHOLOGY; LILITH; SEMITIC MYTHOLOGY; SERPENTS AND SNAKES.

Adonis

resurrect to raise from the dead

In Greek mythology, Adonis was an extremely handsome youth who died and was reborn. Like many other mythological figures who are **resurrected,** Adonis became associated with the annual cycle of the seasons in which vegetation dies in the fall and grows again in the spring. Adonis's counterpart in Near Eastern mythology was the god Tammuz.

According to tradition, Adonis was the son of Myrrha and her father, Theias, the king of Assyria. So attractive was the infant

underworld land of the dead

Adonis that Aphrodite (Venus), the goddess of love, fell in love with him. She hid the baby in a box and gave him to Persephone, goddess of the **underworld,** for safekeeping. When Persephone saw Adonis, however, she also fell in love with him and refused to return him to Aphrodite.

Zeus† settled the dispute by ordering Adonis to divide his time between the two goddesses. During spring and summer, the time of fertility and fruitfulness, Adonis stayed with Aphrodite. He spent fall and winter, the period of barrenness and death, with Persephone.

Adonis adored hunting. While out on a chase one day during his time with Aphrodite, he was killed by a wild boar. Some stories say that the boar was Hephaestus (Vulcan)†, Aphrodite's husband, in disguise—or perhaps it was Ares, the god of war and Aphrodite's jealous lover. Beautiful red flowers called anemones grew and bloomed where Adonis's blood fell on the soil.

Each year in ancient Greece, the worshipers of Adonis, mostly women, celebrated his rebirth by planting "gardens of Adonis" for festivals held in his honor. The god has become a symbol of male beauty, and a handsome young man is sometimes called an Adonis. *See also* **APHRODITE; ARES; GREEK MYTHOLOGY; PERSEPHONE; VULCAN.**

Aegir

primeval from the earliest times
deity god or goddess

In Norse† mythology, Aegir, also known as Hlér or Gymir, was the god of the sea, the counterpart of the Greek god Poseidon† and the Roman god Neptune†. Aegir and his wife, Ran, caused death at sea. The Norse, a seafaring people who knew well the sea and its many dangers, valued Aegir highly. They also appreciated him for his reputation as a giver of banquets and a brewer of strong drink. The name *aegir* comes from the Norse word for "sea."

Aegir was a **primeval** god, more ancient than many other Norse **deities.** He often appears in art as a thin old man with clutching hands and long white hair that resembles sea foam, although he is sometimes shown as a giant. Aegir and Ran carried a net with which they could trap seafarers and pull them down to their underwater kingdom. Drowned sailors were said to dine at Aegir's banquet hall. The underwater couple had nine daughters—the ocean waves—with names such as Howler and Grasper. *See also* **NORSE MYTHOLOGY; POSEIDON.**

Aeneas

demigod one who is part human and part god

The hero Aeneas appears in both Greek and Roman mythology. He was a defender of Troy, the city in Asia Minor† that the Greeks destroyed in the Trojan War†. After the war, Aeneas led the Trojans who survived to the land now called Italy. According to Roman versions of the myth, Aeneas and his followers founded Rome, and he became its first great hero and legendary father.

The Setting. Like many legendary heroes, Aeneas was a nobleman and a **demigod** as well. His father was Anchises, a member

† *See* ***Names and Places*** *at the end of this volume for further information.*

of the royal family of Troy. One day Aphrodite, the Greek goddess of love (called Venus by the Romans), saw Anchises on the hills of Mount Ida near his home. The goddess was so overcome by the handsome youth that she seduced him and bore him a son, Aeneas.

Mountain **nymphs** raised Aeneas until he was five years old, when he was sent to live with his father. Aphrodite had made Anchises promise not to tell anyone that she was the boy's mother. Still, he did so and was struck by lightning. In some versions of the legend, the lightning killed Anchises; in others, it made him blind or lame. Later variations have Anchises surviving and being carried out of Troy by his son after the war.

When the Greeks invaded Troy, Aeneas did not join the conflict immediately. Some versions of the myth say that he entered the war on the side of his fellow Trojans only after the Greek hero Achilles had stolen his cattle. Aeneas's reluctance to join the fighting stemmed, in part, from the prickly relationship he had with King Priam of Troy. Some sources say that Aeneas resented the fact that Priam's son Hector was supreme commander of the Trojan forces. For his part, Priam disliked Aeneas because the sea god Poseidon had predicted that the descendants of Aeneas, not those of Priam, would rule the Trojans in the future. Nevertheless, during the Trojan War, Aeneas married Creusa, one of Priam's daughters, and they had a son named Ascanius.

The Greek Tradition. Aeneas appears as a character in the *Iliad,* the **epic** by the Greek poet Homer that tells the story of the Trojan War. The *Iliad* and other Greek sources provide a number of details about Aeneas's role in the war.

According to Greek tradition, Aeneas was one of the Trojans' leaders, their greatest warrior after Hector. An upright and moral man, he was often called "the pious" because of his respect for the gods and his obedience to their commands. In return, the gods treated Aeneas well. Not only his mother, Aphrodite, but also the powerful gods Poseidon and Apollo gave him their protection.

There are various accounts of the last days of the Trojan War. One story relates that Aphrodite warned Aeneas that Troy would fall and that he left the city and took refuge on Mount Ida, where he established a new kingdom. In later years, several cities on the mountain boasted that they had been founded by Aeneas. Another version states that Aeneas fought bravely to the end of the war and either escaped from Troy with a band of followers or was allowed to depart by the victorious Greeks, who respected his honor and **piety.**

In the 700s B.C., the Greeks began establishing colonies in Italy and on the island of Sicily off the Italian coast. Legends often linked Greek heroes to these colonies, whose citizens liked to think of themselves as descended from the characters that Homer had described in his works. By the 400s B.C. if not earlier, a story had taken shape that Aeneas went to Italy after fleeing the destruction of Troy. The next stage of Aeneas's tale, however, would be told by the Romans, not the Greeks.

nymph minor goddess of nature, usually represented as young and beautiful

epic long poem about legendary or historical heroes, written in a grand style

piety faithfulness to beliefs

omen sign of future events

pyre pile of wood on which a dead body is burned in a funeral ceremony

oracle priest or priestess or other creature through whom a god is believed to speak; also the location (such as a shrine) where such words are spoken
underworld land of the dead

The Roman Tradition. By the 300s B.C., Rome was a rising power in the Mediterranean world. As the city grew larger and more powerful, it faced a dilemma. The Romans shared many myths and legends with the Greeks and had considerable respect for Greece's ancient culture. At the same time, however, the Romans did not want to be overshadowed by Greek culture and tradition. They wanted their own connections to the ancient world of gods and heroes.

Roman writers found a perfect link to the legendary past with Aeneas, who was supposed to have come to Italy around the time of the founding of Rome. Furthermore, because Aeneas was a Trojan, he could give the Romans what they wanted—an ancestry that was connected to the ancient heroes yet separate from the Greeks.

Over the centuries, a number of Roman myths developed about Aeneas. According to Roman tradition, Aeneas fought with great courage in Troy until messages from Aphrodite and Hector convinced him to leave the city. Carrying his father on his back and holding his son by the hand, Aeneas led his supporters out of burning Troy. During the confusion, Aeneas's wife, Creusa, became separated from the fleeing Trojans. Aeneas returned to search for Creusa but could not find her.

Aeneas and his followers found safety on Mount Ida, where they began building ships. After several months, they set sail to the west. Dreams and **omens** told Aeneas that he was destined to found a new kingdom in the land of his ancestors, the country today called Italy.

Aeneas's Travels. After surviving many dangers, including powerful storms and fierce monsters, Aeneas and his Trojan followers landed on the coast of North Africa. Along the way, his father died. At this point in Aeneas's tale, Roman storytellers mingled the history of the hero with earlier tales of a queen named Dido, founder of the city of Carthage in North Africa.

According to Roman legend, Dido and Aeneas fell in love soon after the hero arrived in Carthage. Aeneas stayed with the queen until Mercury, the messenger of the gods, reminded him that his destiny lay in Italy. Aeneas sorrowfully but obediently sailed away. When he looked back, he saw smoke and flames. Lovesick and abandoned, Dido had thrown herself onto a funeral **pyre.**

After stopping in Sicily and leaving some of his followers to found a colony there, Aeneas sailed to Italy. Upon his arrival, he sought advice from Sibyl, a powerful **oracle** who took him to the **underworld.** There Aeneas saw the ghost of Dido, but she turned away and would not speak to him. Then he saw the ghost of his father, Anchises, who told him that he would found the greatest empire the world had ever known.

Founder of an Empire. Heartened by his father's prophecy, Aeneas went to Latium in central Italy. He became engaged to Lavinia, the daughter of the king of the Latins. Turnus, the leader

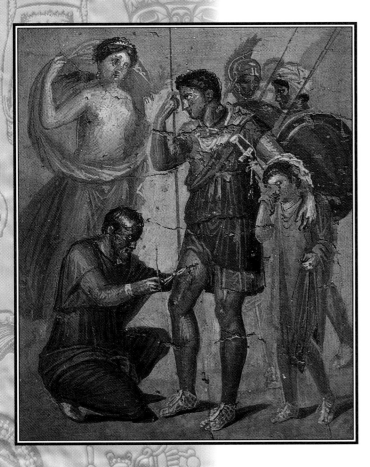

Aeneas was wounded while fighting the Rituli, a tribe in Italy. The goddess Venus cured him, and he returned to battle to fight with new vigor and emerge victorious. Here Venus watches as a physician attends to Aeneas's wound.

of another tribe called the Rutuli, launched a war against the Trojan newcomers. Some of the Latins also fought the Trojans, but Aeneas had finally arrived at his **destiny** and could not be defeated. First he killed Turnus and married Lavinia. Then he founded the city of Lavinium, where Latins and Trojans were united.

After Aeneas's death, his son Ascanius ruled Lavinium and founded a second city called Alba Longa, which became the capital of the Trojan-Latin people. These cities formed the basis of what came to be ancient Rome. Some legends claim that Aeneas founded the city of Rome itself. Others assign that honor to his descendant Romulus.

Later Roman historians altered the story of Rome's origins to make Ascanius the son of Aeneas and Lavinia, thus a Latin by birth. Ascanius was also called Iulus, or Julius, and a clan of Romans called the Julians claimed descent from him. Julius Caesar and his nephew Augustus, who became the first Roman emperor, were members of that clan. In this way, the rulers of Rome traced their ancestry—and their right to rule—back to the demigod Aeneas.

destiny future or fate of an individual or thing

Aeneas in Literature. Although many ancient authors wrote about Aeneas, the most complete and influential account of his life and deeds is the *Aeneid,* a long poem composed around 30 to 20 B.C. by the Roman writer Virgil. Using a style similar to that of the Greek epics the *Iliad* and the *Odyssey,* Virgil reshaped in Latin the legends and traditions about Aeneas to fit Rome's view of its own destiny. In the poem, Virgil tells the story of Aeneas's journey from Troy to Italy.

Like other figures from Greek and Roman mythology, Aeneas appears frequently in Western literature. In *The Divine Comedy,* written in the early A.D. 1300s by Italian poet Dante Alighieri, Aeneas is shown in Limbo, a realm of the afterlife where virtuous **pagans** dwelt. In British mythology, Brutus, Britain's legendary first king, is considered the great-grandson of Aeneas. Generally, Aeneas represents duty and piety, but some authors have portrayed him less favorably. In his play *Cymbeline,* for example, William Shakespeare refers to the "false Aeneas" who abandoned Dido. Shakespeare also mentions Aeneas in his plays *Troilus and Cressida* and *Julius Caesar.* **See also** AENEID, THE; APHRODITE; DIDO; GREEK MYTHOLOGY; HOMER; ILIAD, THE; ROMAN MYTHOLOGY; ROMULUS AND REMUS; TROJAN WAR.

pagan term used by early Christians to describe non-Christians and non-Christian beliefs

Aeneid, The

epic long poem about legendary or historical heroes, written in a grand style
destiny future or fate of an individual or thing
imperial relating to an emperor or empire

pious faithful to one's beliefs

patron special guardian, protector, or supporter

In about 30 B.C., the Roman poet Virgil began composing the *Aeneid*, an **epic** about the legendary hero Aeneas and the founding and **destiny** of Rome. Woven from strands of myth, history, and **imperial** pride, the *Aeneid* summed up everything the Romans valued most about their society. At the same time, it offered tales of adventure featuring gods and goddesses, heroes and ghosts, and warriors and doomed lovers. Virgil died before finishing the work, but it established his reputation as the foremost poet of the Romans.

Creating a Roman Heritage. The *Aeneid* tells the story of Aeneas, a hero of Troy, the city in Asia Minor† that the Greeks destroyed during the Trojan War†. According to legend, Aeneas survived the war and led a group of Trojans on a journey to the kingdom of Latium in central Italy, where Rome eventually arose.

The story of Aeneas was much older than Rome. The hero appears as a character in the *Iliad*†, an epic about the Trojan War by the Greek poet Homer. However, as Rome was emerging as the leading power in the Mediterranean world in the 200s B.C., the Romans became eager to claim Aeneas and the Trojans as their ancestors. Some Romans even visited Ilium, a Roman city in Asia Minor said to stand on the ancient site of Troy.

Aeneas was an ideal figure to serve as the legendary founder of Rome. As the son of Aphrodite (Venus), the goddess of love, and Anchises, a member of the Trojan royal family, he had both divine and royal parents. In addition, the ancient tales portrayed Aeneas as dutiful, **pious,** brave, and honorable—virtues that the Romans felt characterized their culture. Finally, Aeneas was part of the Greek heritage so admired by the Romans. Because he was a Trojan rather than a Greek, however, he provided the Romans with a distinct identity that was not Greek but equally ancient and honorable.

A number of Roman writers contributed to the story of how Aeneas came to Italy so that his descendants could build Rome. However, the person who assembled the elements of the legend into a great national epic was Publius Vergilius Maro, known as Virgil. His **patron,** Augustus, the first emperor of Rome, considered himself a direct descendant of Aeneas. Virgil's *Aeneid* glorified not just Rome but also Augustus, whose reign was portrayed as the fulfillment of the grand Roman destiny that the gods had predicted to Aeneas long ago.

Structure and Style. Virgil modeled the *Aeneid* on the *Iliad* and the *Odyssey,* Homer's two much-admired epics of ancient Greece. Like the Greek poems, the *Aeneid* features the Trojan War, a hero on a long and difficult journey, and stirring descriptions of hand-to-hand combat between heroic warriors. It is also similar in form to the Greek epics, which are composed in dactylic hexameter, a verse that has 18-syllable lines with the first of every 3 syllables accented. The epic consists of 12 books.

Yet the *Aeneid* differs from Homer's epics in ways that reflect the different circumstances in which it was created. Literary scholars

† *See **Names and Places** at the end of this volume for further information.*

are still debating Homer's existence. There may or may not have been an individual author who put the *Iliad* and the *Odyssey* into the form in which they have been handed down. In any case, storytellers told and retold the Greek epics over a long period before they were written down. Many features of their style, such as the frequent repetition of phrases and images, reflect the traditional methods used by oral storytellers. Virgil, by contrast, was an educated man writing a poem for readers. He could study the traditional legends of Greece and Italy, determine his plot, and polish his language.

Virgil first wrote the entire *Aeneid* in **prose** and then turned it into verse a few lines at a time. As he lay dying, Virgil requested that the manuscript of his still unfinished work be destroyed. Nevertheless, the emperor Augustus preserved the work and had it published after Virgil's death in 19 B.C.

The Story and Its Significance. In Book 1 of the *Aeneid*, Aeneas and his followers arrive in Carthage in North Africa after escaping a storm sent by Juno (Hera), the queen of the gods. Early in the story, Virgil establishes the fact that Juno does her best to ruin Aeneas's plans because of her hatred for the Trojans, while Venus supports him. Jupiter, the king of the gods, reveals that Aeneas will ultimately reach Italy and that his descendants will found a great empire. This is the first of many **prophecies** in the *Aeneid*. Their meaning is clear: Rome rules the world because it is fated to do so and has the support of the gods.

In Book 2, Aeneas tells Dido, the queen of Carthage, about the Greek victory in the Trojan War and how he escaped the city. This story within a story continues in Book 3, as Aeneas describes to Dido the earlier attempts by the Trojan survivors to found a city. Book 4 reveals that Dido is in love with Aeneas, and the two become lovers. Fate has other plans for the Trojan leader, however. Jupiter sends Mercury, the messenger of the gods, to remind Aeneas that his destiny lies in Italy. After Aeneas and his followers leave Carthage, Dido kills herself in despair. This episode shows Aeneas's willingness to sacrifice his own desires to obey the will of the gods. It also creates a legendary explanation for the very real hostility between Carthage and Rome.

In Book 5 of the *Aeneid*, the Trojans reach Sicily, an island off the coast of Italy, and Aeneas organizes funeral games to honor the death of his father, Anchises. While the games are in progress, Juno attempts to destroy the Trojan fleet, but Jupiter saves most of the ships and the Trojans depart. In Book 6, the Trojans arrive at Cumae in Italy, and Aeneas visits the shrine of the Cumaean Sibyl, a famous **oracle.** She leads him on a visit to the **underworld,** where he meets the ghost of his father. Another prophecy reveals to Aeneas the greatness that Rome will achieve in the future.

Books 7 through 11 tell of the Trojans' arrival in Latium, the kingdom of the Latins in western Italy. The newcomers are welcomed at first, but then war breaks out between the Trojans and the Latin tribes, sparked by the meddling of Juno. Venus helps

prose language that is not in poetic form

Epics and Nationalism

The *Aeneid* demonstrated that an epic poem could express a people's values and glorify its history. After 1800 when Europe saw a rise in nationalism—a strong loyalty and devotion to national identity combined with commitment to furthering a nation's interests—European writers began producing national epics based on folktales, legends, and history. Many of these writers used the *Aeneid* and the ancient Greek epics of Homer as their models. Among the most famous national epics written at this time were the Finnish *Kalevala* (1835), by Elias Lönnrot; the Estonian *Kalevipoeg* (1857–1861), by F. R. Kreutzwald; the German *Nibelunge* (1868–1874), by Wilhelm Jordan; and the Latvian *Lacplesis* (1888), by Andrejs Pumpurs.

prophecy foretelling of what is to come; also something that is predicted

oracle priest or priestess or other creature through whom a god is believed to speak; also the location (such as a shrine) where such words are spoken

underworld land of the dead

omen sign of future events

This painting by Federico Barocci shows Aeneas fleeing the city of Troy and carrying his father on his shoulders. One of Aeneas's most notable qualities as a hero is his devotion to his father.

Aeneas by giving him a new set of armor and weapons bearing images of Rome's future glory. Jupiter then forbids the gods to interfere further.

The final book of the *Aeneid* recounts the mighty single combat between Aeneas and the Latin hero Turnus, the Trojans' chief opponent. Aeneas wins the fight and is free to marry Lavinia, daughter of the Latin king Latinus. Their marriage symbolizes the union between the Latin and Trojan peoples, and their descendants are the first Romans.

The Influence of the Aeneid. Whatever Virgil may have thought about his work while he lay on his deathbed, others quickly recognized that the *Aeneid* was a masterpiece. Romans loved the poem. It gave them an impressive history and justified the proud expectation that they were destined to rule the world. Yet even after the Roman empire fell, people continued to read and admire the *Aeneid.*

During the Middle Ages, many Europeans believed that Virgil had been a magician and that the *Aeneid* had magical properties, perhaps because the story contained so many **omens** and prophecies. People would read passages from the work and search for hidden meanings or predictions about the future. So admired was Virgil that the Italian poet Dante Alighieri, who wrote during the late 1200s and early 1300s, made him a central character in his own religious epic, *The Divine Comedy.* In Dante's work, Virgil guides the narrator through Hell and Purgatory, but he is not able to enter Heaven because he was not a Christian.

The *Aeneid* influenced English literature as well. Poets Edmund Spenser and John Milton wrote epics that reflect the work's influence. Poet John Dryden was one of many who translated the *Aeneid;* his 1697 version is one of the best English translations. By contrast, the poets Samuel Taylor Coleridge, Percy Bysshe Shelley, and Lord Byron disliked Virgil's work—perhaps because it celebrates social order, religious duty, and national glory over the Romantic qualities that they favored—passion, rebellion, and self-determination.

The *Aeneid* served as inspiration for musical composers as well as writers. Many operas have been based on Virgil's work. Among the best known are *Dido and Aeneas* (1690), by English composer Henry Purcell, and *The Trojans* (1858), by the French composer Hector Berlioz. ***See also*** AENEAS; ILIAD, THE; VENUS.

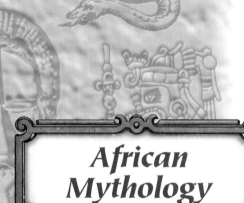

Aeolus

epic long poem about legendary or historical heroes, written in a grand style

Ancient Greek mythology included two characters named Aeolus. One of them was king of the region known as Thessaly in northern Greece. He and his two brothers, the sons of a ruler named Hellen, were the legendary ancestors of the Greek, or Hellenic, people.

Another Aeolus appeared in Homer's *Odyssey,* the Greek **epic** that told the adventures of a warrior named Odysseus and his companions. This character was a skilled sailor whom Zeus, chief of the gods, placed in charge of all the winds. Aeolus kept the winds in a cave on the floating island of Aeolia, releasing them according to the gods' requests or his own wishes. He helped Odysseus by giving him a bag containing all the winds that might prevent him from reaching home, a gift that backfired when Odysseus's men opened the bag. Later writers, including the Roman poet Ovid, occasionally confused or combined the two Aeoluses. ***See also*** ODYSSEY, THE.

African Mythology

Islam religion based on the teachings of the prophet Muhammad; religious faith of Muslims

A vast and geographically varied continent, Africa is home to a great many cultures and to a thousand or more languages. Although no single set of myths and legends unites this diverse population, different culture groups and regions share some common elements.

Like myths from other parts of the world, those of the African peoples reflect beliefs and values. But while the mythologies of many cultures are carefully preserved relics of ancient times, African myths and legends are still a meaningful part of everyday life. Some African myths deal with universal themes, such as the origin of the world and the fate of the individual after death. Yet many spring from the continent's own settings, conditions, and history.

Roots of African Myths and Legends

The Sahara runs from east to west across the widest part of Africa, a vast desert dividing the continent into two main regions. North Africa consists of the Mediterranean coast from Morocco to Egypt and includes the valley of the Nile River as far south as Ethiopia. With strong ties to the Mediterranean and Arab worlds, North Africans felt the influence of Christianity by the A.D. 300s, and in the 700s, much of the area came under the influence of **Islam.**

13

indigenous native to a certain place

This wooden headrest from Zaire portrays twins, which had a special significance in African mythology. They were thought to represent the balance between opposing forces that existed in the natural world.

South of the Sahara is the region inhabited by black Africans. Before the modern era, they had relatively little contact with the rest of the world. Islam entered Africa south of the Sahara very slowly, compared with its sweep across North Africa, and Christian missionaries were not very active there until the 1800s. Since then, the spread of Islam and Christianity has weakened the **indigenous** religions, myths, and legends of sub-Saharan Africa. However, the traditional beliefs have not disappeared. In some places, they have blended with new religions from other cultures, so that an African Muslim might combine Islam with the traditional practice of ancestor worship.

Myths and legends developed over thousands of years in Africa south of the Sahara. Among the influences on their development were the mass migrations that took place from time to time. About 7,000 years ago, the ancestors of the Hottentot and the Bushmen began moving from the Sahara toward southern Africa. Five thousand years later, people who spoke Bantu languages began spreading out from Cameroon, on Africa's west coast, until they eventually inhabited much of sub-Saharan Africa. Such migrations caused myths and legends to spread from group to group and led to a mixing of myths and legends. The migrations also gave rise to new stories about events in the history of those peoples. For instance, as Bantu groups settled in new homelands, they developed legends to explain the origins of their ruling families and the structure of their societies.

The peoples of Africa did not use written language until modern times. Instead, they possessed rich and complex oral traditions, passing myths, legends, and history from generation to generation in spoken form. In some cultures, professional storytellers—called griots—preserved the oral tradition. Written accounts of African mythology began to appear in the early 1800s, and present-day scholars labor to record the continent's myths and legends before they are lost to time and cultural change.

Main Gods and Spirits

African mythologies include supernatural beings who influence human life. Some of these beings are powerful **deities.** Others are lesser spirits, such as the spirits of ancestors.

Deities. Most African traditional religions have multiple gods, often grouped together in family relationships. Nearly every culture recognizes a supreme god, an all-powerful creator who is usually associated with the sky. Various West African peoples refer to the highest god as Amma or Olorun, while some East Africans use the name Mulungu. Africans who have adopted Christianity or Islam sometimes identify the supreme deity of those faiths with the supreme deity of traditional African religion and mythology.

In most African religions, the supreme god is a distant being no longer involved in day-to-day human life. People rarely call on this

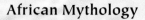

African Deities

Deity	People and Region	Role
Ala	Ibo, Nigeria	mother goddess, ruler of the underworld, goddess of fertility
Amma	Dogon, Mali	supreme god
Cagn	Bushmen, Southwestern Africa	creator god
Eshu	Yoruba, Nigeria	trickster and messenger god
Katonda	Buganda, East Africa	creator god, father of the gods, king and judge of the universe
Kibuka	Buganda, East Africa	war god
Leza	Bantu, Central and South Africa	creator and sky god
Mujaji	Lovedu, South Africa	rain goddess
Nyame	Ashanti and Akan, Ghana	creator god associated with the sun and moon
Ogun	Yoruba, West Africa	god of war and iron
Olorun	Yoruba, West Africa	sky god and supreme deity

deity god or goddess

pantheon all the gods of a particular culture

deity. Instead, they address lesser gods, many of whom have distinct functions. The Yoruba people of Nigeria, for example, worship a storm god, Shango, who controls thunder and lightning.

The number of gods and goddesses varies from culture to culture. The Buganda of east central Africa have one of the largest **pantheons,** with 20 or more deities. Many peoples regard the earth, sun, and moon as gods. In the Congo River region, the most densely wooded part of Africa, the forest itself is a deity—or else a mysterious otherworld where spirits dwell.

Spirits. African mythology is filled with spirits, invisible beings with powers for good or evil. Spirits are less grand, less powerful, and less like humans than the gods, who often have weaknesses and emotions. Many spirits are associated with physical features such as mountains, rivers, wells, trees, and springs. Nations, peoples, and even small communities may honor local spirits unknown outside their borders.

All humans, animals, and plants have spirits, as do elements such as water and fire. Some spirits are helpful, others harmful.

ritual ceremony that follows a set pattern

cult group bound together by devotion to a particular person, belief, or god

People may worship spirits and may also try to control them through magical means, usually with the aid of a skilled practitioner—sometimes called the medicine man or woman or the witch doctor—who leads **rituals.** People thought to have evil spirits are considered dangerous witches.

Ancestors. Many Africans believe that human spirits exist after death. According to some groups, these spirits dwell underground in a world much like that of the living—but upside down. The spirits sleep during the day and come out at night. Other groups place the realm of the dead in the sky. The Bushmen of southern Africa say that the dead become stars.

Many African groups believe that the spirits of dead ancestors remain near their living descendants to help and protect them—as long as these relatives perform certain ceremonies and pay them due respect. Believing that the spirits of chieftains and other important characters offer strong protection, the Zulu hold special ceremonies to bring them into the community. In some cultures, it is said that the soul of a dead grandfather, father, or uncle can be reborn in a new baby boy. Another common belief is that dead souls, particularly those of old men, may return as snakes, which many Africans regard with respect.

Ancestor **cults** play a leading role in the mythologies of some peoples, especially in East and South Africa. The honored dead—whether of the immediate family, the larger clan or kinship group, the community, or the entire culture—become objects of worship and subjects of tales and legends. An example occurs among the Songhai, who live along the Niger River. They honor Zoa, a wise and protective ancestor who long ago made his son chieftain.

Many groups trace their origins, or the origins of all humans, to first ancestors. The Buganda say that the first ancestor was Kintu, who came from the land of the gods and married Nambe, daughter of the king of heaven. The Dinkas of the Sudan speak of Garang and Abuk, the first man and woman, whom God created as tiny clay figures in a pot.

Rulers and Heroes. Ancestral kings and heroes may be transformed into minor deities for communities or entire nations. The line between legend and history is often blurred. Some mythic ancestors began as real-life personages whose deeds were exaggerated over time, while others are purely fictional. The Yoruba storm god Shango, for example, may originally have been a mighty warrior king.

The Shilluk, who live along the Nile in the Sudan, trace their ancestry to Nyikang, their first king. Later kings were thought to have been Nyikang reborn into new bodies, and the well-being of the nation depended on their health and vigor. The first king of the Zulu was supposed to have been a son of the supreme god. Many African peoples traditionally regarded their rulers as divine or semidivine.

Other legends involve culture heroes who performed great feats or embodied important values. The Soninke people of Ghana

epic long poem about legendary or historical heroes, written in a grand style

cosmology set of ideas about the origin, history, and structure of the universe

trickster mischievous figure appearing in various forms in the folktales and mythology of many different peoples

Gods and Tricksters Cross the Sea

Between the 1500s and the 1800s, many thousands of Africans were brought to the Americas as slaves. Their myths and legends helped shape the black cultures that developed in the Caribbean islands and the United States. The Caribbean religion known as vodun or voodoo, for example, involves the worship of the vodu, West African gods. Enslaved blacks also told traditional stories about the spider Anansi and the trickster hare. Anansi came to be called Anancy, and the hare became Brer (Brother) Rabbit, the character who appears in the Uncle Remus animal fables that were collected by Joel Chandler Harris in the late 1800s.

immortal able to live forever

in West Africa have an **epic** song cycle called *Dausi.* In part of it, *Gassire's Lute,* a hero must choose between his own desires and his duty to society.

The Mandingo people built a large empire in Mali. Their griots recited tales of kings and heroes. *Sunjata,* a story of magic, warfare, kingship, and fate, is known over large portions of West Africa.

Main Types of Myths and Legends

The myths of people living along the Nile and on the fringes of the Sahara, as well as the Bantu around the Niger and Congo Rivers, are generally concerned more with the origins of social institutions such as clans and kingships than with cosmic themes such as the creation of the world. In contrast, the non-Bantu groups of the Niger River area, especially the Dogon, Yoruba, and Bambara, have complex and lengthy **cosmologies.** Fables, folklore, and legends about **tricksters** and animals are found in nearly all African cultures.

How Things Came To Be. Many myths explain how the world came into existence. The Dogon say that twin pairs of creator spirits or gods called Nummo hatched from a cosmic egg. Other groups also speak of the universe beginning with an egg. People in both southern and northern Africa believe that the world was formed from the body of an enormous snake, sometimes said to span the sky as a rainbow.

The Fon people of Benin tell of Gu, the oldest son of the creator twins Mawu (moon) and Lisa (sun). Gu came to earth in the form of an iron sword and then became a blacksmith. His task was to prepare the world for people. He taught humans how to make tools, which in turn enabled them to grow food and build shelters. The San people (Bushmen) of the south say that creation was the work of a spirit named Dxui, who was alternately a man and many other things, such as a flower, a bird, or a lizard.

Myths from across Africa tell how death came into the world. The supreme god meant for humans to be **immortal,** but through an unlucky mistake, they received death instead of eternal life. Some stories relate that the god told a cautious chameleon to carry the news of eternal life to earth, but a faster lizard with news of death arrived first. The Mende people of Sierra Leone say that a toad with the message "Death has come" overtakes a dog with the message "Life has come" because the dog stops to eat along the way.

Other myths explain that death came into the world because people or animals angered the gods. The Nuer people of the Sudan blame death on a hyena who cut the rope that connected heaven and earth. Their neighbors the Dinkas say that a greedy woman, not satisfied with the grain the high god gave her, planted more grain. She hit the god in the eye with her hoe, and he cut the connecting rope. A tale told by the Luyia people relates that a chameleon cursed people with death because a man broke the laws of hospitality by refusing to share his food with the chameleon.

Twins. Many African peoples regard twins as special, almost sacred, beings. Twins represent the duality—the tension or balance between paired or opposing forces—that is basic to life. Some groups, such as the non-Bantu peoples of the Niger and Congo regions, believe that twins of opposite sexes are symbols of this duality.

Twins appear in many African myths and legends. In some stories, they are brother and sister who unite in marriage; in others, they seem to be two sides of a single being. The supreme god of the Fon people of West Africa is Mawu-Lisa, usually described as brother and sister twins who became the parents of all the other gods, also born as twins.

Tricksters and Animal Fables. Many African myths feature a trickster. The trickster may be a god, an animal, or a human being. His pranks and mischief cause trouble among gods, among humans, or between gods and humans.

West Africans tell many tales of a wandering trickster spirit known as Eshu among the Yoruba and as Legba among the Fon. This trickster is associated with change and with quarrels; in some accounts, he is the messenger between the world and the supreme god.

Animal tricksters are often small, helpless creatures who manage to outwit bigger and fiercer animals. Anansi, the spider trickster of the Ashanti people, is known throughout West and Central Africa. Tortoises and hares also appear as tricksters. In one such tale, the hare tricks a hippopotamus and an elephant into clearing a field for him.

Other stories about animals show them helping humans. The San Bushmen say that a sacred praying mantis gave them words and fire, and the Bambara people of Mali say that an antelope taught them agriculture. A popular form of entertainment is the animal fable, a story about talking animals with human characteristics. Many fables offer imaginative explanations of features of the natural world, such as why bats hang with their heads downward or why leopards have spots. ***See also*** ALA; AMMA; ANANSI; ANIMALS IN MYTHOLOGY; BRER RABBIT; CAGN; ESHU; ILE-IFE; KATONDA; KIBUKA; LEBE; LEZA; MUJAJI; MULUNGU; MWINDO; NUMMO; NYAME; OGUN; OLORUN; SUNJATA; TRICKSTERS.

Afterlife

Cultures the world over recognize that every life will end in death. However, many claim that some invisible but vital part of the human being—the spirit or soul—continues to exist after death. In some traditions, the individual possesses more than one soul, and each of these may have a separate fate.

Religions throughout the ages have included a belief in an afterlife, a state of being that people enter when they die or a place to which they or their souls go. Myths, legends, and religious texts offer varying visions of the afterlife. These images reveal much about each culture's hopes and fears for the afterlife and often contain lessons about how people should live their lives.

*† See **Names and Places** at the end of this volume for further information.*

The World Beyond

In some cultures, the afterlife is regarded as a place of pleasure and joy. In others, it is a gloomy shadow of earthly existence, a slow fading away, or a remote and unknowable realm. Expectations about the organization of the afterlife also differ. In some societies, everyone is thought to meet the same fate. In others, people are believed to take different paths, depending on the events of their earthly lives. Sometimes a judgment determines the individual's final **destiny.**

destiny future or fate of an individual or thing

underworld land of the dead

Visions of Life After Death. Some cultures have associated the afterlife with a geographic location. The notion of an **underworld** beneath the world of the living is common. The peoples of ancient Mesopotamia†, for example, thought the dead lived on in a dusty, bleak underworld called the Dark Earth. Any pit, cave, or pond could be an entrance to that place. People on the islands of Melanesia in the southeastern Pacific Ocean imagine an underground world that is the mirror image of the upper world. Stories from the island of New Guinea describe an underworld that lies beneath the ocean. Divers have claimed to see the souls of the dead laboring in undersea gardens. In Navajo mythology, the dead descend into a watery underworld. According to the Ibo of Nigeria, the underworld is ruled by the goddess Ala, who receives the dead into her womb.

Other cultures have placed the afterlife in the sky or among the stars. The Pueblo Indians of the American Southwest believe that the dead become rain clouds. Some Native Americans of the Southeast say that the souls of the dead dwell either in the heavens or in the west.

The west has often been associated with the afterlife of the spirits. Polynesian islanders locate their ancestral island in the west and believe that spirits of the dead can return there. The Celtic† people pictured an otherworld that was sometimes underground or under the sea and sometimes an island in the west.

In most accounts, the Celtic otherworld was a magical place filled with enjoyable activities such as feasting and, for heroic warriors, fighting. Some descriptions, though, indicate that the land of the dead had a grim and dangerous side. Annwn, the king of the dead, could be fearsome. Less frightening was Valhalla of Norse† mythology, a vast palace where warriors slain in battle spent the afterlife

Cerberus, the many-headed watchdog of Greek mythology, greeted souls when they arrived in the underworld. He also attacked them if they tried to escape. His image was a popular one with medieval artists. This sculpture of Cerberus can be found on Notre Dame Cathedral in Paris, France.

19

feasting, singing, and indulging in playful combat. Their afterlife was not eternal, however. One day Valhalla and the world would be swept away in the gods' last battle. Not all warriors went to Valhalla. Freya, goddess of love and death, took half of them to her own palace in the afterworld.

In contrast to vivid, lively, and joyous visions of the world beyond, the afterlife pictured by the peoples of the ancient Near East was dim and shadowy. The early Jews called their dismal, ghostly underworld Sheol. The spirits who dwelled in the Mesopotamian underworld felt neither pain nor pleasure but lived a pale, washed-out version of life on earth, complete with a royal court ruled by Nergal and Ereshkigal, the king and queen of the dead. The Mesopotamian **epic** of *Gilgamesh* contains a description of the afterlife in which the hero's dead friend Enkidu returns as a spirit to describe existence in the "house of dust."

Different Fates. Peoples of the ancient Near East such as the Mesopotamians and the early Jews believed that the afterlife was the same for everyone. Other cultures, however, have expected the dead to be divided into different afterworlds. The Polynesians believe that the souls of common people, victims of black magic, and sinners are destroyed by fire. The souls of the upper classes, by contrast, journey to a spirit world where they live among their ancestors. Some ancient Chinese people believed that the afterlife was different for good and bad people. The souls of good people rose to the court of Tien, or heaven, while the souls of bad people descended into one of the 18 levels of hell, depending on their crimes in the world.

The Maya people of Central America believed that the souls of the dead went to an underworld known as Xibalba. To escape and go to heaven, the souls had to trick the underworld gods. Among the Aztecs of Mexico, slain warriors, merchants killed during a journey, and women who died in childbirth joined the sun in the heavens. The ordinary dead spent four years traveling through the nine layers of an underworld called Mictlan and then vanished on reaching the ninth level.

In Norse mythology, warriors went to heavenly palaces, while other individuals ended up in a cold underworld called Niflheim, or Hel. Among the Inuit or Eskimo people of Greenland, a happy land in the sky is the reward for the souls of people who have been generous or have suffered misfortunes in life. Others go to an underworld ruled by the goddess Sedna. The Pima and Papago peoples of the American Southwest say that the spirits of the departed travel to a place in the east where they will be free from hunger and thirst.

Some cultures hold the view that the souls of the dead face judgment: The good are rewarded in the afterlife, while the evil are punished. The ancient Egyptians, for example, believed that a soul had to convince the gods that he or she had committed no sins in life. The dead person's heart was placed on one side of a set of scales with a feather from the headdress of Maat, the goddess of judgment,

epic long poem about legendary or historical heroes, written in a grand style

The Rain God's Garden

The rain god Tlaloc held an important place in the mythology of the Aztecs and other agricultural peoples of Mexico and Central America. Like many Aztec deities, Tlaloc had both a cruel and a kindly side. The Aztecs believed he was responsible for the deaths of people who died by drowning or of certain diseases such as leprosy. Yet Tlaloc then sent these people to a happy afterlife that ordinary Aztecs did not share. Wall paintings in the ancient Mexican city of Teotihuacán show the garden paradise that welcomed the souls of Tlaloc's dead.

† See **Names and Places** at the end of this volume for further information.

on the other. If the two balanced, the soul was declared sinless. A monster devoured those who failed the test.

The Zoroastrians of ancient Persia† believed that the afterlife held a reward for the virtuous. Those who had lived a just life experienced a form of pure light that was the presence of Ahura Mazda, god of goodness, justice, and order. The ancient Greeks imagined the afterlife as a shadowy realm called the House of Hades, and they also spoke of a deeper pit of hell, Tartarus, to which those who had acted wrongly were sent to receive punishment. In Japanese mythology, the dead go to a land of darkness known as Yomi, where they may be punished for their misdeeds.

After about 200 B.C., the Jewish concept of Sheol gave way to a vision of judgment after death. The good entered the presence of God, while the wicked roasted in a hell called Gehenna. This influenced the Christian and Islamic ideas about hell as a state or place of punishment for evil. Heaven is the union of virtuous souls with God. According to the Roman Catholic Church, there is a state of being between heaven and hell called purgatory, in which tarnished souls are purified on the way to heaven.

The Journey to the Afterlife

Many cultures have regarded death as the beginning of the soul's journey to the afterworld. The Etruscans of ancient Italy pictured sea horses and dolphins carrying souls to Elysium, the Islands of the Blessed. The ancient Greeks undertook a darker journey, asking a boatman named Charon to ferry them across the river Styx, which marked the boundary between the world and Hades.

Many Pacific islanders viewed the journey as a leap. Every island had a *reinga,* or leaping place, from which the soul was thought to depart. For the Maoris of New Zealand, the place is the northernmost point of North Island. A sacred tree was often associated with the *reinga.* The Hawaiians believed that the souls of children lingered near the tree to give directions to the newly dead. Other Pacific peoples thought souls swam to the afterlife and that those weighted with sin would sink.

In some cultures, bridges linked the living world and the afterworld, and the crossing was not always easy. The Norse bridge shook if someone not yet dead tried to cross it before his or her time. The Zoroastrians had to cross a bridge the width of a hair. The just survived the crossing; the unjust fell into hell. Both the rainbow and the Milky Way were thought by various peoples to represent the bridge to the land of the gods or spirits.

The Fiji islanders of the Pacific spoke of a Spirit Path with many dangers, a journey so difficult that the only ones who could complete it were warriors who had died violently. A Native American myth of the far north says that the dead person's shadow must walk a trail that the person made during life. Along the way, the person's ghost tries to keep the shadow from reaching the heavenly afterlife.

The living sometimes attempted the journey to the afterworld in search of the secrets, wisdom, powers, or treasures associated with

Related Entries
Other entries related to the afterlife are listed at the end of this article.

cauldron large kettle

ritual ceremony that follows a set pattern

benevolent desiring good for others

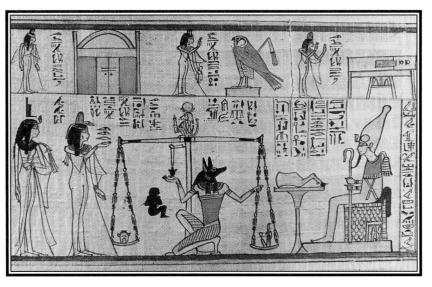

The Egyptians believed that when their souls entered the afterlife, they would be weighed against a feather belonging to Maat, the goddess of justice and truth.

the realm of spirits and of the dead. Welsh heroes entered the realm of Annwn, the king of the dead, to steal his magic **cauldron.** Greek legends tell of the journeys of Orpheus† and Odysseus† to the land of the dead. The Navajo believe that searching for the realm of the dead can bring death to the living.

Return of the Dead

In his play *Hamlet*, William Shakespeare called death "The undiscovered country from whose bourn [boundary]/No traveler returns." Yet myths and legends from around the world say that the dead do interact with the world of the living, one way or another.

In some cultures, the dead are thought to linger near the living as shades or spirits. Southeastern Native Americans believe that newly dead souls remain near their villages hoping to persuade others to join them. In some African myths, in contrast, the souls of the dead stay close to living relatives in order to help and advise them. To consult with their dead ancestors, Mayan rulers performed a bloodletting **ritual** known as the Serpent Vision ceremony.

The belief that the spirits of the dead can do good or ill in the world of the living lies behind some forms of ancestor worship. Ghosts of the dead, whether malicious, helpful, or merely sad, appear in the myths and folktales of many cultures. The Chinese perform ceremonies to honor the spirits of their ancestors and ensure that they will have **benevolent** feelings toward their descendants. Some Native Americans honor the ghosts of their dead with annual feasts. However, the Navajo—who avoid dwelling on death—never mention the dead in their rituals.

The dead sometimes return in another way as well: The soul may be reincarnated—reborn in another body. The notion of multiple rebirths through a series of lifetimes is basic to the Hindu and Buddhist religions. Those who act wrongly in life may be reborn as less fortunate people or as animals or insects. Cultures in some

†See **Names and Places** at the end of this volume for further information.

mummification preservation of a body by removing its organs and allowing it to dry

mortuary having to do with the burial of the dead

areas of Africa also believe that souls are reborn, perhaps after a period spent in the underworld.

Preparation for the Afterlife

In many cultures, rituals associated with death were meant to help the deceased in his or her journey to the afterlife. The Greeks, for example, provided the dead with coins to pay the ferryman Charon. Although the Romans were less certain about the afterlife than the Greeks, they often followed the same custom and sometimes added treats for the dead person to offer to Cerberus, the three-headed dog that guarded the entrance to the underworld. The Tibetan *Book of the Dead* gives instructions for the soul to follow on its journey between death and rebirth.

The ancient Egyptians believed that the body had to be preserved after death in order for the spirit to survive, and they went to great lengths to prepare for the afterlife. They built tombs to protect their dead. The most elaborate are the great monuments known as the pyramids. Within the tombs, they placed grave goods, such as food, furniture, and even servants, for the dead person to use in the next life. The Egyptians also developed an elaborate form of **mummification** to keep the body from decomposing after death. The full process could take as long as 200 days and was available only to the upper classes.

The Egyptians provided their dead with written instructions, including advice on how to survive the hazardous journey after death and guidebooks to the afterworld. The afterlife took many forms but was often pictured as a comfortable existence in a luxuriant realm of rivers, fields, and islands, although the royal dead were said to join the god Osiris† in the heavens. Texts inscribed on the walls of royal tombs included prayers, hymns, and magical spells to protect the dead from the dangers of the soul's journey. They were included in the most famous collection of Egyptian **mortuary** writings, the Book of the Dead, copies of which were often buried with the dead.

The Mesopotamians usually made no attempt to preserve the bodies of their dead or to bury them elaborately. One striking exception is a set of royal graves found in the ruins of the ancient city of Ur, in what is now Iraq. The graves contained not only rare and precious goods but also the bodies of servants, dancing girls, charioteers, and animals, all slain to serve the dead in the afterlife. The early Germanic peoples also buried grave goods with their chieftains. A burial mound at Sutton Hoo in England contained an entire ship along with a quantity of gold and silver items.

The grave goods of the Bushmen of Africa consist of the dead man's weapons. People preparing the body for burial coat it with fat and red powder and bend it into a curled sleeping position. Then they place it in a shallow grave facing in the direction of the rising sun. Other South African tribes follow a different practice: They break the bones of dead people before burial to prevent their ghosts from wandering. ***See also*** ALA; AVALON; BOOK OF THE

DEAD, THE; CERBERUS; ELYSIUM; ENUMA ELISH; GILGAMESH; HADES; HEAVEN; HEL; HELL; ORPHEUS; OSIRIS; REINCARNATION; SHEOL; STYX; UNDERWORLD; VALHALLA; VALKYRIES.

Agamemnon

hubris excessive pride or self-confidence

city-state independent state consisting of a city and its surrounding territory

The Price of Hubris

Greek myths reflect a view of life very different from that expressed by the earlier myths of Mesopotamia†. The Mesopotamians regretted the fact that humans could not live forever like the gods. Their mythical heroes sought eternal life even though the gods showed them that they were doomed to fail. By contrast, one of the basic ideas of Greek mythology is that all humans have a fate that cannot be escaped and limits that they should not try to exceed. The Greeks believed that individuals must face their fate with pride and dignity, gaining as much fame as possible. People—such as Agamemnon—who believed they could change fate by their own actions were guilty of hubris. They would eventually be punished by Nemesis, the vengeance of the gods.

seer one who can predict the future

According to Greek mythology, Agamemnon was the king of Mycenae, a kingdom of legendary Greece. The leader of the Greeks in the Trojan War†, he is one of the central figures in the *Iliad,* Homer's epic poem about the war. Greek writers generally portray Agamemnon as courageous but also as arrogant and overly proud, flaws that sometimes cause him misfortune and eventually lead to his death. The story of Agamemnon is often seen as a warning about the dangers of **hubris.**

Agamemnon's Background. Agamemnon was one of two sons of Atreus, the king of Mycenae. While Agamemnon was still a youth, Atreus was murdered by his brother. Agamemnon and his brother, Menelaus, fled to the **city-state** of Sparta, where they found refuge and protection from King Tyndareos. The king gave his daughters to the brothers as wives. One daughter, Clytemnestra, was already married, but Agamemnon killed her husband, Tantalus, and then married her. Menelaus took her beautiful sister Helen as his bride.

Agamemnon later returned to Mycenae, killed his uncle, and reclaimed the throne of his father. He and Clytemnestra eventually had three daughters—Chrysothemis, Electra, and Iphigenia—and a son, Orestes. Meanwhile, Menelaus became king of Sparta after the death of Tyndareos.

Some time later, Paris, the second son of King Priam of Troy, visited Menelaus in Sparta. The goddess Aphrodite† had promised Paris earlier that he would have the love of Helen, the most beautiful woman in the world. When Paris returned to Troy, he took Helen with him. At the time of Menelaus's marriage to Helen, all the rulers of the Greek city-states had promised to come to her defense if necessary. Menelaus reminded them of their promise, and they agreed to go to war against Troy to bring Helen back. Agamemnon was chosen to lead the Greeks in battle.

Agamemnon prepared a fleet of ships to carry the Greeks to Troy. Just before the ships were ready to sail, however, he insulted the goddess Artemis† by boasting that he was a better hunter than she and by killing a sacred stag. As punishment, Artemis caused the winds to die down so that the Greek fleet could not sail.

A **seer** told Agamemnon that he could please Artemis and gain favorable winds by sacrificing his daughter Iphigenia to the goddess. The king tricked Clytemnestra into sending Iphigenia to him by saying that she was to marry the great warrior Achilles†. When his daughter arrived, Agamemnon killed her. Although the sacrifice pleased Artemis and allowed the Greek ships to sail, it would later have terrible consequences for Agamemnon.

*†See **Names and Places** at the end of this volume for further information.*

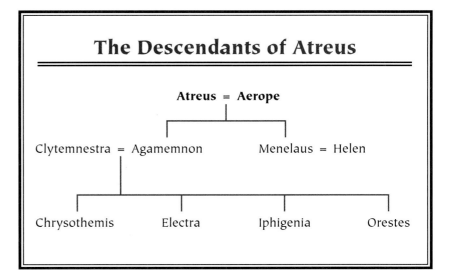

The Descendants of Atreus

Atreus = Aerope

Clytemnestra = Agamemnon   Menelaus = Helen

Chrysothemis   Electra   Iphigenia   Orestes

booty riches or property gained through conquest

The Trojan War. The Greeks fought the people of Troy for nine years and seized many of their cities. However, they failed to capture the city of Troy. This is the point at which the *Iliad* begins, and Agamemnon's arrogance and pride come into play again.

After winning a battle against the Trojans, Agamemnon received a female prisoner named Chryseis as part of his **booty.** The girl was the daughter of Chryses, a priest of the god Apollo†. Chryses begged for the return of his daughter, but Agamemnon refused. Angered, Apollo sent a plague to devastate the Greek forces.

The hero Achilles demanded that Chryseis be returned to her father. Agamemnon still refused. He finally agreed on the condition that he be given Briseis, a female slave of whom Achilles had grown very fond. Achilles became so angry that he laid down his arms and refused to fight any longer. This proved to be a costly mistake because without Achilles the Greeks began to lose badly.

Achilles returned to the battle only after learning of the death of his close friend Patroclus. When he rejoined the Greek forces, the tide of battle turned. The Greeks drove off the Trojans, killed the great Trojan warrior Hector, and went on to defeat the people of Troy and destroy their city. After the war, Agamemnon took the Trojan princess Cassandra back home as a prize. Homer's epic poem the *Odyssey* tells the story of Agamemnon's return to Mycenae.

The Death of Agamemnon. While Agamemnon was away fighting the Trojans, his wife, Clytemnestra, took a lover named Aegisthus. As Agamemnon sailed home from Troy, Clytemnestra was plotting to kill him in revenge for his sacrifice of their daughter Iphigenia.

In the meantime, Cassandra, who had the power to foretell the future, warned Agamemnon that his wife would kill him. However, the gods had put a curse on Cassandra: although she would make accurate predictions, no one would believe them. True to the curse, Agamemnon ignored Cassandra's warning.

When Agamemnon returned home, Clytemnestra welcomed him by preparing a bath in which he could purify himself. As the king stepped out of the bath, however, Clytemnestra wrapped him in a garment or a net that bound his arms so that he could not move. Aegisthus then stabbed Agamemnon to death while Clytemnestra killed Cassandra. It is also said that Clytemnestra herself slew Agamemnon with an ax. Agamemnon's son Orestes eventually avenged the murder by murdering both Clytemnestra and Aegisthus with the help of his sister Electra.

Agamemnon in Literature. Agamemnon is a favorite character in many works of literature besides the *Iliad* and the *Odyssey.* The ancient Greek playwrights Aeschylus, Euripides, and Sophocles wrote a number of plays based on the life of Agamemnon. He was also a popular subject of ancient Roman authors such as Ovid and Seneca. Later writers, including William Shakespeare and French playwright Jean Racine, included Agamemnon as a character in their works. In modern times, Agamemnon has served as a model for characters in works by poet T. S. Eliot and playwright Eugene O'Neill. ***See also*** ACHILLES; APHRODITE; APOLLO; CASSANDRA; CLYTEMNESTRA; ELECTRA; GREEK MYTHOLOGY; HECTOR; HELEN OF TROY; HOMER; ILIAD, THE; IPHIGENIA; MENELAUS; ODYSSEY, THE; ORESTES; PARIS.

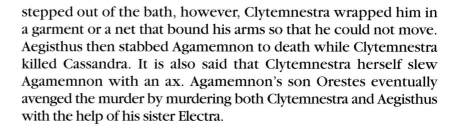

Agnes, St.

patron special guardian, protector, or supporter

martyr person who suffers or is put to death for a belief

pagan term used by early Christians to describe non-Christians and non-Christian beliefs

One of the most popular saints in the Catholic tradition, Agnes is the **patron** saint of virgins and engaged couples. According to early Christian writings, she was a beautiful young Roman girl who lived in the A.D. 300s and died a virgin **martyr** at age 13.

Stories say that a **pagan** Roman fell in love with Agnes and wanted to marry her, but she refused, telling him that she could love only Jesus Christ. At the time, Christians were being persecuted in Rome. Agnes's angry suitor reported her religious beliefs, and she was sent to a house of prostitution as punishment.

Agnes was stripped of her clothes, but God caused her hair to grow long to cover her naked body. He also sent angels to protect her against all who tried to touch her. The one man who dared to do so was killed by an angel. In another version of the story, the man was struck blind, but Agnes healed him.

Agnes was killed later during a period of harsh persecution. She is often depicted in works of art with a lamb, because her name resembles *agnus,* the Latin word for lamb. Each year on January 21, her feast day, two white lambs are blessed in the Church of Santa Agnese in Rome. Wool from these lambs is woven into a garment called a pallium, worn by archbishops of the church.

Ahriman

chaos great disorder or confusion

Ahriman was the god of evil and darkness in Persian mythology and in Zoroastrianism, a religion that attracted a large following in Persia around 600 B.C. Often called Druj ("the Lie"), Ahriman was the force behind anger, greed, envy, and other negative and harmful emotions. He also brought **chaos,** death, disease, and other ills into the world. In the Islamic religion, he is identified with Iblis, the devil.

Originally, Ahriman was the Persian god Angra Mainyu, a destructive spirit whose twin brother, Spenta Mainyu, was a **benevolent** spirit. Humans and gods alike had to choose which spirit to serve. As the Zoroastrian religion developed, Angra Mainyu became Ahriman, and Spenta Mainyu turned into Ahura Mazda, the "Wise Lord." The history of the world was seen as a struggle between these two forces. Ahura Mazda had the backing of the *yazatas* (angels), while Ahriman created a host of demons called *daevas* to spread his evil influence by appealing to the envy, greed, and desire for power of human beings.

In the **dualistic** beliefs of early Zoroastrianism, good and evil fought for control of the world—Ahura Mazda from the heavens and Ahriman from the **underworld.** The two forces were evenly matched, and each in turn gained supremacy. Ahura Mazda represented fire, sunlight, and life. Ahriman was the lord of darkness and death. Zoroastrians later came to view Ahura Mazda as the supreme ruler who would one day achieve final victory over Ahriman. ***See also*** AHURA MAZDA; ANGELS; DEVILS AND DEMONS; PERSIAN MYTHOLOGY.

benevolent desiring good for others

dualistic consisting of two equal and opposing forces
underworld land of the dead

Ahura Mazda

deity god or goddess
patron special guardian, protector, or supporter

Ahura Mazda, whose name means "wise lord," was the most important god in ancient Persian mythology. When the religion known as Zoroastrianism became widespread in Persia around 600 B.C., Ahura Mazda became its supreme **deity.** The Persians considered him to be the creator of earth, the heavens, and humankind, as well as the source of all goodness and happiness on earth. He was known to later Zoroastrians as Ohrmazd.

Ahura Mazda appears in Persian art and texts as a bearded man wearing a robe covered with stars. Dwelling high in heaven, he had the sun for an eye. In the Zoroastrian religion, Ahura Mazda was associated with light and fire, the emblems of truth, goodness, and wisdom. He created six divine beings, or angels, to help him spread goodness and govern the universe. One of the most important angels was Ahsa Vahishta ("Excellent Order" or "Truth"), the **patron** of fire and spirit of justice. Vohu Manah ("Good Mind") was a symbol of love and sacred wisdom who welcomed souls to paradise.

The early Zoroastrians had a dualistic system of belief in which two opposing and equal forces—good and evil—battled for control of the world. Ahura Mazda (originally called Spenta Mainyu) represented light, truth, and goodness. His great

Ancient Persians associated the god Ahura Mazda with royalty, as well as with light and fire. Darius I believed that Ahura Mazda had made him king. In this stone relief, the god gives a crown to the Persian king Ardechir I.

enemy was his twin brother, Angra Mainyu (also known as Ahriman), the god of darkness, anger, and death. Later Zoroastrians considered Ahura Mazda to be the more powerful force, who would ultimately triumph over the evil Ahriman. **See also AHRIMAN; ANGELS; PERSIAN MYTHOLOGY.**

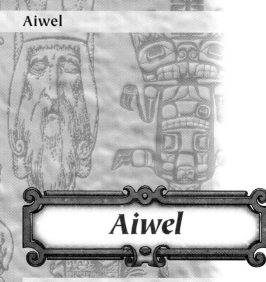

Aiwel

hereditary passed on from parent to child

In African mythology, Aiwel was the founder of a **hereditary** priesthood known as the spear masters among the Dinka people of the Sudan. He was the son of a human mother and a water spirit. While still a child, Aiwel lost his mother and went to live with his water-spirit father in a river. When he grew up, he returned to his village with a multicolored ox named Longar. From then on, the man was known as Aiwel Longar.

There was a drought and many cattle died. Aiwel told the people of the village to follow him to a promised land where they would find plentiful water and grass. The people did not believe him at first and refused to leave the village. Later they changed their minds and tried to follow. Angry, Aiwel killed some of them with his spear as they crossed a river to join him. Eventually, he allowed the people to come across. He gave fishing spears to the first group to cross, and these people became founding members of the spear-master clans. To others who came later, Aiwel gave war spears, and they founded the warrior clans. **See also AFRICAN MYTHOLOGY.**

Ajax

epic long poem about legendary or historical heroes, written in a grand style

Ajax (also known as Aias) was one of the greatest of the Greek heroes who fought in the Trojan War†. He was the son of Telamon, the king of Salamis and a friend of Hercules†. Before the birth of Ajax, Hercules prayed to Zeus† and asked him to give Telamon a brave son. Ajax was named after an eagle *(aietos)* that Telamon had seen before his birth.

According to Homer's **epic** the *Iliad†*, only Achilles† was a greater warrior than Ajax. Of great size and stature, Ajax supposedly looked like a tower when he went into battle holding his shield. He was courageous and good-hearted but spoke very slowly and preferred to let others talk while he fought.

Ajax competed with other Greek warriors to win the hand in marriage of Helen†, one of the most beautiful women of the time. Helen finally married Menelaus, the king of Sparta. Yet Ajax and the other former suitors promised to help defend the marriage.

The Trojan War. While Menelaus was away from home, Prince Paris of Troy persuaded Helen to accompany him to Troy. The Greeks vowed to rescue her, and Ajax contributed 12 ships and many men to the Greek army sent to battle the Trojans.

Ajax proved to be an outstanding warrior during the war that followed. When Achilles left the battle because of a dispute, Ajax fought Hector, the Trojans' champion. During their duel, Hector

†*See **Names and Places** at the end of this volume for further information.*

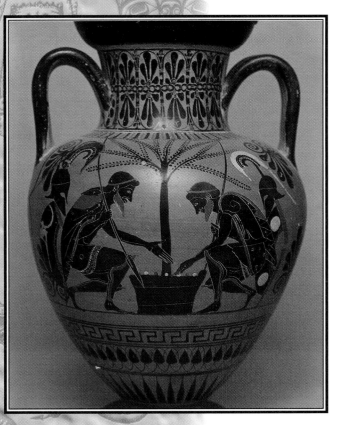

As a warrior, Ajax was second only to Achilles, and the two men were close friends. A painting on a Greek jar shows Ajax and Achilles playing dice, perhaps during a lull between battles.

threw his lance at Ajax, but it struck the belts that held Ajax's shield and sword and bounced off harmlessly. Ajax then picked up a huge stone that no other warrior could lift and hurled it at Hector, striking him in the neck and knocking him to the ground. After the battle, the two heroes exchanged gifts to show their respect for each other. Hector gave Ajax a sword, and Ajax presented Hector with a purple sword belt.

Ajax was one of the Greeks sent to convince the great warrior Achilles to return to the battle. Despite their efforts, Achilles refused to fight, and the Trojan army forced the Greeks to retreat to their ships. During the battle that followed, Ajax fought bravely and saved the life of the Greek hero Menestheus.

When the Trojans attacked the Greek ships, Ajax led the defense by using a huge pole to fight off the enemy. His enormous size made him a target for many Trojan lances and arrows. Ajax was unable to save the fleet by himself, but the Trojan attack was turned back by the timely arrival of additional Greek troops led by Achilles' close friend Patroclus. Hector killed Patroclus and took his armor. Ajax covered the naked corpse with his shield. At the funeral games held in honor of Patroclus, Ajax competed in a number of events, including a wrestling contest with Odysseus that ended in a tie.

The Death of Ajax. Achilles was killed by Paris, and Ajax brought the great champion's body back to the Greek camp and rescued his armor while Odysseus† fought off the Trojans. The armor led to a dispute between Ajax and Odysseus. Both heroes felt entitled to it. To settle the matter, the Greeks decided to take a vote, and they awarded the armor to Odysseus.

Enraged by this decision, Ajax planned an assault on the Greek troops that night. However, Athena, the goddess of wisdom, drove Ajax temporarily insane, and he attacked a flock of sheep instead. After recovering his senses, he was so ashamed that he killed himself with the sword Hector had given him.

According to tradition, a hyacinth flower grew where Ajax's blood fell on the ground. On its petals could be traced the letters *AI*—the first letters of his Greek name and a word in Greek that means "alas." A statue and temple were built in Salamis to honor Ajax, and a festival called the Aianteia was celebrated in his honor each year. According to later Greek mythology, after his death, Ajax went to the island of Leuce with his close friend Achilles. ***See also*** ACHILLES; HECTOR; HELEN OF TROY; HERCULES; HOMER; ILIAD, THE; MENELAUS; ODYSSEUS; PARIS.

Ajax the Lesser

A second Ajax also fought for the Greeks in the Trojan War. He was a small man known as Ajax the Lesser. Despite his size, this Ajax fought bravely and was known for his skill with a spear and his swiftness.

After the Greek victory over the Trojans, Ajax the Lesser dragged Cassandra, the daughter of King Priam of Troy, away from the temple of the goddess Athena and assaulted her. As punishment, Athena caused Ajax and his fleet to be shipwrecked on their voyage home from the war. The sea god Poseidon rescued him, but then when Ajax boasted that he had escaped death against the will of the gods, Poseidon became angry and drowned him.

Ala

underworld land of the dead

deity god or goddess

Ala is a goddess of the Ibo, African people of eastern Nigeria. The daughter of the great god Chuku, she is the mother goddess of the earth, ruler of the **underworld,** guardian of the harvest, and goddess of fertility for both people and animals.

According to Ibo beliefs, Ala makes a child grow within its mother's womb. She remains near and watches over the child as the child grows into an adult. Later when the individual dies, Ala receives him or her into her womb, known as the pocket of Ala. The goddess is also a lawgiver who shows people how to live a good life. Her laws emphasize moral values such as honesty.

Throughout the Ibo region, Ala is worshiped in large square houses with open sides. These structures, called Mbari, contain life-sized mud figures of the goddess painted in bright colors. Usually, Ala is surrounded by sculptures representing other **deities,** animals, and humans.

According to Ibo tradition, Ala sends a sign such as a snake or a bee's nest to tell her priests where to build a Mbari. Groups of men and women work together to assemble and decorate the structure. Construction can take years and is considered a sacred act. However, once built, the Mbari houses are left alone to decay. For this reason, new houses must continually be produced, which ensures that the Mbari tradition will be carried on by younger members of the group. *See also* AFRICAN MYTHOLOGY.

Aladdin

supernatural related to forces beyond the normal world; magical or miraculous
genie spirit that serves the person who summons it
sorcerer magician or wizard

sultan ruler of a Persian or an Arabic state

Aladdin, a character from the folktales of Persia†, appears in the collection of stories known as the *Thousand and One Nights (or the Arabian Nights).* Legends from Europe to China often contained characters like Aladdin—ordinary people who came into possession of magical devices and through them acquired wealth and power. Aladdin's magical tools were a ring and a lamp that controlled **supernatural** beings known as **genies.**

Aladdin was the lazy, irresponsible son of a poor tailor. A **sorcerer** tricked him into entering a treasure-filled cave to seize a magical lamp and gave him a ring that would protect against evil. Aladdin found the lamp, but he refused to give it to the sorcerer until he was outside the cave. The sorcerer blocked the entry to the cave, imprisoning Aladdin within.

Through a series of accidents, Aladdin discovered that rubbing the ring brought forth powerful genies, who released him from the cave. He also discovered he could summon the spirits by rubbing the lamp. The genies offered to fulfill Aladdin's every wish. He asked for and received a magnificent palace and the hand of the **sultan's** daughter in marriage.

The sorcerer, meanwhile, was determined to gain control of the magic lamp. He tricked Aladdin's wife into exchanging the lamp for a new one and then commanded the genie of the lamp to move Aladdin's palace to Africa. In time, Aladdin and his wife defeated the sorcerer and recovered the lamp. Then they had to prevent the sorcerer's wicked younger brother from seizing it. After

†See **Names and Places** at the end of this volume for further information.

various adventures, the couple returned home, where Aladdin became sultan and lived a long and happy life. *See also* GENIES; PERSIAN MYTHOLOGY; THOUSAND AND ONE NIGHTS.

Alcestis

underworld land of the dead

In Greek mythology, Alcestis was the beautiful daughter of Pelias, the king of Iolcus in Thessaly. Pelias promised his daughter in marriage to any man who came to get her in a chariot pulled by a lion and a boar. Admetus, the king of Pherae in Thessaly, performed this feat—with the help of the god Apollo†. In punishment for angering Zeus†, Apollo had been sent to work as a shepherd for Admetus. Because the king had treated him well, Apollo agreed to help him win Alcestis.

When Admetus was near death, Apollo asked the Fates to save his life. They agreed, as long as someone else would volunteer to die in his place. Everyone refused but Alcestis, who offered to sacrifice herself to save her husband. Some stories say that Persephone, goddess of the **underworld,** intervened and allowed Alcestis to live because she admired the woman's devotion to Admetus. Other tales relate that the hero Hercules†, a guest at Admetus's palace, wrestled with Death when it came to take Alcestis. He won, forcing Death to let her live. *See also* APOLLO; FATES; HERCULES; PERSEPHONE; ZEUS.

Alfred

King Alfred the Great is an example of a historical figure who, with the passage of time, became a figure of legend. From A.D. 871 until 899, Alfred ruled the Anglo-Saxon kingdom of Wessex in southwestern England. His achievements won the admiration and affection of his subjects during his reign. Long afterward, English people told tales about his victories and his wisdom.

Alfred's main political achievement was to defend Wessex against the invading armies of the Danes. One of the legends that arose from this campaign involved his powers of concentration. At one point, Alfred was on the run, fleeing his enemy, and took refuge in a cottage. The woman of the house asked the disguised monarch to watch some cakes that were baking in her oven while she stepped out. However, Alfred was so deep in thought that he allowed the cakes to burn.

Alfred is credited with leaving a lasting mark on the English countryside. To celebrate his victory over the Danes, he had the shapes of white horses cut into the chalk hills of Wessex, where they remain to this day.

Amaterasu

imperial relating to an emperor or empire

Amaterasu, goddess of the sun and of fertility, is one of the most important figures in Japanese mythology and in the religion known as Shinto. According to legend, she is the first ancestor of the **imperial** family of Japan.

Daughter of the creator god Izanagi, Amaterasu taught humans to plant rice and weave cloth. In one story, her brother, Susano-ô,

This print by Taiso Yoshitoshi shows Amaterasu, the Japanese sun goddess, emerging from a heavenly cave and bringing light back to the world. Amaterasu's shrine at Ise is regarded as one of Japan's most important Shinto shrines.

taboo prohibition against doing something that is believed to cause harm
deity god or goddess

angered the goddess by interfering with her activities. He destroyed rice fields and violated **taboos,** spreading filth in her sacred buildings and dropping a skinned horse through the roof of the weavers' hall. Furious at Susano-ô's actions, Amaterasu went into a cave and locked the entrance. Her withdrawal plunged the earth into darkness and prevented the rice from growing.

To lure the sun goddess out, the other gods gathered outside the cave with various sacred objects, including a mirror and some jewels. A young goddess began dancing, causing the others to burst into laughter. Wondering how they could make merry in her absence, Amaterasu peeked out to see what was amusing them. The gods spoke of another **deity** more brilliant than Amaterasu. Curious, the goddess looked—and saw her reflection in the mirror. The image of her own brilliance so astonished her that she stepped out of the cave. One of the gods hung a rope across the cave to prevent her from returning to it and depriving the world of her light. Today a mirror in Amaterasu's shrine at Ise is considered one of Japan's three imperial treasures, along with jewels and a sword. *See also* IZANAGI AND IZANAMI; JAPANESE MYTHOLOGY; SUSANO-Ô.

Amazons

In Greek mythology, the Amazons were a nation of fierce female warriors, descendants of Ares, the god of war. The Amazons were usually pictured fighting on horseback with bows and arrows, spears, and axes and carrying a crescent-shaped shield.

Scholars disagree on the meaning of the name *Amazon.* Some say that it means "breastless." This comes from the belief among the Greeks that the Amazons cut off the right breast of each girl so that she could handle a bow and arrow more easily. Other scholars believe that the name may mean "without grain" (or bread) and may have come from the Greek word for barley, *maza.* They reason that the Amazons, as hunters, ate only meat and did not make bread.

Origins. The legendary Amazons, an all-female society, lived in southern Russia or northern Asia Minor†. From time to time, the women had relations with men from surrounding tribes and bore children. The Amazons kept and raised only the girls, killing or making slaves of the male children or sending them to their fathers.

The legend of the Amazons may have come from the possibility that women in some ancient societies took part in battle. In many

†*See **Names and Places** at the end of this volume for further information.*

In this painting from the 400s B.C., two Amazons attack a male soldier. A warlike tribe of women, the Amazons were thought to be descendants of Ares, the Greek god of war.

cases, these were **matriarchal** societies, in which a family's name and property passed down through the mother's side of the family. To the Greeks, with their **patriarchal** society, this practice seemed unnatural and barbaric. They therefore created stories about fierce, man-hating women. In many Greek tales, the Amazons are defeated and killed by male warriors as punishment for taking a role considered appropriate only for men.

matriarchal describing a society in which women hold the dominant positions
patriarchal describing a society in which men hold the dominant positions

Amazon Legends. The Amazons appeared frequently in Greek myth and legend. One of the 12 labors of Hercules† was to capture the belt of the Amazon queen Hippolyta. When Hercules reached the land of the Amazons, Hippolyta received him warmly and agreed to give him her belt. But Hera, queen of the gods, convinced the rest of the Amazons that Hercules was kidnapping Hippolyta, and they took up arms and attacked him. Believing the queen had tricked him, Hercules killed her before sailing back to Greece with the belt.

In another Greek tale, the hero Theseus† attacked the Amazons and carried off their queen. The Amazons responded by going to war against Athens, but Theseus defeated them after a terrific struggle.

During the Trojan War†, the Amazon queen Penthesilea brought extra troops to help the Trojans after the death of the warrior Hector†. For this, the Greek hero Achilles† killed her and then fell in love with her corpse. The Amazons also appear in works by the Greek writers Herodotus and Apollodorus.

The legend of the Amazons lived on long after the time of the ancient Greeks and Romans. In the 1500s, the Spanish explorer Francisco de Orellana claimed to have met a tribe of female warriors while exploring the Marañon River in South America. He supposedly renamed the river the Amazon in their honor. To this day, aggressive women are often referred to as Amazons. *See also* ACHILLES; AENEID, THE; HERA; HERCULES; ILIAD, THE; THESEUS.

The Slavic Amazons

Powerful female warriors also appeared in the folktales of Slavic peoples from southeastern Europe. Led by the warrior Vlasta, these women lived in a castle by the Vltava River. They were aggressive not only in their battles with men but also in their pursuit of them. In one story, Šarka, one of these women, fought the Slavic hero Dobrynia. She grabbed him by his hair, pulled him off his horse, and put him in her pocket. She released him only after he promised to marry her. In most of the stories, the female warriors ended up either dead or married to a hero.

Ambrosia

immortal able to live forever
deity god or goddess

In Greek mythology, ambrosia was a honey-flavored food eaten by the gods that allowed them to remain **immortal.** With the ambrosia, they often drank a honey-flavored drink called nectar. According to legend, each day doves brought ambrosia to Zeus, the king of the gods, to distribute among the other **deities.**

Humans who ate ambrosia grew faster, stronger, and more beautiful, all qualities that were considered divine. Eating ambrosia also made humans immortal. In one Greek myth, a son of Zeus named Tantalus was punished for crimes that included stealing ambrosia from heaven and giving it to humans.

anoint to bless by applying oil or some other substance

cosmic large or universal in scale; having to do with the universe

immortal able to live forever

The gods used ambrosia in another way, applying it to their bodies and hair. The ancient Greeks gave the name to an oil used for **anointing** corpses, which they believed kept the bodies from decaying. In Homer's *Iliad*†, the god Apollo† anoints the body of the dead Trojan hero Sarpedon with ambrosia before handing it over for burial. *See also* APOLLO; GREEK MYTHOLOGY; TANTALUS; ZEUS.

American Indian Mythology

See *Native American Mythology.*

Amma

Amma is the supreme god in the mythology of the Dogon people of Mali in West Africa. Amma created a "**cosmic** egg," which was the source of the universe. The egg vibrated and then opened to reveal a creator spirit. The spirit fell to earth, followed by a female twin and four more pairs of creator spirits. These spirits made the sky and world, the seasons, day and night, and human society.

In another version of this myth, Amma made the stars, the sun, and the moon. Then he became lonely and mated with the earth. This union produced divine twins called the Nummo—one male, one female—who represented water and light. The twins were born with the power of speech, which they gave to the earth. Next, Amma created man and woman. They had four more pairs of twins, who were the ancestors of the Dogon people. *See also* AFRICAN MYTHOLOGY; NUMMO; STARS; SUN.

Amphitryon

In Greek mythology, the hero Amphitryon was the son of King Alcaeus of Tiryns and the grandson of Perseus†. Alcaeus's brother Electryon, the king of Mycenae, asked Amphitryon to take over his kingdom when he went to battle the Taphians, who had killed his eight sons. Before leaving, Electryon promised his daughter Alcmene to Amphitryon as a bride.

When Electryon returned from war, Amphitryon accidentally killed him while throwing a club at some cattle. Forced to flee, the hero went with Alcmene to Thebes, where King Creon cleared him of guilt for the killing. However, Alcmene refused to become Amphitryon's wife until he avenged the death of her eight brothers. Creon agreed to help if Amphitryon would rid Thebes of the Teumessian fox, a beast sent by the gods.

After overcoming the fox, Amphitryon set out with an army to battle the Taphians. The Taphian king had golden hair that made him **immortal** and his city unconquerable. But when his daughter, Comaetho, saw Amphitryon, she fell in love with him and cut her father's golden hair. The king immediately died. The city fell to Amphitryon, who then killed Comaetho for betraying her father and her city.

†*See **Names and Places** at the end of this volume for further information.*

While Amphitryon was away, the god Zeus† disguised himself as the hero and visited Alcmene. Believing Zeus to be Amphitryon, Alcmene slept with him and became pregnant. Amphitryon returned home the next day and learned from the blind **prophet** Tiresias that Alcmene had slept with Zeus and would give birth to a great hero. That night Amphitryon slept with Alcmene, and she became pregnant by him as well. Alcmene later gave birth to twins. One twin—Iphicles, the son of Amphitryon—was a mortal. The other was Hercules†, the son of Zeus. *See also* GREEK MYTHOLOGY; HERCULES; PERSEUS; ZEUS.

prophet one who claims to have received divine messages or insights

Amun

pantheon all the gods of a particular culture
deity god or goddess
cult group bound together by devotion to a particular person, belief, or god

pharaoh ruler of ancient Egypt

For much of the history of ancient Egypt, Amun was honored as the supreme god in the Egyptian **pantheon.** However, he was originally a local **deity** in Hermopolis, a city in southern Egypt, with power over the air or wind. By 2000 B.C. Amun's **cult** had reached the capital of Thebes, and rulers began to honor him as the national god of Egypt. However, after invaders known as the Hyksos conquered northern Egypt in the 1700s B.C., only people in the south continued to worship Amun.

The Egyptians drove out the Hyksos in the 1500s B.C., and Amun's influence expanded rapidly. So did the size and splendor of his temples. Two of the largest temples of ancient Egypt, located at Luxor and Karnak, were devoted to the worship of Amun, and his cult controlled great wealth.

At first Amun was only one of many deities worshiped by the Egyptians. As he became more important, he was combined with the sun god Ra to form a new deity called Amun-Ra. Egyptians honored Amun-Ra as king of the gods and creator of the universe. They also believed him to be the father of the **pharaohs,** a deity who would help these rulers triumph in battle.

Amun usually appears in Egyptian art as a bearded man with a headdress containing two ostrich feathers, a broad necklace, and a close-fitting garment. In one hand, he has an ankh, the Egyptian symbol of life, and in the other, he holds a scepter, a symbol of authority. He is often portrayed sitting on a throne like a pharaoh. As Amun-Ra, the god is sometimes shown with the head of a hawk topped by a golden disk representing the sun, which is encircled by a serpent.

The cult of Amun-Ra remained strong throughout Egypt until almost the time of Jesus. The ancient Greeks associated Amun-Ra with Zeus, their own supreme god. *See also* EGYPTIAN MYTHOLOGY; RA (RE); ZEUS.

This painting of Amun, one of the creator gods in Egyptian mythology, decorates a tomb in Luxor, Egypt. Amun often appears as a human figure with a ram's head.

Anansi

Anansi, the spider, is one of the most popular animal tricksters from West African mythology. Tricksters are mischievous figures who often oppose the will of the gods, resulting in some kind of misfortune for humans. Like many trickster figures, the wily Anansi can change his appearance to look like a human, a rabbit, a fox, or other animals.

West Africans originally considered Anansi to be the creator of the world. He often acted as a go-between for humans in their dealings with the sky god Nyame, and he supposedly persuaded Nyame to give both rain and the night to people. In most stories, however, Anansi is a crafty and cunning trickster who makes life more enjoyable for himself (or more difficult for others) by fooling humans, other animals, and even the gods themselves, often using his cleverness and knowledge of his victims' ways of thinking to trick them and achieve his purpose.

In one well-known tale, Anansi asks God for an ear of corn and promises to repay with 100 servants. He takes the corn to a village and tells the people that it is sacred. During the night, Anansi feeds the corn to chickens. The next morning, he accuses the villagers of stealing the corn, and they give him a bushel of it to make up for the lost ear.

Anansi next meets a man on the road and exchanges the corn for a chicken. He visits another village and tells the people that the chicken is sacred. That night he kills the chicken, and the next morning the frightened villagers give him ten sheep to replace it. Anansi later exchanges the sheep for a corpse, which he takes to a third village and tells the people that it is the sleeping son of God. When the villagers cannot wake the corpse the next morning, Anansi says they have killed God's son. The terrified villagers offer him 100 of their finest young men, and Anansi takes them to God to fulfill his part of the bargain.

There are many other tales about Anansi. Some of them were brought to the West Indies, South America, and North America by African slaves in earlier centuries. In some parts of North America, Anansi became known as Aunt Nancy or Miss Nancy in African American folklore. *See also* AFRICAN MYTHOLOGY; NYAME; TRICKSTERS.

Anat

deity god or goddess

underworld land of the dead

Anat was one of the chief **deities** of the Canaanites, a people of Syria and Palestine in the ancient Near East. A goddess of love, fertility, and war, she was the sister and wife of the god Baal†. Although best known as a warrior goddess, Anat was also worshiped as the queen of heaven and as a mother goddess. In art, she often appears as a young woman wearing a helmet and armed with a shield, battle ax, and spear.

Canaanite myths show Anat as a fierce and pitiless warrior who destroyed Baal's enemies. According to one tale, Baal was taken to the **underworld** and killed by Mot, the god of death. Furious, Anat descended to the underworld and killed Mot, ripped his body

† *See **Names and Places** at the end of this volume for further information.*

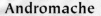

apart, and scattered the pieces over the earth. Her efforts restored Baal to life, and they emerged together from the underworld.

Anat became a favorite goddess of the Egyptian **pharaoh** Ramses II because of her warlike nature and her role as a protector in battle. Various ancient cultures worshiped similar goddesses, including the Semitic Astarte, the Sumerian Inanna, and the Babylonian Ishtar. Anat's counterpart in Greek mythology was Athena†. ***See also*** Athena; Baal; Ishtar.

pharaoh ruler of ancient Egypt

Androcles

According to legend, Androcles was a Roman slave who lived in Africa in the first century A.D. After escaping from his cruel master, Androcles hid in a cave. While there, a lion with a thorn stuck in its paw entered the cave. The lion showed its swollen paw to Androcles, who carefully removed the thorn and befriended the animal.

Some years later, Androcles was captured and thrown into an arena to be killed by lions. One of the lions, however, was the same animal that Androcles had helped in the cave. The lion recognized Androcles and refused to hurt him. The animal even protected Androcles from the other wild beasts. When the spectators in the arena saw what was happening, they demanded that Androcles be set free.

The legend of Androcles appeared in *Noctes Atticae* (Attic Nights), a story by Roman author Aulus Gellius written around A.D. 150. Much later, the legend became the inspiration for the play *Androcles and the Lion,* written by Irish author George Bernard Shaw in 1912. ***See also*** Animals in Mythology.

Andromache

epic long poem about legendary or historical heroes, written in a grand style

Andromache was the wife of Hector, the son of King Priam of Troy and the greatest of the Trojan warriors. In the *Iliad,* the **epic** of the Trojan War† by the Greek poet Homer, Andromache is shown as a devoted wife and mother as well as a symbol of the tragic suffering that war causes innocent people.

During the war, Hector is killed by the Greek hero Achilles†. When Troy finally falls, the Greeks kill Andromache's infant son by throwing him from the walls of the city. Andromache is taken captive by Neoptolemus, the son of Achilles, who makes her his wife. Together they have three sons—Molossus, Pielus, and Pergamus. Neoptolemus later takes a second wife, Hermione, who becomes very jealous of Andromache.

Neoptolemus is murdered, and Andromache marries Hector's brother Helenus, who rules a kingdom in the land of Epirus. After Helenus's death, Andromache returns with her son Pergamus to an area near Troy, where she eventually dies.

The suffering of Andromache provided inspiration for generations of writers, artists, and musicians. Her troubles with Hermione were the subject of plays by the ancient Greek writer Euripides† and the French playwright Racine, who lived in the 1600s. ***See also*** Achilles; Hector; Homer; Iliad, The; Trojan War.

Andromeda

nymph minor goddess of nature, usually represented as young and beautiful

oracle priest or priestess or other creature through whom a god is believed to speak; also the location (such as a shrine) where such words are spoken

Gorgon one of three ugly monsters who had snakes for hair, staring eyes, and huge wings

In Greek mythology, Andromeda was the beautiful daughter of King Cepheus and Queen Cassiopea of Joppa, a kingdom often called Ethiopia by ancient writers. Cassiopea once boasted that Andromeda was more beautiful than the Nereids, a group of sea **nymphs.** Offended by this boast, the Nereids complained to the sea god Poseidon, who punished Joppa by sending a flood and a sea monster to ravage the land.

An **oracle** of Zeus† told Cepheus that the only way to save his kingdom was to chain Andromeda to a rock at the foot of a cliff and let the sea monster devour her. Cepheus did so, and Andromeda awaited her fate. While passing by, the hero Perseus† saw the chained Andromeda and fell in love with her. He asked Cepheus for her hand in marriage, and Cepheus agreed as long as Perseus would slay the sea monster.

As it happened, Perseus had just killed the **Gorgon** named Medusa and had her snake-entwined head in a bag. He showed the head to the sea monster, which immediately turned to stone. Unknown to Perseus, Cepheus had already promised Andromeda to her uncle Phineus. At the marriage feast for Perseus and Andromeda, Phineus showed up with a group of armed supporters and demanded that Andromeda be given to him. However, Perseus once again used the head of Medusa and turned Phineus and his men to stone.

Perseus and Andromeda remained together for the rest of their lives, and they had six children. According to the Greek historian Herodotus, the kings of Persia were descended from their first son, Perses. When Andromeda and Perseus died, the goddess Athena† placed them in the sky as constellations, along with Andromeda's parents and the sea monster. *See also* ATHENA; CASSIOPEA; GORGONS; GREEK MYTHOLOGY; MEDUSA; NYMPHS; PERSEUS; POSEIDON; ZEUS.

Angels

destiny future or fate of an individual or thing

In many of the world's religions, angels are spiritual beings who act as intermediaries between God and humans. Messengers of God, angels may serve any of a number of purposes. Their role may be to teach, command, or inform individuals of their **destiny.** Angels may also act to protect or help people.

The word *angel* comes from the Greek word *angelos,* meaning "messenger." In Western religions, the word specifically describes a kind, or benevolent, being. However, in most other religions, the line separating "good" angels from "bad" angels is not always clear. An angel may act benevolently in one situation but with evil intent in another.

Differing Views

Over the centuries, people have described the function of angels in various ways. The role of angels is developed in greatest detail in religions based on revelation—the disclosure or communication of

†*See **Names and Places** at the end of this volume for further information.*

Through the centuries, artists' representations of angels have emphasized the perfection of their spiritual natures. Here an angel is portrayed as a beautiful young woman with a halo and wings.

cosmos the universe, especially as an orderly and harmonious system

divine truth or divine will to human beings. These religions include Judaism, Christianity, and Islam, as well as Zoroastrianism, a faith founded by the ancient Persian prophet Zoroaster.

In religions based on revelation, God and humans are distant from each other. Angels help bridge the gap. Angels praise God, carry out God's will, and reveal divine word. They may also help people attain salvation or receive special favors. Furthermore, acting for God, angels may influence human affairs through such deeds as rewarding faithful believers, punishing people who do evil, and helping people in need.

Angels tend to play a lesser role in religions with many gods. The gods themselves may carry out angelic functions, often taking human forms. In religions based on the belief that all the **cosmos** is sacred and that the divine and the human share one essence, angels are less important. They are not needed to bridge a gap between the gods and humankind. However, even in these religions angel-like spiritual beings may help people relate to the divine.

The Nature of Angels. The world's religions have had different views about the nature of angels. Some regard angels as divine beings who deserve to be worshiped rather than just as messengers of God. Disagreement also exists about the bodies of angels. Some think that angels have actual physical bodies. Others insist that angels only appear to have such bodies. Still others believe that angels are purely spiritual beings but that they can assume material bodies.

Zoroastrianism and Judaism. The view of angels in Judaism was influenced by Zoroastrianism. Zoroastrian mythology describes a cosmic clash between Ahura Mazda and Ahriman—forces of good and evil with their armies of angels and devils. Like Ahura Mazda, the Old Testament god Yahweh has an army of angels. These warrior angels battle against evil forces led by Satan, who resembles Ahriman.

Following the Zoroastrian view, Judaism divides the universe into three parts: earth, heaven, and hell. Earth is the home of humans. Heaven is reserved for God and his angels. Hell is the dark world of Satan and his followers. Angels fulfill a similar role in the two religions, linking heaven with the world of humans and revealing God's plans and laws. Their function is to serve God and carry out his will. They reward goodness and punish wickedness and injustice. They also help people understand God's will, and they take the souls of righteous individuals to heaven.

Christianity. The Christian concept of a three-part universe came from Judaic and Zoroastrian ideas, as did Christian ideas of angels and their functions. In the Christian view, angels are God's messengers. Angels proclaimed the birth of Christ and continue to play an active role in the daily lives of Christians. They bring strength to those who are weak and comfort to those who suffer and carry the prayers of faithful Christians to God. According to legend, guardian angels watch over children.

Islam. The Islamic idea of angels is similar to Judaic and Christian views. God is in heaven, and the angels serve him and carry out his will. However, while Judaism and Christianity generally divide spiritual beings into those who are with or against God, Islam divides such beings into angels, demons, and djinni, or genies. The djinni may be either good or harmful. According to Islamic folklore, they were created out of fire, can be visible or invisible, and can assume various human or animal shapes.

Hierarchies of Angels

Angels in different orders, or levels, were a part of the mythology of ancient Mesopotamia. Later in the A.D. 400s, the Greek philosopher Dionysius the Areopagite described a **hierarchy** of angels. Based on his writings, angels are traditionally ranked in nine orders. The highest order of angels is the seraphim, followed by the cherubim, thrones, dominions (or dominations), virtues, powers, principalities, archangels, and angels.

According to this system, the first circle of angels—the seraphim, cherubim, and thrones—devote their time to contemplating God. The second circle—the dominions, virtues, and powers—govern the universe. The third circle—principalities, archangels, and angels—carry out the orders of the superior angels.

Representation of Angels

At first, artists struggled with the problem of how to represent angels. Written descriptions were not very helpful. They tended to be vague or bizarre or did not draw a clear distinction between angels and human beings.

Artists tried various approaches before arriving at the image of a young male figure. Later they added two feathery wings to the figure. The wings suggested that angels were spiritual beings elevated above humans and associated with heaven. Besides wings, angels were sometimes shown with halos, long hair, and flowing white robes.

The idea of representing spirits as winged figures dates back many thousands of years. The ancient Egyptians portrayed the sun god Horus as a winged disk. Other winged beings can be found in ancient Greek and Roman art.

Over time, artists came to depict the different orders of angels in distinct ways. For instance, seraphim sometimes were shown

hierarchy organization of a group into higher and lower levels

Fallen Angels

Fallen angels were angels who had once been close to God but "fell" to a lower position. They tried to interfere with the relationship between human beings and God by encouraging individuals to sin. Fallen angels were also believed to cause such disasters as famine, disease, war, and earthquakes.

In Christian belief, the leader of the fallen angels was Satan. He led a rebellion against God, for which he and the other fallen angels were cast into hell.

with six wings and holding shields. Around the seraphim, flames burned to symbolize their devotion to God. Artists often portrayed the dominions bearing swords and spears, symbolizing God's power. *See also* AHRIMAN; AHURA MAZDA; PERSIAN MYTHOLOGY; SEMITIC MYTHOLOGY.

Animals in Mythology

trickster mischievous figure appearing in various forms in the folktales and mythology of many different peoples
mediator go-between
shaman person thought to possess spiritual and healing powers
dualistic consisting of two equal and opposing forces

underworld land of the dead

Since the beginning of human history, people have lived in close contact with animals—usually as hunters and farmers—and have developed myths and legends about them. All kinds of creatures, from fierce leopards to tiny spiders, play important roles in mythology. A myth can give special meaning or extraordinary qualities to common animals such as frogs and bears. However, other creatures found in myths—many-headed monsters, dragons, and unicorns—never existed in the real world.

Animals may serve as stand-ins for humans or human characteristics, as in the African and Native American **trickster** tales or the fables of the Greek storyteller Aesop. In some legends, animals perform heroic deeds or act as **mediators** between heaven and earth. They may also be the source of the wisdom and power of a **shaman.**

Animals often have a **dualistic** quality in mythology. They can be helpful to humans or harmful—sometimes both. They provide people with food, but at the same time, they can be dangerous. As sources and symbols, animals represent the mystery and power of the natural world, which can create or destroy.

Animals and People

Many myths explore relationships between humans and animals. People may talk with animals, fight them, or even marry them. Sometimes animals perform services for humans, such as guiding them through the **underworld** or helping them complete tasks. One large group of myths involving animals concerns transformations, or changes, between the human and animal states. Other myths focus on the close connection between people and animals.

Transformation. A princess kisses an enchanted frog, and he becomes a handsome prince with whom, the fairy tale tells us, she will live "happily ever after." Such transformations—in which people turn into animals or animals turn into people—take place in stories from around the world. Transformation myths are about crossing the boundaries that set humans apart from the rest of the world.

Native American mythologies describe a time in the past when the boundaries between people and animals were less sharply drawn and beings changed form (known as shape shifting) freely. Bears were especially close to humans, and in some Native American stories, bears appear as humans wearing coats made of bearskins. The Tsimshian people of the northwestern coast of the United States tell about Asdiwal, a young man who follows a white

41

Totem Poles and Animal Ancestors

The Native Americans of the north-western United States and Canada believe that each clan or kinship group is descended from a particular animal, such as a whale, wolf, or bear. This animal has become the group's totem, a powerful symbol of its identity. People display their identity and status with totem poles—tall standing logs carved with images of mythical animals. Totem poles mark the approaches to villages and the burial sites of chieftains and stand at the entrance of each clan house.

sorcerer magician or wizard

supernatural related to forces beyond the normal world; magical or miraculous

ritual ceremony that follows a set pattern

bear up a mountain to the sky. He discovers that the beast is actually a beautiful woman dressed in a bear skin, and he marries her.

The ancient Greeks and Romans believed that the gods could blur the boundaries between different classes of beings. Ovid's *Metamorphoses* is a collection of Greek and Roman legends about mortals whom the gods turned into animals and plants. Both Chinese and Slavic mythologies include tales of people who, under some evil force, turn into werewolves.

The Scots have stories about silkies—imaginary sea creatures resembling seals that take on human form, marry men and women, and then return to the sea. In fact, the theme of animal wives or husbands comes up over and over again in mythology. Native Americans tell of girls marrying bears and men marrying deer. Eskimo and Chinese tales mention beautiful, seductive women who turn out to be foxes in disguise. In one Eskimo story, a woman enters the home of a hunter while he is out. She cooks for him and stays for some time, but eventually she puts on her fox skin and disappears. The well-known fable of Beauty and the Beast is a modern version of the myth of the animal husband whose beastly form cannot disguise his noble soul.

Sometimes transformations are forced on people by cruel or wicked **sorcerers** or as punishment for offending the gods. When people voluntarily seek transformation, however, the change can be a sign of power. In many societies, individuals called shamans were thought to have **supernatural** abilities, including the power to communicate with animals or to transform themselves into animals. South American shamans were said to be able to change themselves into jaguars.

Connections. Myths, legends, and folktales often highlight the close links between people and animals. West Africans and Native Americans, for example, believe that each person has a magical or spiritual connection to a particular animal that can act as a guardian, a source of wisdom, or an inspiration. Among the Plains Indians of North America, individuals had to discover their spirit animal through a mystical experience called a vision quest. Some Native American religions in Central America include *nagualism,* the idea that each person's life is linked to an animal or object called a *nagual.* If the *nagual* is hurt or killed, the person suffers or dies. One myth says that the *naguals* fought on the side of the Native Americans against the invading Spanish centuries ago. Traditional African religions had secret societies in which men believed they took on a leopard's strength by performing **rituals** that involved wearing leopard skins.

In many societies, people believed that shamans had animal helpers who guided them through the supernatural realm. This idea is similar to the common image of a witch's "familiar"—an animal, usually a black cat, that gives the witch certain powers. Animals offer helpful advice to ordinary people in many legends. Generally, those who ignore the animal's advice will fail to achieve their goal.

Sometimes a family, a clan, or a whole society feels a special attachment to a certain kind of animal, usually one that they consider to be an ancestor or protector. This connection, called totemism, defines social groups and their behavior. Hunters are sometimes forbidden to kill their group's totem animal, for example. Among the Native Americans of the Pacific Northwest, the beaver, the eagle, the raven, and the killer whale are all associated with particular clans.

Many cultures have legends of human children raised by animals. The Romans claimed that a wolf mother had fed Romulus and Remus, their legendary ancestors. The story of Tarzan, raised by African apes, is a modern version of this ancient myth.

Roles in Myth and Legend

Animals fill a wide variety of roles in myths and legends. Many stories explain the part that animals played in creating the world or in bringing fire, tools, or farming skills to humans. Animal stories also tell how things came to be the way they are or how animals acquired their appearance or characteristics. A story of the Seneca Indians, for example, says that the chipmunk's stripes were originally bear scratches. In addition, animals may play tricks, symbolize human qualities, and terrorize humans.

Gods, Creators, and Heroes. In some mythological traditions, the gods take on animal form. The ancient Egyptians portrayed their gods as animals or as humans with the heads of animals; Bastet was a cat goddess and Horus a hawk god. Although supernatural animals such as Pegasus, the winged horse of Greek mythology, were not gods themselves, they were often created, given power, or protected by the gods.

Some myths associate animals with the creation of the world. Asian and Native North American traditions place the earth on the back of an enormous turtle. Myths of Africa and elsewhere tell that the earth was formed from or supported by the body of a huge serpent. Some legends say that the earth's features, such as lakes or canyons, were carved by the digging of mythic beasts.

Animals are linked to human origins as well as to the origin of the world. Many Native American clans believed they were descended from animals, and the Yao people of southern China traced their origins to a dog ancestor. Animals also helped shape human existence by acting as messengers to the gods. An African myth tells that the gods sent two animals to earth, one

This wood carving of a frog was made by the Tsimshian people of the northwestern coast of North America. Many stories from Native American mythology give animals important roles and extraordinary qualities.

43

deity god or goddess

chaos great disorder or confusion

with a message of eternal life, one bringing death. The messenger of death arrived first, and that is why people die. The Pima Indians of North America say that a rattlesnake brought death into the world.

Animals can play a positive role as well, bringing people the gifts of civilization. Various African myths, for example, tell of a dog, chimpanzee, wasp, and praying mantis bringing fire to people. The Bambara people of Mali believe that a sacred antelope taught people to farm long ago. Zuni and Navajo myths show animals behaving heroically on behalf of people. In Chinese legends, monkeys perform brave deeds, while in Mayan myth, they possess artistic talent, particularly in writing and sculpture.

Symbols. Animals sometimes appear in myths and legends as symbols of certain characteristics they are believed to represent. Common phrases such as "sly as a fox" or "brave as a lion" are everyday examples of the practice of using animals to represent human qualities. The dog often appears as a symbol of loyalty in myths and legends, and the tiger stands for power and vitality. In Celtic mythology, the boar symbolized war, and its image was carved on helmets and coins. Many cultures have stories in which animal characters representing human qualities present moral lessons.

Animals can also be symbols of the **deities.** Because people traditionally saw owls as wise, Athena, the Greek goddess of wisdom, was often shown with an owl. Dolphins might indicate the presence of the sea god Poseidon (Neptune).

Tricksters. Many myths feature animal tricksters, mischievous and unpredictable beings who use deceit, magic, or cleverness to fool others. Although some tricksters are just playing pranks, others act in harmful ways. Occasionally, the tricksters themselves wind up being tricked or trapped. Their limited magical powers may echo the greater powers of the gods.

In Native American mythology, the best-known trickster is Coyote, who can take on human form. One of his favorite tricks involves masquerading as a hunter in order to sleep with the hunter's wife. Many African legends feature a trickster spider, tortoise, or hare that uses cunning to outwit larger or more powerful animals. African slaves brought tales of the trickster hare to America, where it eventually became known as Brer Rabbit.

Monsters. From the great sea beast called Leviathan in the Bible to the mutant lizard Godzilla of modern science fiction movies, monstrous animals appear in many kinds of myths. Monsters represent our darkest fears: **chaos** and uncontrollable destruction. A monster is more than just a large or fierce animal. It is something abnormal, something that breaks the laws of society.

An animal may be monstrous simply because of abnormal size. The most dreadful monsters, however, do not correspond to anything known in the real world. Often they are hybrids, mixtures of different species—another breaking of natural boundaries. Dragons,

Some important animal characters in world mythology were imaginary combinations of other animals. For example, dragons such as the ones seen here were made up of features from horses, snakes, and birds.

for example, are usually visualized as a snake or reptile with bat's wings and sometimes with a head resembling that of a horse. In some traditions, dragons have multiple heads or can change shape.

Other hybrid creatures include the griffin, a combination of eagle and lion, and the Plumed Serpent, Quetzalcoatl, a god of the Maya, Toltecs, and Aztecs that is part bird and part snake. In addition, the pygmies of Central Africa tell stories about encounters with a living dinosaur, a beast the size of an elephant, with a long neck and brownish-gray skin.

Some hybrids are blends of human and animal. The centaur is half man, half horse; the echidna is a snake woman; the manticore is part human, part lion, part dragon; and the satyr is a manlike being with the lower body of a goat. In mythology, hybrid creatures often have a dualistic nature.

Common Animals in Mythology

Certain animals appear frequently in the myths and legends of different cultures, often with different meanings. Snakes or serpents, for example, can be helpful or harmful. The Romans regarded snake spirits as protection for their homes. The Hopi Indians, who live in a dry part of the American Southwest, have stories about a water snake that is associated with springs. Because the snake sheds its skin as it grows, some cultures have seen it as a symbol of rebirth and have associated it with healing.

However, in the Bible, the snake is a treacherous creature that introduces Adam and Eve to sin. A Japanese myth tells of a huge snake with eight heads that holds a princess prisoner. Snakes and snakelike dragons play a similar evil guardian role in many other tales.

The bull is another animal with a dualistic nature that appears in many myths. It can represent either tremendous energy and power or frightening strength. In Celtic mythology, the bull was a

Related Entries
Other entries related to animals in mythology are listed at the end of this article.

sign of good fortune and fertility. In several Greek legends, bulls were associated with death and destruction. At different times, the hero Theseus† killed both a wild bull that was destroying farmers' fields and the minotaur, a dangerous half-man, half-bull monster. Among Native Americans who traditionally lived by hunting buffalo, myths describe the buffalo's fertility and generosity. The buffalo controls love affairs and determines how many children a woman will bear.

Dogs almost always appear in a positive light. Native American stories generally portray the dog as the symbol of friendship and loyalty. In Greek and Roman mythology, dogs often acted as guardians; the three-headed dog Cerberus, for example, guarded the entrance to the underworld. Many cultures associated dogs with death as well as with protection. Both the ancient Egyptians and the Aztecs of Mexico believed that dogs guided the dead on their journey through the afterlife. Occasionally, dogs appear in negative roles, such as the hellhound Gram in Norse mythology or the fighting dogs belonging to the Greek goddess Hecate.

The goat is another dualistic animal. Male goats are negatively linked with dangerous or uncontrolled sexual lust, while female goats appear as mother figures. In Greek mythology, Zeus† was nursed as a baby by a she-goat. Goat images in mythology are often associated with sexuality and fertility.

Foxes in mythology are usually quick, cunning, and sneaky. In Asia, the fox represented sexual seductiveness. Japanese legends tell of fox spirits called *kitsune* that can turn themselves into people and have the powers of deceitful witches. In yet another example of the dualistic nature of animals, however, Japanese mythology also portrays the fox as the messenger of Inari, the god of rice. The ancient Romans regarded foxes as fire demons, perhaps because of their reddish coats, and in Christian mythology, the fox is associated with the devil.

The frog appears in many transformation stories, most likely because it goes through a transformation of its own, from tadpole to frog. Another animal that undergoes a physical transformation is the butterfly, which begins life as a caterpillar, rests in a cocoon, and emerges as a butterfly to spread its wings. The Greek word for butterfly, *psyche,* is also the word for soul, and in Greek mythology the butterfly was the symbol of the soul's transformation after the death of the body. ***See also*** ANANSI; BASILISK; BIRDS IN MYTHOLOGY; BRER RABBIT; CENTAURS; CERBERUS; DRAGONS; GEORGE, ST.; GORGONS; GRIFFINS; HYDRA; LEVIATHAN; LOCH NESS MONSTER; MANTICORE; METAMORPHOSES, THE; MINOTAUR; MONSTERS; NEMEAN LION; PEGASUS; SACRIFICE; SATYRS; SERPENTS AND SNAKES; TRICKSTERS; UNICORN; WEREWOLVES; WITCHES AND WIZARDS.

The Battle of Ireland's Bulls

To the Celtic people, bulls stood for strength and power. Irish mythology tells of two famous beasts, the White-Horned Bull of Connacht and the Brown Bull of Ulster. The rulers of Connacht and Ulster each boasted of the size of their bulls. However, some said that the gods had sent the bulls to Ireland to cause trouble. Eventually, the two bulls met in a fierce battle that raged across all of Ireland. The Brown Bull won but then died. The death of the two magical bulls brought peace between Connacht and Ulster.

Antaeus

In Greek mythology, Antaeus was a giant who lived in Libya and forced anyone who traveled through the country to wrestle with him. He was the son of Poseidon, god of the sea, and of Gaia, goddess of the earth. Because Gaia was his mother, Antaeus became

†*See **Names and Places** at the end of this volume for further information.*

stronger each time he touched the earth. As a result, he defeated and killed all who wrestled him, and he used their skulls to make a roof for a temple to Poseidon.

One of the labors of the Greek hero Hercules† took him through Libya. Antaeus challenged Hercules to wrestle. At first, Hercules, despite his great strength, could not defeat Antaeus. Then realizing that Antaeus got his strength from the ground, Hercules lifted him off his feet so that he could not touch the earth. Slowly, Antaeus's strength drained away, and Hercules eventually squeezed him to death. ***See also* GAIA; HERCULES; POSEIDON.**

Anthony of Padua, St.

heretic person whose beliefs are contrary to church doctrine

St. Anthony of Padua was a Franciscan monk and a popular preacher in Italy in the 1200s. Born in Portugal, Anthony left his homeland after deciding to become a missionary. He spent a brief time in Morocco, but illness forced him to return to Europe. Settling in Italy, he became a follower of St. Francis of Assisi.

Anthony was noted for his skill as a preacher, for his profound knowledge of the Bible, and for the many stories of miracles that grew up around him. In one such legend, a group of **heretics** refused to pay attention to him when he was preaching, so he went to the water and spoke to the fishes. The fishes held their heads out of the water and listened closely, which turned the heretics into believers.

Anthony is the patron saint of Portugal as well as of the Italian city of Padua, where he is buried. He is traditionally called on for help in locating lost property.

Antigone

oracle priest or priestess or other creature through whom a god is believed to speak; also the location (such as a shrine) where such words are spoken

In Greek mythology, Antigone was the daughter of Oedipus, king of Thebes, and Jocasta. A faithful daughter and sister, Antigone was the main character in a tragedy by the Greek playwright Sophocles†. Euripides†, another dramatist of ancient Greece, presented a different, and happier, version of her life. In more recent times, Antigone has been the inspiration for several playwrights and composers.

Background to the Story. In Sophocles' earlier play, *Oedipus Rex,* Oedipus had unknowingly murdered his father and married his mother, Jocasta. When they discovered what they had done, Jocasta hanged herself and Oedipus blinded himself. His sons, Eteocles and Polynices, drove Oedipus from Thebes and took over the kingdom.

Antigone and her sister Ismene accompanied their blind father during his wanderings around Greece. Meanwhile, Eteocles broke his promise to share power with Polynices and drove him from the kingdom as well. Polynices decided to lead an army against Thebes to regain the throne.

Their uncle, Creon, supported Eteocles in the conflict with his brother. An **oracle** told Creon that whoever gave shelter to Oedipus would win the battle for Thebes. Creon therefore asked Oedipus,

prophet one who claims to have received divine messages or insights

who had taken refuge in the city of Colonus, to return. When Oedipus refused, Creon sent soldiers to seize Antigone and Ismene to force their father to come back. Theseus†, king of Athens, rescued Antigone and Ismene, but soon afterward, Oedipus died and his daughters returned to Thebes.

The Story of Antigone. Polynices attacked Thebes, and in the battle that followed, the two brothers met in combat and killed each other. Creon became king. He gave Eteocles a hero's burial but refused to let anyone bury Polynices, whom he considered a traitor. Antigone, mindful of her duty to her brother, secretly crept out at night to bury Polynices. She was caught by Creon's soldiers and condemned to death for her disobedience. To avoid direct responsibility for her death, Creon ordered that Antigone be sealed alive in a cave with food and water. Creon's son Haemon, who was engaged to Antigone, pleaded in vain for her life.

A **prophet** then came to see Creon. He warned that the king had angered the gods by sealing up Antigone and refusing burial to Polynices. Creon immediately ordered that Polynices be buried and went to the cave to release Antigone. On opening the cave, however, he found that Antigone had hanged herself. Haemon was overcome with grief. He tried to kill his father and then stabbed himself to death. When Creon's wife, Eurydice, learned of her son's suicide, she took her own life.

Euripides' version of the story has a happier ending. In his play, Creon instructed Haemon to carry out Antigone's sentence. Haemon pretended to seal Antigone away as ordered but actually took her to the countryside. The couple stayed in hiding for many years, raising a son. After the son grew up, he went to Thebes to take part in an athletic event. There he stripped off his clothes to run in a race and revealed a birthmark that was found only on members of Antigone's family. Creon recognized the mark and sentenced Haemon and Antigone to death for disobeying his orders. The god Dionysus (Bacchus)† pleaded with Creon to spare their lives (in some versions of the story, Hercules† is the one who pleaded for them). Creon agreed, and the lovers were formally married.

Sophocles used the story of Antigone to comment on the conflict between the laws of the state and the laws of the gods. Creon's decree against burying Polynices is shown to be unjust and against the gods' wishes. Antigone's decision to perform her religious duty to her brother wins the sympathy of the audience.

Literature and Art. Sophocles and Euripides were the first of many to create works of art based on the story of Antigone. Among those who wrote plays about her were the European playwrights Jean Cocteau, Jean Anouilh, and Bertholt Brecht. An Italian translation of the Greek play was the basis for an opera of the 1700s called *Antigono*. More recently, German composer Carl Orff wrote a "tragic play with music" about Antigone in the 1940s. ***See also*** EURYDICE; GREEK MYTHOLOGY; JOCASTA; OEDIPUS.

† See **Names and Places** at the end of this volume for further information.

Anu

pantheon all the gods of a particular culture

destiny future or fate of an individual or thing

Anu, the god of the sky in many cultures of the ancient Near East, was the creator god in the Near Eastern **pantheon.** He was father of the gods as well as of demons and evil spirits. He led a trio of gods that included Enlil, god of the sea, and Ea, god of storms or war. According to one tradition, he was married to Uras, the earth goddess. Sumerian† mythology said he was the husband of Nintu; the Babylonians† gave him Antu for a wife.

The Babylonians revered Anu as the ancestor of kings, the main creative force in the universe, and the ruler of **destiny.** The Sumerian equivalent of Anu, known as An, dates back to at least 3000 B.C. Despite his importance, Anu plays only a small part in Near Eastern mythology and is rarely pictured in works of art. Sometimes he appears as a bull or as a man with bull's horns, which suggests that he was at one time a god of herders. *See also* DEVILS AND DEMONS; ENLIL; PERSIAN MYTHOLOGY; SEMITIC MYTHOLOGY.

Anubis

underworld land of the dead

embalm to treat a corpse with oils or chemicals to prevent or slow down the process of decay
jackal small, doglike mammal native to Asia and Africa

In the early days of ancient Egypt, Anubis (or Anpu) was the god of the dead. Later, when Osiris took over this role, Anubis became the god who oversaw funerals. He was also the guardian of the **underworld,** where he escorted the dead to the hall of judgment and helped weigh each person's heart against the feather of truth before presenting the soul to Osiris.

Anubis was the son of the goddess Nephthys, who had tricked her brother Osiris into fathering her child. The goddess's husband, Set (Seth), hated Osiris and planned to murder the child when he was born. Nephthys therefore decided to abandon the infant at birth. She hid him in the marshes by the Nile River, where he was found by Isis, the wife of Osiris. Isis raised Anubis, and when he reached adulthood, he repaid her by becoming her protector.

Later, when Osiris set out to conquer the world, Anubis accompanied him. Osiris was murdered by his old enemy Set, who tore his body to pieces. Anubis helped find the pieces of Osiris's body and **embalmed** the body so well that it never decayed. Anubis is said to have performed the first Egyptian burial rites and to have introduced the practice of embalming the dead.

Images of Anubis depict him as a **jackal** or as a man with the head of a jackal. Jackals prowled Egyptian cemeteries at night, looking for food and even eating corpses. The Egyptians believed that Anubis, in the form of a jackal, would keep jackals away and protect the dead. The Greeks and the Romans also worshiped Anubis, whose name is actually the Greek form of the Egyptian name *Anpu. See also* EGYPTIAN MYTHOLOGY; ISIS; OSIRIS; SET.

Aphrodite

The Greek goddess Aphrodite, one of the 12 Olympian **deities,** was associated with love, beauty, and fertility. Myths about Aphrodite probably originated in West Asia and reached Greece by way of the island of Cyprus. The Romans later incorporated her into their **pantheon** and renamed her Venus.

Aphrodite

deity god or goddess
pantheon all the gods of a particular culture
Titan one of a family of giants who ruled the earth until overthrown by the Greek gods of Olympus

underworld land of the dead

Major Myths. According to one account, Aphrodite was born when the **Titan** Cronus cut off the sex organs of his father, Uranus, and threw them into the sea. Aphrodite emerged from the foam (her name comes from *aphros,* the Greek word for foam) that gathered on the surface of the water. Some sources say that she washed ashore in Cyprus, an important center of her worship.

Aphrodite's connection with love is reflected in the numerous stories about her romantic affairs. She was married to Hephaestus (Vulcan), the lame god of metalworking. However, her frequent relationships and the children she had with various other gods—including Ares†, Hermes†, Poseidon†, and Dionysus†—angered her husband. After learning about Aphrodite's love for Ares, Hephaestus created a fine metal mesh to catch the lovers in bed. When the indignant husband called the other gods to see the guilty pair, most of them laughed with him. Among Aphrodite's many children were Deimos (terror) and Phobos (fear), fathered by Ares, and Eryx, the son of Poseidon.

The handsome youth Adonis was another of Aphrodite's great loves. Persephone, the goddess of the **underworld,** also developed a passion for Adonis, leading to a bitter dispute between the two goddesses. Zeus† resolved the conflict by instructing the youth to divide his time between them.

Aphrodite's role as the goddess of beauty was one of the factors that led to the outbreak of the Trojan War†. Zeus forced the Trojan prince Paris to decide which of three goddesses—Hera†, Athena†, or Aphrodite—was the fairest. Each goddess tried to bribe Paris with generous gifts, but he found Aphrodite's offer to give him the most beautiful woman in the world the best. Paris declared Aphrodite the fairest of the goddesses, and she kept her promise by helping him gain the love of Helen, the wife of King Menelaus of Sparta. Paris took Helen to Troy with him, and the Greeks' attempts to reclaim her resulted in the Trojan War.

Aphrodite continued to influence events during the ten years of the war. At various stages during the conflict, she assisted the Trojan soldiers, particularly Paris. Meanwhile, Hera and Athena—still offended by Paris's choice of Aphrodite as the fairest—came to the aid of the Greeks. Aphrodite was also closely linked with the Trojan cause through her son, the brave leader Aeneas. His birth resulted from Aphrodite's love for the Trojan Anchises.

Depictions in Literature and Art. Aphrodite appears in the works of many ancient writers. The legend of her birth is recounted in Hesiod's† *Theogony.* Aphrodite and her son Aeneas are central to the action of Virgil's† epic poem, the *Aeneid.* Euripides† included the story of the judgment of Paris in his play *The Trojan Women,* and Homer† described her role in the Trojan War in the *Iliad.*

Aphrodite was also the subject of the most famous work by the Greek sculptor Praxiteles, who completed the *Aphrodite of Cnidos* in about 350 B.C. Although this statue is now lost, it is known through the many copies made of it during Roman times. Aphrodite has also been portrayed as the Roman goddess Venus in

†*See **Names and Places** at the end of this volume for further information.*

works such as *Venus de Milo* from around 200 B.C. and *The Birth of Venus,* painted by Italian artist Sandro Botticelli about 1482. ***See also*** ADONIS; AENEAS; AENEID, THE; ARES; CRONUS; GREEK MYTHOLOGY; PARIS; TROJAN WAR; VENUS; VULCAN.

Apollo

Titan one of a family of giants who ruled the earth until overthrown by the Greek gods of Olympus

prophecy foretelling of what is to come; also something that is predicted

oracle priest or priestess or other creature through whom a god is believed to speak; also the location (such as a shrine) where such words are spoken

cult group bound together by devotion to a particular person, belief, or god

The Sacred Laurel

One of Apollo's tragic loves was Daphne, daughter of the river god Peneus. Apollo fell in love with Daphne, but she did not return his affection. When Apollo chased her through the woods, she became so frightened that she cried out for her father to save her. Peneus turned Daphne into a laurel tree so that she could avoid Apollo's advances. The disappointed Apollo broke off a branch of laurel. He twisted it into a wreath to wear on his head in memory of Daphne. Thereafter, the laurel tree became sacred to the cult of Apollo, and a laurel wreath became a mark of honor to be given to poets, victors, and winners in athletic contests.

The most widely worshiped of the Greek gods, Apollo was the son of Zeus† and the **Titan** Leto and the twin brother of Artemis (Diana), the goddess of the hunt. Apollo had many roles in Greek mythology, including god of the sun, god of the arts (especially music, poetry, and dance), god of medicine, protector of herdsmen and their flocks, and god of **prophecy.** His **oracle** at Delphi was the most famous in the world, and his **cult** spread far beyond the Greek world.

Origins. The worship of Apollo began outside of Greece. Early cults associated with the god developed in Asia Minor† and in the lands north of Greece. Several tales link him to the city of Troy†. One credits him with helping the sea god Poseidon build the walls of Troy.

Scholars think that Apollo's original role may have been as protector of herdsmen and shepherds. He is often pictured holding a lyre (a type of harp), and shepherds were known for playing music to pass their idle hours. Apollo's identification as god of music, archery, and medicine came after his oracle was established at Delphi. Only much later did he become the sun god.

According to legend, Apollo was born on the Greek island of Delos and grew to adulthood in just four days. To escape the island, he changed himself into a dolphin and caused a great storm on the sea. Apollo then threw himself on the deck of a ship in distress and led it safely to shore. Having reached the mainland, Apollo set off for Pytho, the site of an important oracle of Gaia, the earth goddess. A monstrous serpent named Python not only guarded the place but also spoke the oracle's prophecies. Apollo killed Python and took the oracle for himself. The name of the site was changed to Delphi because Apollo had become a dolphin (*delphis* in Greek) in order to reach it.

The Cult of Apollo. Delphi became the most famous and frequently visited oracle in the ancient world. Its location was considered to be the geographic center of the earth.

The oracle's words were inspired by Apollo and delivered by a local woman, over the age of 50, who was called the Pythia in honor of Python. As she spoke, priests interpreted the prophecies and wrote them down. The priests of Apollo claimed to be descended from the sailors aboard the ship that Apollo had led to safety in the storm.

The worship of Apollo was widespread not only in Greece but also throughout the ancient world. Shrines could be found in places from Egypt to Anatolia (now northwestern Turkey). The Romans built their first temple to Apollo (Phoebus) in 432 B.C.,

The Apollo Belvedere, believed to be the work of the sculptor Leochares, is one of the best-known images of the Greek god of the sun. The patron of youth and male beauty, Apollo was often represented as a handsome young man.

and he became a favorite Roman god. The Roman emperor Augustus was a devoted worshiper because the battle of Actium, in which he gained political supremacy, was fought near a temple of Apollo.

The Loves of Apollo. Apollo was considered the ideal of male beauty, and he had many love affairs and fathered many children. Yet there are numerous stories of his failure to win a woman he desired or of his lovers being unfaithful to him.

One of the most famous concerns Cassandra, daughter of King Priam of Troy. Apollo fell in love with her and gave her the gift of prophecy to win her favor. When she rejected him anyway, Apollo punished her by declaring that her prophecies would be accurate but that no one would believe her. In another story, he courted the **nymph** Sinope, who asked him to grant her a favor before she accepted his proposal. When Apollo agreed, she asked to remain a virgin until her death. Perhaps the most famous tale of Apollo's unfulfilled love involved his pursuit of Daphne, who turned into a laurel tree to escape his advances.

Some of Apollo's romantic misfortunes involved animals that became associated with him. One myth explains how the crow's feathers turned from white to black. Apollo asked the crow to watch over the princess Coronis, who was pregnant with his son. Nevertheless the crow failed to prevent Coronis from having an affair with another man. Angry at the crow, Apollo turned its feathers from white to black. He then asked his sister Diana to kill Coronis. When Coronis lay burning on the funeral **pyre**, Apollo pulled his unborn son Asclepius from her body. The boy later became the god of healing. Apollo was also associated with the wolf, the dolphin, the raven, the serpent, and other animals.

Literature and Art. Like many important figures in myth and legend, Apollo is a favorite subject of art and literature. He first appears in Greek literature in the *Iliad,* Homer's† **epic** about the Trojan War†. In the poem, Apollo is Troy's most consistent and enthusiastic champion against the Greeks. The *Iliad* opens with Apollo's anger against Agamemnon†, who had taken the daughter of a Trojan priest of Apollo captive. Despite the priest's pleas and offers of ransom, Agamemnon refuses to return the girl. As punishment, Apollo sends a plague on the Greek army. After the events described in the *Iliad,* Apollo kills the great Greek hero Achilles† by guiding the flight of an arrow shot by the Trojan warrior Paris.

nymph minor goddess of nature, usually represented as young and beautiful

pyre pile of wood on which a dead body is burned in a funeral ceremony

epic long poem about legendary or historical heroes, written in a grand style

†*See **Names and Places** at the end of this volume for further information.*

Ancient sculptures show Apollo as a handsome youth. One of the most famous is the *Apollo Belvedere,* a marble version of an ancient bronze statue found in Rome. The great German artist Albrecht Dürer used the proportions of the statue for his "ideal male" figure. Apollo is typically portrayed holding a bow and arrow, symbols of his role as the god of death and disease, or a harp, representing his role as god of music and the arts or of shepherds. Apollo is featured in poetry by Percy Bysshe Shelley and Algernon Charles Swinburne, and he was the inspiration for a ballet by Igor Stravinsky. More than 20 operas have had Apollo as a central figure. *See also* ACHILLES; AGAMEMNON; ASCLEPIUS; CASSANDRA; DELPHI; GREEK MYTHOLOGY; ILIAD, THE; ZEUS.

Arachne

In Greek mythology, Arachne was a peasant girl who became an expert spinner and weaver of cloth. No human could spin or weave as well as Arachne or produce finer cloth. She became famous throughout Greece.

Arachne grew arrogant about her skill, boasting that she was better than Athena, the goddess of wisdom, who invented spinning and weaving. At first, Athena laughed off Arachne's claims. Then many people began to believe them and to stay away from Athena's temples and from festivals held in her honor. Athena decided she had to teach the boastful girl a lesson.

Disguised as an old woman, the goddess came to earth and challenged Arachne to a weaving contest. The cloth that Athena wove showed the power of the gods and the fate of humans who dared to challenge them. Arachne's tapestry contained scenes of the foolish romantic misadventures of the gods. Arachne's work was the equal of Athena's, and the goddess was impressed by its quality. However, Arachne could not resist boasting that her weaving surpassed that of Athena.

At that moment, the goddess revealed her true identity. She tore apart Arachne's weaving and beat her with the shuttle from her weaving loom. In despair, Arachne took a rope and hanged herself. Out of pity, Athena changed the rope into a web and turned Arachne into a spider, an animal known for its spinning and weaving skills. Today the class of animals to which spiders belong is called Arachnida, after the girl who could weave so well. *See also* ATHENA; GREEK MYTHOLOGY.

Arcadia

Arcadia, a mountainous region in central Greece, was represented in Greek and Roman mythology as an earthly paradise. It was the land of Pan, the god of woods, fields, and flocks.

Cut off from the rest of Greece by mountains, the people of ancient Arcadia could pursue their simple way of life, based on agriculture and herding, without interruption or influence from the outside world. But the land fell into decay after being conquered by the Romans.

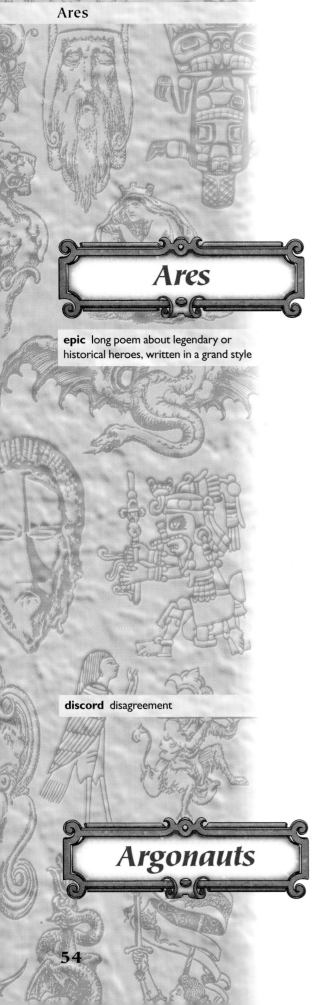

The image of Arcadia as an ideal state of peace and simplicity has been used by poets and artists through the ages. Ancient authors such as Theocritus and Virgil† sang its praises. It appears in later works of literature such as *Arcadia* by the Italian poet Sanazaro and *The Shepherd's Calendar* by English poet Edmund Spenser. However, another English poet, William Cowper, attacked the idea of using Arcadia to symbolize an ideal state that never really existed, especially for poor country people.

Ares

epic long poem about legendary or historical heroes, written in a grand style

In Greek mythology Ares, the son of Zeus† and Hera†, waged battle as the god of war. The Romans identified him with their own war god, Mars, although the two gods were quite different in character.

Generally described as bloodthirsty, cruel, and a troublemaker, Ares was not a popular god. In Homer's **epic** the *Iliad*†, Zeus tells Ares, "You are to me the most hateful of the gods. . . . For dear to you always are strife and wars and battles." However, another ancient text, the *Hymn to Ares,* offers a different view of the god:

> Shed down a kindly ray from above upon my life, and strength of war, that I may be able to drive away bitter cowardice from my head and crush down the deceitful impulses of my soul. . . . O blessed one, give me boldness to abide within the harmless laws of peace, avoiding strife and hatred and the violent fiends of death.

Although Ares was not a major figure in Greek mythology, some stories tell of his love affairs with the goddess Aphrodite† and with human women. Some of his sons became kings, warriors, and in one case a bandit. In one myth Poseidon's† son raped a daughter of Ares, and Ares struck the youth dead. Poseidon insisted that the gods try Ares for murder at the place where the rape and the killing had occurred, on a hill outside the city of Athens. The gods found Ares not guilty. From that time on, Athenians referred to the hill outside their city as the Areopagus, "Ares' hill."

discord disagreement

Vultures, who feed on the flesh of the dead on battlefields, were regarded as Ares' sacred birds. Ares liked to storm around the battlefields accompanied by his sister Eris, the goddess of **discord;** Enyo, a war goddess; and his twin sons Phobos (fear) and Deimos (terror). Despite Ares' fierce behavior, however, the goddess Athena† often defeated him in battle. *See also* GREEK MYTHOLOGY; MARS.

Argonauts

In Greek mythology, the Argonauts were a band of heroes who sailed with Jason in his quest for the Golden Fleece†. Their journey took them through numerous adventures and required the help of many different gods. Among the Argonauts were the sons of kings and of gods. According to some sources, one of the Argonauts was a woman, the huntress Atalanta.

†*See **Names and Places** at the end of this volume for further information.*

centaur half-human, half-animal creature with the body of a horse and the head, chest, and arms of a human

nymph minor goddess of nature, usually represented as young and beautiful

prophet one who claims to have received divine messages or insights

The Quest for the Fleece

Jason was the son of Aeson, the rightful king of Iolcus. When Aeson was overthrown by his brother Pelias, he sent Jason to be raised by the wise **centaur** Chiron. Later Jason returned to Iolcus to claim the throne. Pelias agreed to give it to him if he first found and brought back the Golden Fleece from Colchis—which Pelias knew to be an almost impossible task.

The Golden Fleece was the hide of a golden ram sent by the gods to save Phrixus and Helle, two royal children of the land of Iolcus whose lives were threatened by their stepmother. As the ram carried them to safety, Helle fell into the sea and drowned. The area where she fell (the Dardanelles in present-day Turkey) became known as Hellespont. Phrixus reached Colchis safely. There he sacrificed the ram to the goddess Hera†, his protector. The fleece was hung on a tree in a sacred grove and guarded by a serpent that never slept.

The Call for Heroes. Jason ordered a ship, the *Argo,* to be built and sent messengers throughout Greece asking others to join him in his quest for the Golden Fleece. After assembling a group of 50 heroes, Jason set off. The Argonauts' first adventure was on the island of Lemnos, which was populated only by women. As a result of a dispute between husbands and wives, the women had killed all the men. The women received the Argonauts with great hospitality, and the heroes began to forget their quest. One of the Argonauts stood firm, however. This was Hercules (Heracles)†, a hero known for his strength. Hercules persuaded the other Argonauts to return to the ship.

In another adventure, Hercules defended the ship against six-armed giants who attacked while the others were on land. Later, in a rowing contest, Hercules broke his oar. While cutting wood for a new oar, his squire was kidnapped by a water **nymph.** Hercules went in search of the boy and, eventually, was left behind by the Argonauts.

When the heroes stopped at the land of the Bebryces, the king, Amycus, challenged them—as he did all visitors—to a fight to the death. Pollux, the son of Zeus†, took up the challenge and killed Amycus.

The Argonauts then stopped to see Phineus, the blind king of Thynia. Phineus was a **prophet,** and the travelers needed advice on how to proceed. Phineus agreed to help them if they would rid him of the Harpies, fierce, part-woman, part-bird creatures who stole and spoiled his food. Jason ordered a feast to be prepared. When the Harpies arrived to ruin the feast, two of the Argonauts— Calais and Zetes (winged sons of Boreas, the North Wind)—pursued them. Eventually, Zeus sent a message that the Harpies should be spared but that they should leave Phineus in peace.

After reaching the entrance to the Black Sea, the Argonauts had to go through the Symplegades. These were huge rocks that crashed together and destroyed any ship that tried to sail through them. Following Phineus's advice, the Argonauts released a dove

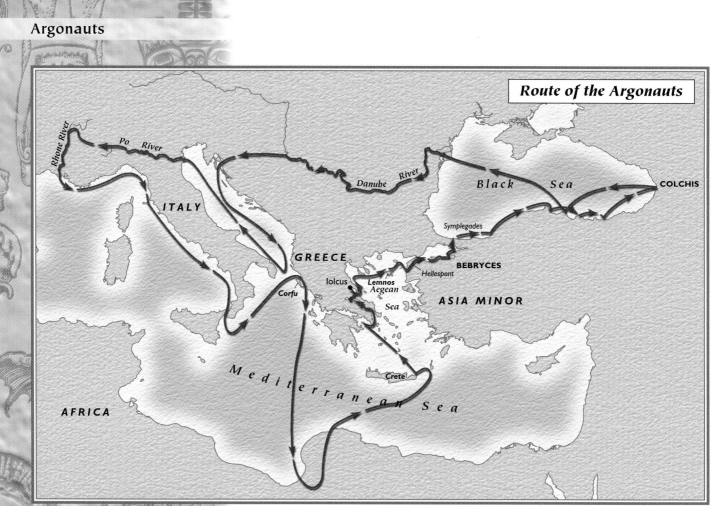

Route of the Argonauts

and watched its course as it flew between the rocks. The dove made the passage, losing only a single tail feather. As soon as the rocks began to come apart, the Argonauts pulled hard on their oars, following the path of the dove. When they had almost passed through, a great wave held them back. At that point, the goddesses Athena† and Hera gave them a push, and the ship made it to safety. Forever after, the Symplegades remained separated.

Help from Medea. After more adventures, the Argonauts finally reached Colchis. Jason and several companions went to the court of King Aeëtes to request the Golden Fleece. The first to see Jason was Medea, the king's daughter. Aphrodite (Venus), the goddess of love, made her fall in love with Jason. Medea was a witch and could help him with the difficulties ahead.

Aeëtes had no intention of handing over the Golden Fleece, but he pretended to agree if Jason could pass several trials. Jason was to yoke two fire-breathing bulls to a plow and sow a field with dragon's teeth. The teeth would yield armed men whom Jason would then have to kill. Medea gave Jason a magic ointment that he rubbed on himself to protect him from the fiery bulls. Next she told Jason to throw a boulder in the midst of the soldiers to confuse them and make them fight one another. Then he would have to fight only the survivors. Following her directions, Jason succeeded in defeating the warriors.

† See **Names and Places** at the end of this volume for further information.

Aeëtes told Jason he would hand over the Fleece the next day, but Jason and Medea did not believe him. Promising to marry her, Jason once again obtained Medea's help. That night, she led him to the sacred grove and put the serpent to sleep with her magic. Jason then took the Fleece and with Medea and the Argonauts set sail across the Black Sea.

The Return Home

Accounts of the Argonauts' journey home vary. According to the writer Apollonius, Medea's brother Apsyrtus blocked the mouth of the Black Sea so the Argonauts had to find a different route for returning to Iolcus. Several versions of the legend agree that the heroes crossed the Black Sea to the Danube River. After sailing up the Danube, they traveled along various rivers and seas before reaching the Mediterranean Sea. Some sources say that the Argonauts went north to the Baltic Sea; others relate that they followed the Rhine River to the Atlantic Ocean or that they reached the Adriatic Sea. At the entrance to the Adriatic, they met Apsyrtus, who tried to convince Jason to give up Medea. Jason refused and killed Apsyrtus.

The Argonauts sailed up the Po River and down the Rhone. Having almost reached Greece, the *Argo* was blown off course to Libya. There a great wave stranded the crew in the desert. On the advice of the gods, the Argonauts carried the ship across the desert until the sea god Triton helped them launch it back on the Mediterranean.

As they sailed past the island of Crete, Talos, the bronze man appointed by King Minos to protect the island, threw rocks at the Argonauts. Medea killed Talos with her witchcraft. The Argonauts' adventures continued. Nearing Greece, the ship was enveloped in a darkness so great that they lost their way. Apollo† sent a blazing arrow that showed them the way to an island where they could wait until the light returned.

At last, the *Argo* arrived home in Iolcus. The Argonauts were held in great honor throughout Greece, and many noble families later claimed to be descended from them. Jason presented the Golden Fleece to Pelias, but he never became king.

The Argonauts in Literature

Many writers have been inspired by the subject of the Argonauts and the quest for the Golden Fleece. Among the ancient Greek works are Pindar's *Pythian Ode,* Apollonius Rhodius's **epic** *Argonautica,* and Euripedes' play *Medea.* The Roman poet Ovid mentioned the Argonauts in the *Metamorphoses.* In the Middle Ages, Chaucer retold the story in the *Legend of Good Women,* and in the 1800s, William Morris wrote a long narrative poem *Life and Death of Jason.* Robert Graves's novel *Heracles, My Shipmate* was published in 1944. ***See also* ATALANTA; HARPIES; HERA; HERCULES; JASON; MEDEA.**

A Magic Ship

Jason's ship, the *Argo,* was made from the wood of a sacred oak and had the ability to think, to speak, and even to prophesy. The ship had one oar for each of the Argonauts, who rowed themselves to their adventures. When it was first built, the *Argo* refused to descend to the sea until the musician Orpheus sang to it and played his lyre. During the quest, the ship traveled under the protection of Athena and Apollo. Afterward, the *Argo* was dedicated to Poseidon† and placed near his temple in Corinth. Eventually, the gods turned the ship into a constellation in the sky.

epic long poem about legendary or historical heroes, written in a grand style

Argus

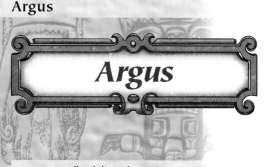

satyr woodland deity that was part man and part goat or horse

In Greek mythology, Argus was a giant with 100 eyes. Some accounts say the eyes were all in his head; others say they were all over his body. Known as Panoptes or "all seeing" because some of his eyes always remained open while the others slept, Argus was very powerful. He killed Echidna, a monster who was half woman, half serpent and who crushed her victims with her tail. Argus also killed a bull that was destroying Arcadia, a land of shepherds, and a **satyr** who stole cattle.

The goddess Hera† appointed Argus to watch over Io, a priestess whom Zeus† had turned into a cow. Zeus sent his son Hermes† to free Io. Hermes told stories and played music for Argus until he succeeded in making all 100 eyes go to sleep at the same time. Hermes wasted no time and slew the giant. Hera took Argus's eyes and placed them on the tail of her sacred bird, the peacock. *See also* **Io.**

Ariadne

immortal able to live forever

In Greek mythology, Ariadne was the daughter of King Minos of Crete and of his queen, Pasiphae. She fell in love with the Athenian hero Theseus when he came to Crete. Theseus was one of a group of youths and maidens who were to be fed to the Minotaur. Half bull and half man, the Minotaur was kept in a maze called the Labyrinth. Before Theseus entered it, Ariadne helped him by giving him a ball of yarn. He used the yarn to leave a trail by which he could find his way out. Theseus succeeded in killing the Minotaur and escaping the Labyrinth. Ariadne then fled with Theseus when he sailed back to Athens.

There are different versions of the rest of Ariadne's story. In one version, she was abandoned by Theseus on the island of Naxos while she slept on the shore. There Dionysus (Bacchus)† found her and decided to make her his wife. In another version, after arriving on Naxos, Ariadne was killed by Artemis† but then found by Dionysus, who asked Zeus† to make her **immortal** so that he could marry her. Dionysus and Ariadne were married on Naxos. Two festivals were held in honor of Ariadne: one celebrating her marriage and one mourning her death. The couple had three sons. *See also* **DIONYSUS; MINOTAUR; THESEUS.**

Ariel

cabalistic referring to a system of mystical thought based on a secret interpretation of the Hebrew Scriptures

In the Bible's book of Isaiah, *Ariel* is a symbolic name for Jerusalem. By the Middle Ages, it had become the name of one of seven water spirits who were led by the archangel Michael, according to the **cabalistic** Jewish tradition. Among the common folk, it was simply the name of an air or water spirit.

Ariel is also the name of several different spirits in English literature. In William Shakespeare's *The Tempest,* Ariel is a mischievous spirit who had been imprisoned by a witch and freed by the magician Prospero. Ariel helps Prospero reconcile with his enemies, regain his throne, and marry off his daughter. In John Milton's *Paradise Lost,* Ariel is one of the fallen angels who accompany Satan. In Alexander Pope's *The Rape of the Lock,* he is one of the comic protectors of the heroine Belinda. *See also* **SATAN.**

†See **Names and Places** at the end of this volume for further information.

Ark of the Covenant

cherubim winged lions; in later times, angels portrayed as winged human figures

The Ark of the Covenant was the gold-covered wooden box that held the tablets on which the Ten Commandments were written. Its lid, called the Mercy Seat, had two gold statues of **cherubim** kneeling in prayer. The Ark was carried by placing poles through the two rings on each side.

The Ark was a symbol of the covenant, or agreement, between God and the Hebrew people. God promised to protect them; they agreed to obey his commandments. According to the Bible, the Ark guided the Hebrews to Canaan†, the Promised Land. During their years of wandering, the Hebrews set up a Tabernacle, or house of worship, for the Ark at each stopping point. This was a tent with an inner room called the holy of holies for the Ark. It was believed that the spirit of God dwelled there and sat upon the Mercy Seat.

According to the first book of Samuel in the Bible, the Philistines captured the Ark at one point and carried it from town to town. Wherever the Ark went, however, the people were struck with plagues. On the advice of Philistine priests and soothsayers, the Ark was placed on a cart and sent back to Canaan.

King David of Israel had the Ark moved to Jerusalem. His son, King Solomon, ordered a great temple to be built and placed the Ark within the holy of holies. In the 500s B.C., the Babylonians† conquered the Hebrews and took the treasures from the temple. The fate of the Ark is not explained in the Bible, but it was probably lost or destroyed. *See also* SEMITIC MYTHOLOGY.

Armageddon

In the Christian tradition, Armageddon is where the final battle will take place between the forces of God and the forces of Satan. The battle, in which evil will finally be defeated, will be followed by the Day of Judgment. On that day, all souls will be judged by Christ, who will decide whether to send them to heaven or to hell. Armageddon is mentioned just once in the Bible, in the sixteenth chapter of the New Testament book of Revelation.

The term *Armageddon* means "hill of Megiddo," which was an ancient town in what is now northern Israel. Megiddo stood at the crossroads of military and trade routes that connected Egypt, Israel, Phoenicia, Syria, and Mesopotamia†. Numerous battles were fought at Megiddo because of its strategic location. Over time, the word *Armageddon* began to be used to mean any great battle. *See also* SATAN.

Artemis

deity god or goddess
chastity purity or virginity
Titan one of a family of giants who ruled the earth until overthrown by the Greek gods of Olympus

The Greek goddess Artemis, one of the 12 **deities** who lived on the slopes of Mount Olympus†, was the twin sister of Apollo†. Fond of hunting, archery, and wild animals, she was also associated with childbirth, the harvest, and the moon. As a virgin goddess, Artemis was considered the guardian of **chastity** and protector of maidens and small children. She was also worshiped by the Romans, who called her Diana.

Artemis and Apollo were the children of Zeus† and the **Titan** Leto. When Leto was about to deliver the twins, Zeus's jealous

59

wife Hera declared that she would not allow them to be born in any land where the sun shone. For this reason, Zeus led Leto to a floating island and caused a wave to shade the shore, creating a place for the birth that was above ground but hidden from the sun.

Many myths about Artemis relate to her vengeful nature. She was known for punishing humans who offended or angered her. In one story, a young hunter named Actaeon came upon Artemis while she was bathing in a stream. Although he knew better than to spy on a goddess, he was captivated by her beauty. Artemis caught sight of Actaeon and, not wanting him to boast of having seen her naked body, changed him into a stag. His own hounds then attacked and killed him.

In another myth, Artemis and Apollo defended the honor of their mother, Leto. A woman named Niobe, who had six sons and six daughters, boasted that her offspring outshone Leto's two children. Outraged, Leto sent Artemis and Apollo to punish Niobe. The twins shot Niobe's children with their arrows, killing all of them.

In works of art, Artemis is often shown carrying her bow and arrows and surrounded by her hounds. She appears in many literary works including Homer's† *Iliad,* Ovid's† *Metamorphoses,* and one play of Euripides†. ***See also*** APOLLO; DIANA; GREEK MYTHOLOGY; ZEUS.

Arthur, King

chivalry rules and customs of medieval knighthood

medieval relating to the Middle Ages in Europe, a period from about A.D. 500 to 1500

King Arthur was a legendary ruler of Britain whose life and deeds became the basis for a collection of tales known as the Arthurian legends. As the leading figure in British mythology, King Arthur is a national hero and a symbol of Britain's heroic heritage. But his appeal is not limited to Britain. The Arthurian story, with its elements of mystery, magic, love, war, adventure, betrayal, **chivalry,** and fate, has touched the popular imagination and has become part of the world's shared mythology.

Sources

King Arthur was born somewhere in the misty region where history and imagination meet. The original legends may have been based on a real person, but scholars have yet to determine who that person was. Whether real or imaginary, the story of Arthur has been shaped by the ancient myths and literary creations that developed around him, and the courtly **medieval** king who appears in the best-known versions of Arthur's story is a creation of a later time.

Historical Clues. Was there a real Arthur? Almost 1,500 years after the first known written reference to Arthur, scholars still debate this question. Some believe that King Arthur may be based on a war leader, possibly named Artorius, who defended the native Celtic† people of Britain against Anglo-Saxon invaders after Rome withdrew its troops from the British Isles in A.D. 410. References to this hero appear in a book written around 550 by a Celtic monk named Gildas; in a work by Nennius, a Celtic historian of around

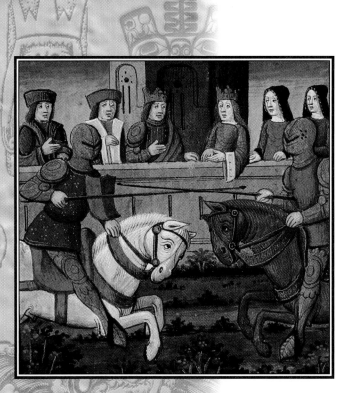

The fellowship of the knights in King Arthur's court, Camelot, was symbolized by a round table. This illumination from a French manuscript portrays two knights of the Round Table fighting before King Arthur and Queen Guinevere in a tournament.

800; and in a history of Wales compiled around 955. According to these accounts, Artorius fought a series of battles against the Saxons sometime between 500 and 537.

A researcher named Geoffrey Ashe proposed a different identity for Arthur. He based his theory on a letter that a Roman nobleman wrote around 460 to a British king named Riothamus. Linking this letter with medieval accounts of Arthur's deeds in France, Ashe suggested that Riothamus, who led a British army into France, was the source of the Arthur legend.

Mythological Connections. A historical figure may have contributed to the Arthur legend, but so did Celtic lore. The Celts blended stories of the warrior Arthur with those of much older mythological characters, such as Gwydion, a Welsh priest-king. Old Welsh tales and poems place Arthur in traditional Celtic legends, including a hunt for an enchanted wild pig and a search for a magic **cauldron.** In addition, Arthur is surrounded by a band of loyal followers who greatly resemble those associated with the legendary Irish hero Finn.

cauldron large kettle

pagan term used by early Christians to describe non-Christians and non-Christian beliefs

As time went on, the old **pagan** and Celtic features of King Arthur's story were buried under new layers of myth. Some versions claimed that Arthur was descended from Aeneas†, the legendary founder of Rome. This detail connected British mythology with that of ancient Greece and Rome. As Britain came under Anglo-Saxon rule, Arthur became an idealized leader, a symbol of national identity who had once united all the warring kingdoms of the British Isles. In some accounts, he led his armies across Europe, a mighty conqueror like Alexander the Great of the ancient world.

Christianity also played a role in the stories about Arthur. Some commentators have compared Arthur, a good man who was betrayed by those closest to him, to Jesus, who was betrayed by his trusted disciple Judas. In time, Arthur's story could be interpreted as a tale of Christian virtues and vices.

Literary Development. Modern scholars can trace the changes in King Arthur's story through the works of particular medieval writers. The most important of these writers was Geoffrey of Monmouth, who lived and worked between about 1100 and 1155. His *History of the Kings of Britain* contains the most detailed account of King Arthur written up to that time. Geoffrey drew upon Welsh folklore and possibly upon earlier histories, but his Arthur—a conquering national hero—is mainly his own literary creation.

Geoffrey's work introduced King Arthur to a wider audience. Soon English and European writers were producing their own

61

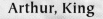

versions of his life and adding new characters, adventures, and details. Sir Thomas Malory, an English writer, wove various strands of the story into a lengthy volume called *Le Morte D'Arthur* (The Death of Arthur) that placed King Arthur firmly in the medieval world. Published in 1485, it became the best-known and most widely read account of the legendary king. Modern images of Arthur, from books to movies, comic books, and cartoons, are largely based on Malory's story.

Arthur's Life and Deeds

King Arthur's life includes many features found in myths from around the world, from his secret parentage to his final voyage to a paradise across the waters. Although supernatural elements such as magic, wizards, and giants play key roles in the story, at its heart is the simple drama of a man struggling to live by the highest standards in a world with human weakness.

Birth and Upbringing. According to Malory, Arthur was the son of a king named Uther Pendragon, who fell in love with Igraine, wife of Duke Gorlois of Cornwall. With the aid of a wizard named Merlin, Uther disguised himself as Gorlois and conceived a child with Igraine. (Some versions say that Uther married Igraine after Gorlois died.) Their child, born at Tintagel Castle in Cornwall, was named Arthur.

Merlin took charge of the boy's upbringing, arranging for a knight named Sir Hector to raise Arthur as his foster son. When King Uther died, he left no known heir to the throne. It was said that the person who succeeded in pulling the magical sword Excalibur from the stone that held it would be the next king. The greatest knights in the land accepted the challenge, but none managed to pull out the sword. When Sir Hector brought the young Arthur to London, he was able to withdraw the sword with ease, thus proving that he was meant to be king of England. At a later point in Arthur's story, however, Malory says that he received the sword from a mysterious figure called the Lady of the Lake. Either way, Arthur became king and gained possession of Excalibur. The wise Merlin helped him defeat the rebellious kings and nobles who opposed his kingship.

In time, King Arthur was visited by Morgause, wife of King Lot of the Orkney Islands. Morgause, a daughter of Igraine, was Arthur's half sister. Among her children was Gawain, Arthur's nephew, who became a loyal supporter of the king. Morgause then bore a much younger son, Mordred or Modred. In some versions of the story, Mordred was Arthur's child, the result of an incestuous relationship and thus, perhaps, destined to be the seed of Arthur's destruction.

The Fate of the King. Arthur fell in love with Guinevere, daughter of King Leodegran of Scotland. But Merlin said that Arthur must fight a campaign in France before he could marry. Once

Arthur's Tomb?

King Arthur has long been linked with Glastonbury in southwestern Britain. Old traditions claimed that early British Christians founded an abbey church in Glastonbury in A.D. 166. The church stood until a fire destroyed it in 1184. According to legend, Arthur and his queen, Guinevere, were buried nearby. Arthur's tomb bore these words: "Here lies Arthur, king that was, king that shall be." Some chronicles say that King Henry II ordered the tomb opened in 1150 and that it contained Arthur's skeleton and sword. Modern scholars, though, have been unable to disentangle fact from legend.

†See **Names and Places** at the end of this volume for further information.

Arthur returned in triumph from France, the wedding took place. As a present, Guinevere's parents gave Arthur a large round table for the knights who made up his court. This Round Table became the symbol of the fellowship of the brave knights who undertook quests to defeat evil, help those in danger, and keep the land free. Among their quests was the search for the **Holy Grail.**

King Arthur made Camelot the seat of his court, and Merlin built a castle with a special chamber for the Round Table. After a time, though, trouble arose in the realm. Queen Guinevere and Lancelot, Arthur's friend and champion knight, became lovers. Mordred had the queen accused of **adultery.** Lancelot defended her honor, but the conflict destroyed the unity of the court. Some knights sided with Arthur, others with Mordred. After several battles, Guinevere returned to Arthur.

At a later time, Arthur left Mordred in charge of the kingdom while he went off to fight a military campaign. While the king was away, Mordred plotted against him, planning to marry Guinevere and take over as ruler of Britain. When Arthur returned and learned of the plot, he went to battle with Mordred.

The armies of Arthur and Mordred met near the town of Salisbury. While the two commanders discussed peace terms, someone saw a snake in the grass and drew his sword. In a flash, all the knights drew their weapons and set upon one another. Arthur killed Mordred but was gravely wounded. He asked the sole survivor, Sir Bedivere, to throw Excalibur into a lake. At first, Sir Bedivere hesitated, but eventually he did as instructed. A hand rose from beneath the water—the hand of the Lady of the Lake—and caught the sword. Then a mysterious barge appeared. Sir Bedivere placed King Arthur on the barge, which carried him away to Avalon, a sacred island in the west. There he would be cared for by Morgan Le Fay and healed of his wounds. Legend said that he would return one day when England's need of him was great. ***See also*** Arthurian Legends; Avalon; Camelot; Celtic Mythology; Excalibur; Guinevere; Holy Grail; Lady of the Lake; Lancelot; Merlin; Morgan Le Fay; Round Table.

Arthurian Legends

The Arthurian legends, stories that revolve around the character of King Arthur, form an important part of Britain's national mythology. Arthur may be based on a historical person, possibly a Celtic† warlord of the A.D. 400s. The legends, however, have little to do with history. A blend of Celtic mythology and medieval **romance,** they feature such well-known elements as the magic sword Excalibur, the Knights of the Round Table, and the search for the **Holy Grail.**

Major Elements

The Arthurian legends exist in numerous versions and can be interpreted in a variety of ways. They include tales of adventure filled with battles and marvels, a tragic love story, a Christian **allegory,** an examination of kingship, and an exploration of the conflict between

Holy Grail sacred cup said to have been used by Jesus Christ at the Last Supper

adultery sexual relationship between a married person and someone other than his or her spouse

romance in medieval literature, a tale based on legend, love, and adventure, often set in a distant place or time
Holy Grail sacred cup said to have been used by Jesus Christ at the Last Supper
allegory literary and artistic device in which characters represent an idea or a religious or moral principle

The Arthurian legends were popular subjects in art and literature for many centuries. This drawing by Aubrey Beardsley from 1894 shows Merlin receiving baby Arthur into his care. Merlin played an important role in Arthur's life, first overseeing his childhood and later serving as his adviser.

love and duty. The legends tell the story of a mighty king who brought order to a troubled land. He might have gone on to rule the world if passion and betrayal had not disrupted his perfect realm and led to his death.

The King and His Knights. At the center of the legends is King Arthur. Like many heroes of myth and legend, he is of royal birth. But until he comes of age and claims his throne, his parents are unknown. Arthur must overcome many enemies to establish his claim to the throne, and some of the kings and noblemen he defeats are so impressed by him that they swear loyalty to him.

When Arthur finally falls in battle he is carried away to Avalon, a sacred island, to be healed of his wounds so that he can return to Britain during a future crisis. Some scholars have seen in Arthur echoes of **pagan** sun gods who die and sink into the west only to be reborn.

pagan term used by early Christians to describe non-Christians and non-Christian beliefs

Like Finn, the legendary Irish hero, Arthur is surrounded by a band of devoted followers. In early versions of the tales, these were warriors and chieftains, but once the setting of the tales was fixed in the Middle Ages, his followers became courtly knights. Their number varies from a dozen to more than a hundred depending on the source. A few of the knights—especially Gawain, Galahad, and Lancelot—emerge as distinct personalities with strengths and weaknesses.

Not all the legends focus on King Arthur. Many deal with the Knights of the Round Table, who ride out from the court at Camelot to do good deeds and perform brave feats. The most honorable and difficult of all their actions is the search for the Holy Grail. Only Galahad is pure enough to succeed in this quest.

Magical Power and Human Weakness. **Supernatural** beings and events abound in the Arthurian legends. Even before Arthur's birth his destiny is shaped by the wizard Merlin, who later serves as the king's adviser and helper. Another powerful magical figure is the witch Morgan Le Fay, who works for good in some versions of the legends and for evil in others. She is sometimes referred to as Arthur's half sister.

supernatural related to forces beyond the normal world; magical or miraculous

Arthur becomes king by gaining possession of the enchanted sword Excalibur, a token of power similar to many magical devices in mythology. Other supernatural elements in the Arthurian legends include the giants and monsters that Arthur and the knights frequently battle.

The tragic aspect of the legends, however, arises not from wicked sorcerers or vicious enemies but from the people closest to the king. Guinevere, his queen, and Lancelot, his beloved friend and champion knight, betray the king by becoming lovers. Like the appearance of the serpent in the Garden of Eden, their **adultery** introduces discord and deception into what had been a perfect world.

Mordred, Arthur's jealous nephew, uses Guinevere's affair to tear the comradeship of the Round Table apart, and he eventually goes to war against Arthur. Some versions of the story make Mordred the son of Arthur and his half sister Morgause, placing part of the blame for the fall of Camelot on the king's youthful sin of incest.

Development of the Legends

The Arthurian legends took shape over hundreds of years. The versions that survive today reflect a number of sources and influences.

Early Sources. The earliest forms of the Arthurian legends blended Celtic history and myth. Scholars have not been able to determine whether King Arthur is based on a historical personage who really existed, although several early histories of Britain mention him. He may have been a Celtic war leader who helped defend Britain against Anglo-Saxon invaders in the A.D. 400s or 500s.

The role of Celtic mythology in the early Arthurian legends is much more definite. Many of the characters and adventures associated with Arthur come from older myths. Arthur himself may be based on the legendary Welsh priest-king Gwydion, and Merlin clearly comes from Myrddin, who appears as both a prophet and a madman in Welsh and Scottish lore. Scholars believe that the Arthurian legends took shape sometime after about 500, when the Celts began to attach familiar myths to new stories about a war hero named Arthur.

Medieval Literary Influences. Writers during the Middle Ages created new versions of the Arthurian legends. In the early 1100s, an Englishman named Geoffrey of Monmouth produced the *History of the Kings of Britain,* which presented Arthur as a national hero.

New influences, such as Christianity, entered the legends. An old Celtic tale about a search for a magic **cauldron,** for example, became transformed into the quest for the Holy Grail. Another key influence was the medieval concept of **chivalry,** the code of conduct that inspired the courtly behavior of the Knights of the Round Table.

Numerous versions of the Arthurian legends were produced during the Middle Ages. French writer Chrétien de Troyes wrote poems on Arthurian subjects between 1155 and 1185. He focused on magic and marvels and introduced the theme of the quest for the Holy Grail. The Grail also inspired Wolfram von Eschenbach, a German who wrote around 1200. Other romances of the period

adultery sexual relationship between a married person and someone other than his or her spouse

Irish Arthur

The main Celtic source of the Arthurian legends was Wales, but Arthur also appears in Irish folklore and literature. In early tales, he is the son of the king of Britain. He steals dogs belonging to Finn, a legendary Irish hero drawn from the same ancient Celtic sources as Arthur himself. During the Middle Ages, Irish storytellers and writers produced their own versions of the Arthurian tales. They also used Arthurian characters in new Irish stories. In one such story from the 1400s, Sir Gawain helps the king of India, who has been turned into a dog, recover his proper form.

cauldron large kettle

chivalry rules and customs of medieval knighthood

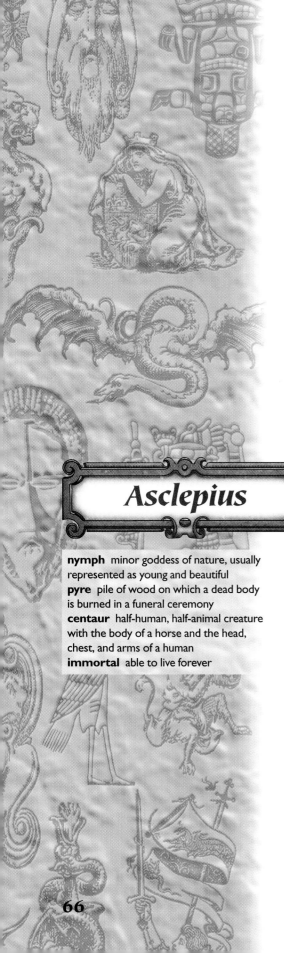

developed the character of Merlin and the romantic entanglement of Lancelot and Guinevere.

In 1485 Sir Thomas Malory, an Englishman, wove together many strands of the Arthurian legends in a volume called *Le Morte D'Arthur* (The Death of Arthur). The best-known version of the legends, Malory's work has been the basis of most modern interpretations.

Modern Versions. Many writers since Malory have adapted the Arthurian legends. In 1859 the English poet Alfred Lord Tennyson published the first part of *Idylls of the King,* a book-length poem about Arthur and his knights. Between 1917 and 1927, the American poet Edwin Arlington Robinson published three poems on Arthurian subjects: "Merlin," "Lancelot," and "Tristram."

One of the most popular modern Arthurian novels is T. H. White's *The Once and Future King* (1958). Other writers, such as Mary Stewart and Marion Zimmer Bradley, have retold the Arthurian story from different points of view, including those of the women in Arthur's life. The legends have also inspired the Broadway musical *Camelot* (1960) and movies such as *A Connecticut Yankee in King Arthur's Court* (1948). ***See also*** ARTHUR, KING; AVALON; CAMELOT; CELTIC MYTHOLOGY; EXCALIBUR; FINN; GALAHAD; GUINEVERE; HOLY GRAIL; LADY OF THE LAKE; LANCELOT; MERLIN; MORGAN LE FAY; ROUND TABLE; SHALLOT, THE LADY OF.

Asclepius

nymph minor goddess of nature, usually represented as young and beautiful

pyre pile of wood on which a dead body is burned in a funeral ceremony

centaur half-human, half-animal creature with the body of a horse and the head, chest, and arms of a human

immortal able to live forever

In Greek and Roman mythology, Asclepius was the god of medicine. He was the son of Apollo† and of the **nymph** Coronis. While Coronis was pregnant with Asclepius, she fell in love with a human. The jealous Apollo arranged for his sister Artemis (Diana)† to kill her. As Coronis's body lay burning on the funeral **pyre,** Apollo removed the child. He gave the baby to the wise **centaur** Chiron, who raised him and taught him medicine. When Asclepius grew up, he began to cure the sick. He became so skilled in medicine that he could even bring the dead back to life. Fearing that Asclepius might make all people **immortal,** Zeus† struck him with a thunderbolt and killed him. Deeply saddened, Apollo asked Zeus to place Asclepius in the sky, where he became the constellation Ophiucus.

Asclepius's family included his daughters, Hygieia, the goddess of health; and Panacea, the goddess of healing. His sons were both skilled physicians who served in the Trojan War†. His symbol was a wooden staff with a single snake wound around it. It is used to the present day with two snakes as the symbol of physicians.

Asclepius was widely worshiped, and his temples were places of healing. Patients would perform ritual baths, sacrifices, and fasting and spend the night in the temple. As they slept, Asclepius would appear to them in dreams. In the morning, his priests would interpret the dreams. It is said that some patients awoke from their dreams completely cured. ***See also*** APOLLO.

† *See **Names and Places** at the end of this volume for further information.*

Ashur

In the ancient Near East, Ashur was originally the main god of the city of Ashur, the capital of Assyria. As Assyria emerged as a great empire, Ashur became the national god of all of Assyria. The Assyrians saw him primarily as a warrior god and believed that he supported them against their enemies.

By about 1300 B.C., Ashur was identified with the supreme Sumerian god Enlil, probably in an effort to portray him as king of the gods. Under Assyria's king Sargon, Ashur became the father of Anu, the Babylonian† god of the sky and the main creative force in the universe. Later, as Assyria and Babylon competed for political and military power, Ashur took on the characteristics of the Babylonian national god, Marduk. Because the qualities of so many other gods were transferred to Ashur, he had little or no clear character or traditions of his own. More than anything, he was a symbol of the people and power of Assyria. ***See also*** ANU; ENLIL; MARDUK.

Astarte

See *Ishtar.*

Astyanax

In Greek mythology, Astyanax was a prince of Troy† and the son of Hector, the great Trojan military leader. His real name was Scamandrius, but he was called Astyanax, or "lord of the city," in honor of his father. After the Greeks killed Hector and overran Troy, Astyanax was saved by his mother, Andromache. However, fearing that Astyanax would avenge the death of his father and restore the city of Troy, the Greek leader Odysseus† ordered that he be killed. Astyanax was thrown from the walls of the city to his death. His father's shield was used as his coffin.

Some sources state that Astyanax survived and returned to rule Troy. Medieval legend claimed that he was the founder of the kingdom of Messina in Sicily and that the emperor Charlemagne was one of his descendants. ***See also*** ANDROMACHE; HECTOR.

Atalanta

prophecy foretelling of what is to come; also something that is predicted
centaur half-human, half-animal creature with the body of a horse and the head, chest, and arms of a human

In Greek mythology, Atalanta was a skilled huntress and swift runner. As an infant, she was abandoned by her father, a king who was disappointed that she was not a boy. The goddess Artemis (Diana)† sent a female bear to nurse the child until some hunters took her in. A **prophecy** foretold that Atalanta would be unhappy if she married, so she decided to remain a virgin and dedicate herself to hunting. While still a girl, she used her bow and arrows to kill two **centaurs** who tried to rape her.

Atalanta gained fame in the Calydonian boar hunt. Meleager, the son of the king of Calydon, organized a great hunt to kill a huge boar. Atalanta joined the hunt, and Meleager fell in love with her. Atalanta was the first to wound the boar; Meleager was the one to kill it. Meleager gave Atalanta the hide, the prize of the hunt, over the protests of the other hunters.

Later Atalanta tried to join Jason† on the quest for the Golden Fleece. Some sources say that she sailed as one of the Argonauts;

other sources state that Jason refused to accept her, fearing that a woman in the crew would create problems among the men.

When Atalanta's fame spread, her father invited her to return home. He wanted to see her properly married, but she made a condition: the suitor would have to beat her in a foot race and forfeit his life if he lost. Many young men tried—and died. Finally, a young man named Hippomenes prayed to Aphrodite† for help, and the goddess gave him three golden apples. By throwing an apple across Atalanta's path at different times during the race, he distracted her and made her run after them. Thus, Hippomenes was able to pull ahead and win. He and Atalanta were married and had a son. Later they angered Aphrodite, who turned them into a lion and lioness. *See also* ARGONAUTS.

Aten

pharaoh ruler of ancient Egypt
monotheism belief in only one god

Aten, or Aton, was an ancient Egyptian god who was worshiped during the reign of the **pharaoh** Akhenaten (1350s to 1330s B.C.). Unlike earlier pharaohs, who had worshiped many gods, Akhenaten claimed that Aten was the one supreme god. This may have been the earliest example of **monotheism** in the ancient Near East. Aten was depicted as a disk, representing the sun. Rays of light ending in hands extended from the disk and reached down to the king, his family, and the natural world.

Originally named Amenhotep, Akhenaten changed his name to mean "right hand of Aten." Akhenaten was determined to promote Aten as the only supreme god and not to honor other gods. To this end, he tried to get rid of images of other gods and to reduce the power of the priests who led the worship of other gods. He built temples to Aten and established a new capital city, called Akhetaten, or Horizon of Aten. Today that city is known as Amarna.

Much of what is known about the worship of Aten comes from the *Hymn to Aten*, a joyful poem inscribed on the walls of some ancient tombs at Amarna. The hymn describes Aten as the only supreme being and the creator of all life. It says that Akhenaten and his wife, Queen Nefertiti, are the only people who can understand the god and express his wishes. The hymn speaks of Aten as a loving god who brings order and beauty to the world.

The worship of Aten as the sole supreme being lasted only for the years of Akhenaten's reign. The Egyptian people could not accept the idea of one supreme god and returned to their old belief in many gods. They destroyed the temples to Aten, and he became a minor god among all the other gods. *See also* AMUN; EGYPTIAN MYTHOLOGY.

This stone relief shows the pharaoh Akhenaten and his family worshiping Aten. According to the *Hymn to Aten*, Akhenaten and his wife, Nefertiti, were the only people who fully understood the god and his wishes.

†*See **Names and Places** at the end of this volume for further information.*

Athena

In Greek mythology, Athena was the goddess of wisdom, of warfare, and of crafts. She ranked as Zeus's† favorite child and one of the most powerful of the 12 Olympian gods. Although Athena was worshiped in many cities, the Athenians considered her to be their special protector and named their city after her. Many rulers sought her wisdom in both government and military matters. The Romans called her Minerva.

Like Artemis (Diana), the goddess of the hunt, Athena was a virgin goddess. Unlike Artemis, she did not reject men. Athena took an active part in the lives of many heroes and enjoyed their bravery in battle.

Athena's Life

Athena was the daughter of Zeus and of the **Titan** Metis, known for her knowledge and wisdom. Metis had tried to avoid Zeus's advances by changing herself into different animals, but her tactic failed, and she became pregnant. Zeus learned from an **oracle** that Metis was expecting a girl. The oracle also predicted that if Metis and Zeus had a male child, the boy would overthrow his father when he grew up, just as Zeus had overthrown his father. To protect himself from this possibility, Zeus swallowed Metis after she changed herself into a fly. Some sources say that Zeus did this mainly because he wanted to possess all her wisdom.

Time passed and one day Zeus developed a terrible headache. He cried out in pain, saying that he felt as if a warrior were stabbing him from inside with a spear. Hephaestus (Vulcan), the god of metalworking, finally understood what was wrong and split Zeus's head open with an ax. Athena sprang out, fully grown and dressed in armor. By all accounts she was a dutiful daughter. For his part, Zeus tended to indulge Athena, which at times made the other gods jealous and angry.

The goddess was active in the lives of many warriors, kings, and heroes. She gave Bellerophon the magic bridle that enabled him to ride Pegasus, the winged horse. She showed the shipbuilder Argus how to build a magic ship for Jason† and then protected the boat on its travels. She helped Perseus† kill the monster Medusa†. She supported Hercules† through the 12 labors.

Athena also played a role in the Trojan War†. She was one of the three goddesses who took part in a beauty contest that led to the war. During the conflict, she fought on the side of the Greeks, inspired Odysseus† with the idea of the wooden horse, and afterward helped him return home.

To become **patron** of Athens, Athena had to win a contest against Poseidon†. The clever Athenians asked each god to devise a gift for the city. With his **trident,** Poseidon struck the Acropolis, the hill in the middle of the city, and a saltwater spring began to flow. Athena then touched the Acropolis with her spear, and an olive tree sprang forth. The people decided that the goddess's gift was the more valuable and chose her as their patron. To avoid angering Poseidon, they promised to worship him too. In ancient

Titan one of a family of giants who ruled the earth until overthrown by the Greek gods of Olympus

oracle priest or priestess or other creature through whom a god is believed to speak; also the location (such as a shrine) where such words are spoken

The Parthenon

The Acropolis is a hill rising 500 feet above the city of Athens. On it stand the remains of some of the finest temples of ancient Greece. The largest and most famous of these temples is the Parthenon, dedicated to Athena. This magnificent white marble building was surrounded by columns. Inside stood a huge statue of Athena, made of gold and ivory. Carvings all around the building showed scenes from the Panathenaean procession.

patron special guardian, protector, or supporter

trident three-pronged spear, similar to a pitchfork

69

Related Entries
Other entries related to Athena are listed at the end of this article.

This Roman statue of Athena as goddess of warfare offers another view of the goddess, usually identified with wisdom and crafts. Although she championed military skill and courage, Athena frowned on violence and bloodshed.

times, visitors to Athens were taken to see Athena's olive tree and the rock that Poseidon had struck.

Despite her virgin status, Athena ended up raising a child. According to one myth, Hephaestus became attracted to her and tried to force his attentions on her. The powerful Athena resisted him, and Hephaestus's semen fell to the ground. From that seed was born the half-man, half-snake Erichthonius. Athena put the baby in a box and gave him to the daughters of Cecrops, king of Athens. She told them to care for him but not to look in the box. Two of the daughters looked inside and, driven mad, jumped off the Acropolis to their deaths. Athena then took Erichthonius to her temple and reared him herself. Later he became king of Athens and honored her greatly.

Although Athena favored the Greeks, she was also important to the people of Troy. They erected a statue of her, called the Palladium, and believed that as long as it remained in Troy, the city could not be conquered. To win the Trojan War, the Greeks first had to creep into the city to steal the statue.

Patron of Crafts, Civilization, and Wisdom

As goddess of handicrafts, Athena created many useful items, such as the potter's wheel, vase, horse bridle, chariot, and ship. She was the patron of architects and sculptors and the inventor of numbers and mathematics, which of course influenced many aspects of civilization. Athena took a special interest in agricultural work, giving farmers the rake, plow, and yoke and teaching them how to use oxen to cultivate their fields. In addition, she helped women by inventing spinning and weaving.

Athena even tried her hand at musical instruments. She created the flute to imitate the wailing of the **Gorgons** when Medusa was killed. However, when the goddess saw her reflection playing this new instrument with her cheeks puffed out, she was disgusted with her appearance. She threw the flute away and put a curse on the first person to pick it up. Marsyus the **satyr** did so and suffered the consequences when he dared challenge Apollo to a musical contest. Some sources say that Athena threw away the flute because the other gods laughed at her for looking so ridiculous.

Nonetheless, in her wisdom, Athena was generally a kindly goddess. She promoted good government, looking after the welfare of kings who asked for her guidance and advising government officials. Athena was a goddess of justice tempered by mercy. Her work led Athens to adopt trial by jury.

Like the other gods, however, Athena did not tolerate lack of respect. She turned Arachne into a spider after Arachne boasted that she could spin more skillfully than Athena. She also blinded Tiresias when he happened upon a stream where she was bathing and saw her nude. Because his fault was accidental, she softened his punishment by giving him the gift of **prophecy.**

Festivals, Art, and Literature

Several festivals, some tied to the growing season, were held in honor of Athena. Processions of priests, priestesses, and other members of society—particularly young girls—often formed part of the celebration. The goddess's most important festival was the Panathenaea. Started as a harvest festival, this annual event gradually changed into a celebration of Athena. A great parade of people from the city and surrounding areas brought the goddess gifts and sacrifices. Athletic competitions, poetry readings, and musical contests rounded out the festival. The Panathenaea came to rival the Olympic Games.

In works of art, Athena is usually portrayed as a warrior. She wears a helmet and breastplate and carries a spear and a shield adorned with the head of Medusa. An owl generally sits on her shoulder or hand or hovers nearby. The Romans frequently depicted the goddess wearing a coat of armor.

Athena inspired numerous paintings and statues. The great Athenian sculptor Phidias produced several works, including a 30-foot bronze piece and an ivory and gold statue that was housed in

Gorgon one of three ugly monsters who had snakes for hair, staring eyes, and huge wings

satyr woodland deity that was part man and part goat or horse

prophecy foretelling of what is to come; also something that is predicted

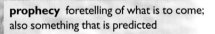

the Parthenon. The statue of Athena kept in the Roman temple of the goddess Vesta was said to be the Palladium of Troy, taken by the Trojan prince Aeneas† when he fled the burning city.

Athena and her stories appear in many literary works as well. In Greek literature, she is a prominent character in the *Iliad* and the *Odyssey,* and her influence is felt throughout the plays of Aeschylus, Sophocles†, and Euripides†. In the works of Roman writers Virgil† and Ovid, the goddess also plays a leading role. ***See also*** Arachne; Artemis; Bellerophon; Helen of Troy; Hercules; Iliad, The; Jason; Medusa; Odysseus; Pegasus; Perseus; Poseidon; Tiresias; Titans; Vulcan; Zeus.

Atlantis

According to the ancient Greeks, Atlantis was an island located in the Atlantic Ocean beyond the Straits of Gibraltar. It was an island paradise that sank into the sea one day. Since ancient times, many people have tried to explain the legend of Atlantis or to find what remains of the island.

Origin of the Legend

The tale of Atlantis comes from the Greek philosopher Plato, who lived in the 300s B.C. In two of his works, the *Timaeus* and the *Critias,* he relates that the famous Athenian lawgiver Solon had heard the story of Atlantis when he visited Egypt. In the very distant past, a great island as large as North Africa and the Near East combined existed in the Atlantic Ocean. The island belonged to Poseidon (Neptune)†, who fell in love with a young woman of the island named Cleito and married her. Poseidon built a city on the island, and on a mountain in the center of the city, he built a palace for Cleito. The couple had ten children, and in time Poseidon divided the island among them, giving each a section to rule.

Atlantis was a paradise: no one had to work hard, every type of wonderful food grew there, and animals were plentiful. Poseidon had created a stream of hot water and a stream of cold water for the island. It had a glorious culture with wonderful palaces and temples. The kings were rich in gold, silver, and other precious metals. The people of Atlantis lived in a golden age of harmony and abundance.

Then things began to change. The gods started to intermarry with humans. The Atlanteans became greedy for more than they had. They decided to conquer the lands around the Mediterranean. Angered by the Atlanteans' behavior, Zeus† sent an earthquake, or perhaps a series of earthquakes, that made Atlantis sink into the sea in the course of one day and one night.

A Lasting Legend

Scholars of the Middle Ages and the Renaissance believed that Plato was recounting a real event. They were curious about the location of Atlantis. After the discovery of the Americas, some Europeans

†*See **Names and Places** at the end of this volume for further information.*

Paradise Lost

Many cultures have stories about a "golden age" in the distant past when people were happy and lived without working. Usually the earthly paradise was lost as a result of greed. The golden age of the ancient Greeks was ruled by Cronus (called Saturn by the Romans). When Zeus took over, the Silver, Bronze, and Iron Ages followed, each less happy and less prosperous than the previous one. In the mythology of Persia†, Masha and Mashyoi lost their paradise when they were fooled by the evil spirit. A Mayan myth tells of perfect people, made out of cornmeal, who became too proud. The gods put a mist before their eyes to weaken their understanding.

made a connection between the newly found lands and Atlantis. Some thought that the Native Americans might be descendants of the people of Atlantis who fled their destroyed island. The legend of Atlantis inspired writers and thinkers. Sir Francis Bacon, an English philosopher of the 1600s, wrote a political fable called *The New Atlantis* that described an ideal world.

In the 1800s, the myth regained popularity. Scholars and popular writers both tried to use scientific evidence to support the existence of Atlantis. Many, however, used only the evidence that supported their ideas and conveniently ignored the rest. Although geological studies of the ocean floor revealed no sunken islands or continents at the bottom of the Atlantic Ocean, the legend persisted. In fact, people from lands as diverse as Scotland, the Basque region of Spain, and Scandinavia have claimed the Atlanteans as their ancestors.

Modern Developments

Since 1960, geological, meteorological, and archaeological studies have tended to support the legend, though not in its original form. Many scientists now think that Atlantis was actually the island of Thera in the Mediterranean Sea, near the island of Crete. Thera (now called Thíra) was one of the colonies of the rich Minoan civilization of Crete. The Minoans built luxurious palaces and temples and traded all over the Mediterranean. Geologists and meteorologists have established that around 1470 B.C. the volcano of Thera erupted, and part of the island sank into the sea. Subsequent earthquakes destroyed much that was on Crete. Archaeologists have studied Thíra and have found the remains of a large Minoan town built around the volcano. The town has a palace and waterways that seem to match the general plan described by Plato. *See also* EDEN, GARDEN OF; POSEIDON.

Atlas

Titan one of a family of giants who ruled the earth until overthrown by the Greek gods of Olympus
nymph minor goddess of nature, usually represented as young and beautiful

In Greek mythology, Atlas was a **Titan,** a son of the Titan Iapetus and the **nymph** Clymene. After the Titans lost a war against Zeus†, Atlas was condemned by Zeus to stand forever holding up the heavens. (A collection of maps has been called an atlas since the 1500s, when the mapmaker Mercator put a picture of Atlas holding up the world—not the heavens—on the title page of his book.) Because the place where Atlas stood to perform his task was the westernmost end of the world known to the ancient Greeks, the ocean near him was called Atlantic in his honor.

Atlas belonged to an illustrious family. One of his brothers was Prometheus, god of fire and creator of mankind. His daughters included the Pleiades (the stars that announced good spring weather), the Hyades (the stars that announced the rainy season), and the nymph Calypso. In addition, he was either the father or the grandfather of the Hesperides, the maidens who guarded a tree bearing golden apples.

In Greek mythology, Atlas was usually responsible for holding up the heavens. This marble relief from a Greek temple shows Hercules holding up the world for Atlas so that Atlas can bring him the golden apples of the Hesperides.

Gorgon one of three ugly monsters who had snakes for hair, staring eyes, and huge wings

prophecy foretelling of what is to come; also something that is predicted

Many different stories are told about Atlas. One of them concerns Perseus, son of Zeus and slayer of the **Gorgon** Medusa. Because of a **prophecy** that a son of Zeus would one day steal the golden apples of the Hesperides, Atlas refused to offer Perseus hospitality when he came to visit. Insulted, Perseus showed him the severed head of Medusa, which had the power to turn all who looked at it into stone. Atlas turned into stone. The stone became the Atlas Mountains in what is now the country of Morocco.

Another story concerns Hercules (Heracles)†, the grandson of Perseus. One of the labors of Hercules was to obtain some of the golden apples that were guarded by the Hesperides. Hercules asked Atlas to help him get the apples. Seeing an opportunity to escape from the burden of holding up the heavens, Atlas asked Hercules to take over the task while he obtained the apples. Hercules agreed. When Atlas returned with the apples, he told Hercules that he would deliver them for him. His intention was to leave Hercules to support the heavens. However, Hercules asked Atlas to take back the heavens for just a moment so that he could adjust his burden. When Atlas did this, Hercules walked away with the apples. *See also* HERCULES; MEDUSA; PROMETHEUS; TITANS.

Attis

Attis was a god of vegetation, associated with death and **resurrection.** He was worshiped in Phrygia, an ancient country of Asia Minor†, and later throughout the Roman empire.

Many different accounts of Attis's life and death exist. According to one story, he was a young, handsome shepherd who was

†*See **Names and Places** at the end of this volume for further information.*

resurrection coming to life again; rising from the dead

nymph minor goddess of nature, usually represented as young and beautiful

loved by Cybele (by some accounts, his mother), the Phrygian goddess of fertility. When Cybele discovered that Attis had been unfaithful to her, she killed the **nymph** he had been with. Driven to madness, Attis then wounded himself under a pine tree and bled to death.

With his death, the earth's plant life ceased to grow. However, the gods agreed that Attis should be resurrected each spring. In this way, he came to be associated with the cycle of the seasons, dying in the winter and being reborn in the spring. As part of an annual spring festival, the Romans would cut down a pine tree in Attis's honor. Worshipers adorned the tree with violets, which they considered to have grown from the blood of Attis. *See also* CYBELE.

Atum

chaos great disorder or confusion

In ancient Egyptian mythology, Atum was a creator god associated with Heliopolis, a city near the Nile River delta that was a center of sun worship. In some accounts, Atum created himself. In others, he was produced by four frogs and four snakes, symbolizing the **chaos** of earliest times.

According to one creation myth, Atum made the first divine couple: Shu, god of air, and Tefnut, goddess of moisture. From the union of this pair came the earth god Geb and the sky goddess Nut. Images of Atum often show him as an elderly bearded man, sometimes wearing the combined crowns of Lower and Upper Egypt. Over time, the myths of Atum merged with those of Ra (Re), the great sun god. Later Ra became linked with Amun, another creator god, emerging as Amun-Ra, an all-powerful supreme being. As a result, Atum became associated with the setting sun. *See also* AMUN; RA (RE).

Aurora

Titan one of a family of giants who ruled the earth until overthrown by the Greek gods of Olympus

Aurora was the Roman goddess of the dawn. The Greeks called her Eos. She was the daughter of the **Titans** Hyperion and Theia and the sister of Helios (the sun god) and Selene (the moon goddess). Every morning, Aurora arose from the sea and rode in her horse-drawn chariot across the sky ahead of the sun, carrying a pitcher from which she sprinkled dew upon the earth.

Aurora's first husband was the Titan Astraeus. They had several sons: the winds Boreas, Eurus, Notus, and Zephyrus as well as the morning star Eosphorus and the evening star Hesperus. Aurora's beauty caused Mars, the god of war, to take an interest in her. This angered Venus (Aphrodite)†, who caused Aurora to fall in love with a number of mortals. She married one of them, Tithonus, and begged Zeus† to make him immortal. Zeus granted her wish, but she had forgotten to ask for Tithonus's eternal youth too. As a result, he continued to age until he became decrepit and shriveled. Aurora shut him away in his room until the gods finally took pity on him and turned him into a cicada. *See also* BOREAS.

Australian Mythology

Australia, a vast land dominated by desert and semidesert landscapes, was first inhabited by the Aborigines. The mythology of Australia comes from these people and has been influenced by their very close relationship with the natural environment. Most of the myths deal with the features of the landscape, how they were created, and their importance to the Aborigines.

In Australian mythology, there are no standard versions of individual myths. Instead, a tale about a particular character varies from region to region. The reason for these variations in the mythology lies in the lifestyle of the Aborigines.

Origins and Influences

The first humans to inhabit Australia may have arrived more than 75,000 years ago. They probably came from the islands to the north that are now known as Indonesia or from islands in the Pacific Ocean. Some historians believe that the earliest inhabitants traveled overland, across a land bridge that once connected Australia and southeastern Asia. Later immigrants arrived by raft or boat after the ocean rose and covered the land route.

The early inhabitants were seminomads who survived by hunting wild animals, fishing, and gathering fruits and plants. Each group had a home territory where their ancestors had originally settled. However, most groups moved with the seasons as they ran out of food and fresh water. This seminomadic lifestyle exposed some Aborigines to different areas and brought various groups into contact with one another.

Types of Myths

Australian myths deal with the creation of the world, floods and drought and other natural disasters, and major events in the life cycle, such as birth and death. Most myths are set in the local terrain and explain the origins of features of the land, including hills and valleys, water holes, and places of safety or danger. Listening to the stories, the Aborigines learn about the local geography while reinforcing their bonds to the group and its heritage.

Storytelling. In Aboriginal culture many types of information, including myths and legends, are transmitted orally. Storytellers rely on techniques such as repetition and special expressions that always take the same form. They use songs, chants, and sand paintings to help tell the tale. Journeys, the subject of many Aboriginal stories, are described by explaining what happened at each place along the way.

Myths fall into different categories. Some are public and may be shared with all members of a group. Others are restricted: only people who have participated in certain special ceremonies may hear them. Some sacred stories may be told by and heard only by men, while others are restricted to women or to the elder members of the community.

End of an Era

For thousands of years, the Aborigines' way of life was touched little by outside influences. Then, in the late 1700s and early 1800s, European colonists began to arrive in Australia. Today the Aborigines make up little more than 2 percent of Australia's population, and few of them maintain their traditional way of life. Aware that the breakdown of their seminomadic lifestyle and oral tradition could lead to a loss of their heritage, some Aborigines are making an effort to collect and record the myths and legends they know for future generations.

Dreamtime. The Aborigines believe that the world began during a mythical period called Dreamtime, or The Dreaming. During this time, ancestral beings that slept beneath the ground emerged from the earth. They created the landscape, made people, established the laws by which people lived, and taught them how to survive. After the ancestral beings' work was done, they returned underground.

The Aborigines actively recall the events of Dreamtime. By participating in certain **rituals,** individuals can reenact the journeys of their ancestors.

ritual ceremony that follows a set pattern

Ritual. As important as the myths themselves are the rituals that accompany their reenactment. The rituals involve singing, dancing, and painting, which according to the Aborigines, nurture the land, the people, and the ancestral beings. The individuals performing the ritual call upon the ancestral beings and later sing a song to return them to their place of emergence.

Rituals also include the creation of mythological designs, such as the body paintings, ground paintings, rock paintings, and engravings found throughout Australia. The Aborigines decorate sacred objects and weapons to represent certain myths. They chant a myth to attach it to the object being decorated. When a sacred object or place is touched, struck, or rubbed, it releases the spirit that inhabits it. Such rituals are preserved and repeated to establish ties between past, present, and future generations.

Main Myths and Mythical Figures

Aboriginal myths often tell of a big flood, with local variations. The Worrorra people in western Australia describe an enormous flood that destroyed the previous landscape. It was caused by ancestral figures called the *wandjina,* who then spread throughout the land, establishing a new society. Other groups say the flood was brought by a great serpent that still exists in deep pools of water or off the coast.

The Tiwi, from islands off the northern coast, tell of the old woman Mudungkala who rose up from the ground carrying three children. These children were the ancestors of all the islands' inhabitants. As Mudungkala walked across the landscape, water

These paintings from Nourlangie Rock in the Northern Territory of Australia are examples of X-ray art, a style practiced by the Aborigines of the region. The works show both the internal organs and the skeletons of the figures.

rose up in her wake and cut the islands off from the mainland. According to some myths, the people of the land were created by two sisters and a brother called the Djang'kawu, who traveled throughout the land. Their journey is recalled in a cycle of more than 500 songs.

Aboriginal beliefs about the origin of death vary. One tale about death says that Crow and Crab argued about the best way to die. Crab crawled off into a hole, shed her shell, and waited for a new one to grow. Crow said that this took too long and that he had a better way. He rolled back his eyes and fell over dead. The Murinbata people have a ritual dance comparing the two types of death, and it shows that Crow's way is the better way.

Other popular mythical figures include the Seven Sisters. According to a version of their story told in central and southern Australia, the sisters fled from central Australia to Port Augusta on the south coast to escape a man named Nyiru who wanted to rape the oldest sister. They traveled over hundreds of miles, and many features of the landscape of today are associated with their journey. For example, legend has it that a low cliff near Mount Conner is a windbreak they constructed, and a cave is a hut they built. One of the wild fig trees nearby is the oldest sister. At the end of the journey, the sisters turned into the constellation called the Pleiades, and Nyiru became some of the stars in the constellation Orion.

Tales about **tricksters** who often cause trouble are believed to be some of the earliest myths. Tricksters typically appear as characters who upset the natural order of things by stealing or by causing humans to fight or engage in other unpleasant behavior. People of the Kimberly region in northwestern Australia say that a race of tricksters called the Wurulu-Wurulu use flowers mounted on sticks to steal honey from bees' nests. An empty nest is said to be a sign that the Wurulu-Wurulu have been there. **See also** ANIMALS IN MYTHOLOGY; CREATION STORIES; DJANG'KAWU; DREAMTIME; TRICKSTERS; WANDJINA.

Ayers Rock

Ayers Rock is a huge dome-shaped rock in central Australia. According to Aboriginal myths, the gullies and holes on the south side of Ayers Rock were battle scars left over from a battle between snake men. To the southwest of the rock are some stands of oak trees. These were said to be young warriors waiting silently to join in the battle.

trickster mischievous figure appearing in various forms in the folktales and mythology of many different peoples

Avalon

In Celtic† mythology, Avalon was an earthly paradise generally described as a land of plenty where eternal spring, health, and harmony reigned. On this island of apple trees, food-producing plants were so abundant that no one ever needed to farm the land. The enchantress Morgan Le Fay and her eight sisters, all expert healers, ruled Avalon.

After King Arthur was mortally wounded, he was taken by boat to Avalon. There, Morgan Le Fay cared for him and healed his wounds. Arthur remained there until it was time for him to return to rule Britain again. Avalon has long been identified with the town of Glastonbury in Somerset, England. Arthur and his wife, Guinevere, are said to have been buried at the abbey there. **See also** ARTHUR, KING; ARTHURIAN LEGENDS; CELTIC MYTHOLOGY; MORGAN LE FAY.

†See **Names and Places** at the end of this volume for further information.

Aztec Mythology

deity god or goddess

city-state independent state consisting of a city and its surrounding territory

pantheon all the gods of a particular culture

The Fiery Birth of the Sun

According to Aztec myth, at the beginning of this world, darkness covered the earth. The gods gathered at a sacred place and made a fire. Nanahuatzin, one of the gods, leaped into the fire and came out as the sun. However, before he could begin to move through the sky, the other gods had to give the sun their blood. This was one of several myths relating how the gods sacrificed themselves to set the world in motion. Through bloodletting and human sacrifice people imitated the sacrifices made by the gods—and kept the sun alive by feeding it with blood.

ritual ceremony that follows a set pattern

The mythology of the Aztec civilization, which dominated central Mexico in the 1400s and early 1500s, described a universe of grandeur and dread. Worlds were created and destroyed in the myths, and splendid gods warred among themselves. Everyday items—colors, numbers, directions, days of the calendar—took on special meaning because each was associated with a **deity.** Aztec religious life ranged from keeping small pottery statues of the gods in homes to attending elaborate public ceremonies involving human sacrifice.

Origins and Influences

The Aztecs migrated to central Mexico from the north in the 1200s. According to their legends, they came from a land called Aztlan, the source of their name. The Aztecs were not a single people but several groups, including the Colhua-Mexica, the Mexica, and the Tenocha. In the early 1300s, these groups formed an alliance and together founded a **city-state** called Tenochtitlán on the site where Mexico City stands today. The people of Tenochtitlán rose to power and conquered a large empire during the 1400s.

The Aztecs were newcomers in a region long occupied by earlier civilizations such as those of the Olmecs and the Toltecs, who had developed a **pantheon** of gods and a body of myths and legends. The Aztecs absorbed deities, stories, and beliefs from these earlier peoples and from the Maya of southern Mexico. As a result, Aztec mythology contained religious and mythological traditions that many groups in Mexico and Central America shared. However, under the Aztecs certain aspects of the religion, notably human sacrifice, came to the forefront.

Major Themes and Deities

In the Aztec view of the universe, human life was small and insignificant. An individual's fate was shaped by forces beyond his or her control. The gods created people to work and fight for them. They did not offer favors or grant direct protection, although failure to serve the gods properly could lead to doom and destruction.

Main Themes. The idea that people were servants of the gods was a theme that ran through Aztec mythology. Humans had the responsibility of keeping the gods fed—otherwise, disaster could strike at any time. The food of the gods was a precious substance found in human blood. The need to satisfy the gods, especially the sun god, gave rise to a related theme: human sacrifice.

Priests conducted ceremonies at the temples, often with crowds in attendance. With song and dance, masked performers acted out myths, and the priests offered sacrifices. To prepare for the ceremonies, the priests performed a **ritual** called bloodletting, which involved pulling barbed cords across their tongues or other body parts to draw blood. Bloodletting was similar to a

Coatlicue, the Aztec goddess of the earth, wore a skirt made out of snakes and a necklace of human hearts. She was usually portrayed with clawed hands and feet. This monumental statue of Coatlicue measures more than 8 feet tall.

predetermined decided in advance
destiny future or fate of an individual or thing
divination act or practice of foretelling the future

primal earliest; existing before other things

Mayan ceremony known as the Vision Quest. Peoples before the Aztecs had practiced human sacrifice, but the Aztecs made it the centerpiece of their rituals. Spanish explorers reported witnessing ceremonies in which hundreds of people met their deaths on sacrificial altars. The need for prisoners to sacrifice was one reason for the Aztecs's drive to conquer other Indians, although it was certainly not the only reason.

Sacrifice was linked to another theme, that of death and rebirth. The Aztecs believed that the world had died and been reborn several times and that the gods also died and were reborn. Sometimes the gods even sacrificed themselves for the good of the world. Though death loomed large in Aztec mythology, it was always balanced by fertility and the celebration of life and growth.

Another important idea in Aztec mythology was that a **predetermined** fate shaped human lives. The Aztec ball game, about which historians know little, may have been related to this theme. Aztec temples, like those of other peoples throughout Mexico and Central America, had walled courts where teams of players struck a rubber ball with their hips, elbows, and knees, trying to drive it through a stone ring. Some historians believe that the game represented the human struggle to control **destiny.** It was a religious ritual, not simply a sport, and players may have been sacrificed after the game.

The theme of fate was also reflected in the Aztecs' use of the calendar. Both the Aztecs and the Maya developed elaborate systems of recording dates with two calendars: a 365-day solar calendar, based on the position of the sun, and a 260-day ritual calendar used for **divination.** Each day of the ritual calendar was influenced by a unique combination of gods and goddesses. Divination involved interpreting the positive or negative meanings of these influences, which determined an individual's fate. Priests also used the ritual calendar to choose the most favorable days for such activities as erecting buildings, planting crops, and waging war.

The 365-day and 260-day cycles meshed, like a smaller wheel within a larger one, to create a 52-year cycle called the Calendar Round. At the end of a Calendar Round, the Aztecs put out all their fires. To begin a new Calendar Round, priests oversaw a ceremony in which new fires were lit from flames burning in a sacrificial victim's chest.

A third key theme of Aztec myth was that of duality, a balance between two equal and opposing forces. Many of the Aztec gods and goddesses were dualistic, which meant that they had two sides or roles. Deities often functioned in pairs or opposites. In addition, the same god could appear under multiple names or identities, perhaps because the Aztecs had blended elements of their myths from a variety of sources.

Major Deities. Duality was the basic element of the **primal** deity Ometecuhtli, who had a male side called Ometeotl and a female side known as Omecihuatl. The other gods and goddesses were their offspring. Their first four children were Tezcatlipoca, Quetzalcoatl, Huitzilopochtli, and Xipe Totec, the creator gods of Aztec mythology.

Aztec Deities

Deity	Meaning of Name	Role
Coatlicue	Lady of the Serpent Skirt	earth goddess
Huitzilopochtli	Hummingbird of the South	sun and war god
Ometecuhtli	Dual Lord	creator god
Quetzalcoatl	Feathered Serpent	god of twins and learning
Tezcatlipoca	Lord of the Smoking Mirror	god of the night sky
Tlaloc	Growth-maker	god of rain and fertility
Xipe Totec	Flayed Lord	god of vegetation, torture, and sacrifice

Originally a Toltec god, Tezcatlipoca (Lord of the Smoking Mirror) was god of the night sky. The color black and the direction north were associated with him. He possessed a magical mirror that allowed him to see inside people's hearts, and the Aztecs considered themselves his slaves. In his animal form, he appeared as a jaguar. His dual nature caused him to bring good fortune sometimes and misery at other times.

Tezcatlipoca's great rival and opponent in **cosmic** battles, as well as his partner in acts of creation, was Quetzalcoatl (Feathered Serpent), an ancient Mexican and Central American deity associated in Aztec mythology with the color white and the direction west. Some stories about Quetzalcoatl refer to him as an earthly priest-king, suggesting that there may have been a Toltec king by that name whose legend became mixed with mythology.

As a god, Quetzalcoatl had many different aspects. He was the planet Venus (both a morning and an evening star), the god of twins, and the god of learning. The Aztecs credited him with inventing the calendar. A peaceful god, Quetzalcoatl accepted sacrifices of animals and jade but not of human blood. When he was defeated by Tezcatlipoca, Quetzalcoatl sailed out into the Atlantic Ocean on a raft of serpents. The legend arose that he would return over the sea from the east at the end of one of the Aztec 52-year calendar cycles. When the white-skinned Spanish invader Hernán Cortés landed in Mexico in 1519, some Aztecs thought he was Quetzalcoatl come again—a belief Cortés encouraged.

Huitzilopochtli (Hummingbird of the South), a deity that originated with the Aztecs, was the sun and war god. The souls of warriors who died in battle were said to become hummingbirds and follow him across the sky. Blue was his color and south his direction.

cosmic large or universal in scale; having to do with the universe

81

cult group bound together by devotion to a particular person, belief, or god

The Loss of the Ancients

Many stories told of the Loss of the Ancients, the mythic event in which the first people disappeared from the earth. One version says that Tezcatlipoca stole the sun, but Quetzalcoatl chased him and knocked him back down to earth with a stick. Tezcatlipoca then changed into a jaguar and devoured the people who lived in that world. The Aztecs combined versions of this story to explain the disappearance of people at the end of each of the four worlds that had existed before theirs. Carvings on a stone calendar found in 1790 tell how jaguars, wind, fire, and flood in turn destroyed the Ancients.

The Aztecs claimed that an idol of Huitzilopochtli had led them south during their long migration and told them to build their capital on the site where an eagle was seen eating a snake. The **cult** of Huitzilopochtli was especially strong in Tenochtitlán, which regarded him as the city's founding god.

Xipe Totec (Flayed Lord) had a dual nature as well. He was a god of vegetation, of life-giving spring growth, and at the same time, a fearsome god of torture and sacrifice. His double meaning reflected the Aztec vision of a universal balance in which new life had to be paid for in blood. Xipe Totec's color was red, his direction east.

The Aztecs took up in addition the worship of Tlaloc, an important god of rain and fertility long known under various names in Mexico and Central America. He governed a host of lesser gods called Tlaloques, who made thunder and rain by smashing their water jars. Other deities, such as Huitzilopochtli's mother, the earth goddess Coatlicue (Lady of the Serpent Skirt), probably played key parts in the religion of the common people, who were mainly farmers. Many deities were associated with flowers, summer, fertility, and corn.

Major Myths

Many Aztec myths tell all or part of the story of the five suns. The Aztecs believed that four suns, or worlds, had existed before theirs. In each case, catastrophic events had destroyed everything, and the world had come to an end.

Tezcatlipoca created the first sun, known as Nahui-Ocelotl, or Four-Jaguar. It came to an end when Quetzalcoatl struck down Tezcatlipoca, who became a jaguar and destroyed all the people. Quetzalcoatl was the ruler of the second sun, Nahui-Ehécatl, or Four-Wind. However, Tezcatlipoca threw Quetzalcoatl off his throne, and together the fallen god and the sun were carried off by a hurricane of wind. People turned into monkeys and fled into the forest.

The third sun, Nahuiquiahuitl or Four-Rain, belonged to the rain god Tlaloc. Quetzalcoatl destroyed it with fire that fell from the heavens. The water goddess Chalchiuhtlicue ruled the fourth sun, called Nahui-Atl or Four-Water. A 52-year flood destroyed that sun, and the people turned into fish.

The Aztecs lived in the world of Nahui-Ollin (Four-Movement), the fifth sun. They believed that the earth was a flat disk divided into north, east, south, and west quarters, each associated with a color, special gods, and certain days. At the center was Huehueteotl, god of fire. Above the earth were 13 heavens; below it were 9 underworlds, where the dead dwelled, making 9 an extremely unlucky number. A myth about Tezcatlipoca and Quetzalcoatl tells how the world was quartered. They made the earth by seizing a woman from the sky and pulling her into the shape of a cross. Her body became the earth, which, angered by their rough treatment, devoured the dead.

Quetzalcoatl, known as the Feathered Serpent, was one of the major gods of Aztec mythology. This carved serpent's head appears on the Temple of Quetzalcoatl in Teotihuacán, Mexico.

Another myth tells of Tezcatlipoca and Quetzalcoatl working together to raise the sky. After the flood that ended the fourth sun, the sky collapsed onto the earth. The two gods became trees, and as they grew, they pushed the sky up. Leaving the trees supporting the sky, one at each end of the earth, they climbed onto the sky and met in the Milky Way.

Quetzalcoatl gave life to the people of the fifth sun by gathering the bones of the only man and woman who had survived the long flood and sprinkling them with his own blood. The gods created the world with blood and required the sacrifice of human blood to keep it intact. One day, however, the fifth sun would meet its end in an all-destroying earthquake.

The Aztec Legacy

The Spanish destroyed as many Aztec documents and images as they could, believing the Aztec religion to be not just **pagan** but devilish. At the same time, however, much of what we know about Tenochtitlán and Aztec customs comes from accounts of Spanish writers who witnessed the last days of the Aztec empire.

The legacy of Aztec mythology remains strong within Mexico. Aztec images and themes have influenced the arts and public life. In the late 1800s, Mexico had won independence from Spain but had not established its own national identity. Civic and cultural leaders of the new country began forming a vision of their past that was linked with the proud and powerful Aztec civilization. Symbols from Aztec carvings, such as images of the god Quetzalcoatl, began to appear on murals and postage stamps. Mexico's coat of arms featured an eagle clutching a snake in its beak, the mythic emblem of the founding of the Aztec capital.

pagan term used by early Christians to describe non-Christians and non-Christian beliefs

83

clay tablet baked clay slab inscribed with ancient writings

underworld land of the dead

During the 1920s, Mexico's education minister invited artists to paint murals on public buildings. The three foremost artists in this group were Diego Rivera, José Clemente Orozco, and David Alfaro Siqueiros. Although their works deal mainly with the Mexican Revolution and the hard life of Indians and peasants, the artists drew upon Aztec mythology for symbols and images to connect Mexico's present with its ancient past. Rivera, for example, once combined the images of the earth goddess Coatlicue and a piece of factory machinery. Aztec mythology has become part of Mexico's national identity. ***See also*** COATLICUE; HUEHUETEOTL; HUITZILOPOCHTLI; MAYAN MYTHOLOGY; QUETZALCOATL; SACRIFICE; TEZCATLIPOCA; TLALOC.

Baal

Baal was one of the most widely worshiped gods in ancient Canaan†, where he was associated with fertility and rain. He was the son of El, the supreme god of the Canaanites, and the husband and brother of Anat, the ferocious goddess of war.

Fertility and Storm God. *Baal* is a common Semitic† word that means "lord" or "owner." The title was given to the local god of nearly every city in Canaan. Because of the importance of rain to life in the dry lands of the Near East, these local gods were usually associated with fertility and the cycle of wet and dry seasons. Baal developed into a single, widely known god, called Lord of the Earth and Lord of the Rain and Dew. **Clay tablets** found at the ruins of the ancient town of Ras es-Shamrah (in present-day Syria) contain a series of stories about how Baal became the rain god and gained power over the waters of earth.

According to the tales, Yam, the sea god, demanded that Baal be made his slave. He sent messengers to Baal, asking him to surrender, but Baal attacked the messengers and drove them away. Baal then fought with Yam and, using two magic weapons, defeated him and seized control of the waters. In the story, Yam represents the destructive nature of water: rivers and seas flooding the land and ruining crops and killing animals. Baal represents water's positive powers: rain and dew providing the moisture needed to make crops grow.

Baal's Battle with Death. Other myths about Baal relate to fertility and the cycle of the seasons. One such story tells of the battle between Baal and Mot, the god of death and infertility. After conquering Yam, Baal complained that he had no house like the other gods did. El agreed to let the crafts god Kothar build Baal a fine house. When it was finished, Baal held a great feast—but he did not invite Mot or send him respectful presents. Greatly insulted, Mot asked Baal to come to the **underworld** to dine. Although afraid, Baal could not refuse the invitation. The food served at Mot's table was mud, the food of death, and when Baal ate it, he was trapped in the underworld.

While Baal was in the underworld, famine struck the earth, and El searched for someone to replace Baal. Asherah, the lady of the sea,

†*See **Names and Places** at the end of this volume for further information.*

winnow to separate the chaff, or useless part, of grain from the part that can be used for making flour

Beelzebub, Lord of the Flies

In the New Testament of the Bible, *Beelzebub* is one of the names given to Satan by Jesus. In some places, he is Satan's main assistant rather than Satan himself. The name comes from *Baalzebub,* the name of the god of the Philistine city of Ekron. *Baalzebub,* which means "lord of the flies," is probably a distorted version of *Baal,* or "lord of the house." The origin of the word is unknown.

cult group bound together by devotion to a particular person, belief, or god

convinced El to give Baal's throne to her son Ashtar. But when Ashtar, the god of irrigation, sat on the throne, his feet did not even touch the floor. Realizing he could not fill Baal's place, Ashtar gave up the throne.

Meanwhile, Baal's wife and sister, the fierce goddess Anat, traveled to the underworld. After splitting Mot with her sword, she **winnowed** him with her fan, burned the pieces in a fire, ground them in a mill, and planted them in the ground. These actions brought Baal back to life. Later Mot was also restored to life, and the two gods again battled each other. In the end, the sun goddess Shapath separated them, Baal regained his throne, and the land became fertile again.

Like the story of Yam, this myth emphasizes the importance of rain to the land. Baal represents the fertility of spring rains, while Mot represents the drought of the summer months. The actions taken by Anat against Mot—splitting, winnowing, burning, grinding, and planting—are steps taken by farmers when they harvest wheat. They prepare it for use as food during the winter and sow it to create more crops the next year. By defeating the drought (Mot), the rains (Baal) renew the earth each year and allow life to flourish in the dry Near East.

Baal in Other Ancient Cultures. Worship of Baal was widespread in the ancient Near East. The clay tablets of Ras es-Shamrah date from about 1500 B.C., and Baal was also popular in Egypt from about 1400 to 1075 B.C. In Mesopotamia, Baal was known to the Babylonians and Assyrians, and he was identified with their national gods Marduk and Ashur. The Greeks called the god Belos and identified him with Zeus†.

Like the other inhabitants of Canaan, the ancient Hebrews worshiped local gods called Baal and honored their children with names ending with *baal*—such as Ishbaal, the son of King Saul. In fact, the Hebrew god Yahweh appears to have shared many of Baal's characteristics.

As the worship of Yahweh became more important, Baal took on a negative meaning for the Hebrews. In the 800s B.C., a queen of Israel named Jezebel introduced a **cult** of Baal borrowed from the Phoenicians. She set up the cult as a rival to the official worship of Yahweh. Opposition to Baal grew so strong that over the next century the name *Baal* was replaced with the term *boshet,* meaning shame. In later texts, the name of Saul's son was changed from Ishbaal to Ishbosheth. Later still, Christians considered *Baal* to be a name for a devil. ***See also*** ANAT; DEVILS AND DEMONS; EL; JEZEBEL; SATAN; SEMITIC MYTHOLOGY; UNDERWORLD.

Babel, Tower of

The story of the Tower of Babel is told in the first book of the Old Testament of the Bible. After a great flood, some of Noah's descendants decided to build a city on the plains of southern Mesopotamia† with a tall tower reaching up into the heavens.

Their plan was to gain recognition for themselves as a people and to be able to stay together. When God saw what they were doing, however, he concluded that they were trying to gain more power. To make planning difficult for them, he made them speak many different languages. Unable to communicate with each other at the building site, the people gave up the project and scattered to different lands. The remains of the city became known as Babel.

The story of the tower may have developed from the way that later visitors interpreted the ruins of the old cities of that area. In Hebrew, the word *Babel* is a version of the name *Babylon,* which meant "the gate of God." In fact, researchers have found evidence of one or more tall towers in the ancient city of Babylon. Another Hebrew word, *balal,* means "confusion." Today the image of the Tower of Babel is used to mean confusion and failure to communicate. ***See also*** SEMITIC MYTHOLOGY.

Bacchus

See *Dionysus.*

Badb

In Celtic† mythology, Badb was the goddess of war. Often appearing in the form of a raven or crow, she would confuse and frighten armies by flying over the battlefield and shrieking loudly. In some stories, she belonged to the Morrigan, a trio of war goddesses that included Nemain and Macha.

Badb was also the goddess of death: her appearance seemed to indicate that someone was about to die. In the role of "the washer at the ford," Badb washed the equipment of warriors who were about to die. Some sources say that Badb was a friend and helper of the Irish folk hero Cuchulain. When Cuchulain was killed, Badb flew over his body in the form of a crow. The fact that Cuchulain did not strike out at her proved that he was dead. ***See also*** CELTIC MYTHOLOGY; CUCHULAIN.

Balaam

prophet one who claims to have received divine messages or insights

In the Old Testament of the Bible, Balaam is a **prophet** sent by King Balak of Moab (an area in what is now Jordan) to curse the Hebrews. Balaam agrees to do so but says that he will only speak words inspired by the Hebrew god Yahweh. As Balaam makes his way to see the Hebrews, Yahweh sends an angel to block the way. The angel is invisible to Balaam but not to his donkey, which sees the angel and refuses to go farther. Balaam beats the donkey for refusing to continue. Eventually, after several beatings, the donkey speaks. It asks why it is being beaten and explains that it stopped only because an angel was in the way. Balaam recognizes, from the miracle of hearing the donkey speak, that he is in Yahweh's presence. Yahweh allows Balaam to continue on his journey but commands him to bless the Hebrews instead of cursing them. This Balaam does, despite pressure from King Balak. During the Middle Ages, many Christians believed that the donkey that Jesus rode into Jerusalem was a direct descendant of Balaam's donkey.

†*See **Names and Places** at the end of this volume for further information.*

Balder

In Norse† mythology, Balder (or Baldur) was the son of Odin, king of the gods, and of Odin's wife, Frigg. Balder was the most beautiful of the gods and the one most beloved by Odin. As a youth, he led a happy life and eventually married Nanna. Soon, however, Balder began to suffer from terrible dreams that threatened him with death. Fearing for his safety, Frigg asked everything in creation, whether living or not—including animals, birds, stones, wood, and metal—to take an oath not to hurt Balder. There was only one thing that she did not ask to make such a promise: the mistletoe plant. Frigg thought that the mistletoe was too young to take an oath.

After everyone and everything had taken Frigg's oath, the gods would amuse themselves by throwing things at Balder because they knew nothing could harm him. However, the evil god Loki decided to find a way to hurt Balder. Loki transformed himself into an old woman and went to visit Frigg. The old woman asked if it was true that all things had taken an oath not to hurt Balder. Frigg admitted that she had not asked the mistletoe to take the oath. Loki then went to the place where the mistletoe grew and took a twig from it.

Next, Loki approached Balder's blind brother Höd (or Hodur) and asked why he was not throwing things at Balder like everyone else. Höd replied that he could not see Balder, and besides, he had nothing to throw. Loki then handed Höd a dart he had made from the mistletoe and offered to guide Höd's hand as he threw it. The dart struck Balder and killed him instantly. The gods were shocked and confused. Frigg begged someone to go to the **underworld** and pay a ransom to bring back her son. Hermod, another of Odin's sons, volunteered to go to recover Balder.

Hermod journeyed to the underworld, where he stayed one night. Hel, the goddess of death, told him that if everything under heaven shed a tear for Balder, she would allow him to return. However, if even one thing—living or dead—spoke against Balder or refused to weep for him, he would have to remain in the underworld. The gods sent messengers to every part of world to ask everything to weep for Balder. They thought they had succeeded until they found an old hag named Thökk sitting in a cave. They asked her to weep for Balder, but she refused. Most accounts suggest that Thökk was none other than Loki, the god of evil, in disguise.

***See also* FRIGG; HEL; LOKI; NORSE MYTHOLOGY; ODIN.**

underworld land of the dead

Balder was protected against all living things—except mistletoe. This print shows the evil god Loki guiding the blind god Höd to kill Balder with a branch of mistletoe.

Banshee

Banshee is the English spelling of *bean-sídhe,* the name of a female fairy of Irish and Celtic† folklore. The banshee's nighttime howling warned people that the death of a relative was about to take place. When an important or holy person was about to die, several banshees would wail or sing together. According to some legends, the banshees were accompanied by a large black coach carrying a coffin and pulled by headless horses. When the coach arrived at a house, a basin of blood was thrown at the person who opened the door. However, if a banshee loved a person who was near death, she would sing a gentle song that predicted death but also comforted the dying person and family members. *See also* CELTIC MYTHOLOGY.

Basilisk

In European mythology, the basilisk was a small serpent that could kill any living thing with its glance or breath. It was usually shown as a creature with a dragon's body and wings and a serpent's head. The basilisk first appeared in legends from ancient Greece and Rome. In the 1100s, St. Hildegard wrote of the serpent coming out of an egg sat upon by a toad.

This German woodcut from 1510 represents a mythological creature, the basilisk. It was usually shown with wings, a crested head, and a dragon's body. The basilisk was known as the cockatrice to the Elizabethans.

†*See **Names and Places** at the end of this volume for further information.*

Early myths mentioned weasels and cocks as enemies of the basilisk. It was believed that a basilisk would die if it heard a cock crowing. Another way to destroy a basilisk was to hold a mirror up to its face. The creature would die immediately after seeing its reflection. Travelers often carried cocks, weasels, or mirrors for protection when they traveled to regions where basilisks lived.

Called the king of serpents, the basilisk was often associated with the devil and symbolized the deadly sin of **lust.** Jesus is depicted fighting one in medieval art. The basilisk is also mentioned in literature by the English writers Chaucer and Spenser and is referred to in Shakespeare's plays *Romeo and Juliet* and *Richard III.* ***See also* DEVILS AND DEMONS; SERPENTS AND SNAKES.**

lust strong desire

Baucis and Philemon

Baucis and Philemon, an old couple from the land of Phrygia†, showed hospitality toward the gods and were rewarded. According to Greek myth, the gods Zeus† and Hermes† assumed human form and visited earth disguised as poor travelers. When they reached Phrygia, they looked for shelter but were turned away by everyone except Philemon and his wife, Baucis.

The old couple gladly shared their small amount of food and wine with the strangers. Baucis and Philemon realized that their guests were gods after noticing that the wine jug never ran out and that their poor wine was replaced by wine of the finest quality. Zeus and Hermes led the couple to a hill above Phrygia and sent a flood to destroy the land to punish the people who had turned them away. Only the old couple's house remained undamaged. Zeus made the house a temple to the gods and awarded Baucis and Philemon two wishes: to serve as priest and priestess of the temple and, when the time came, to die together. Many years later, when the moment of their deaths came, Baucis and Philemon were transformed into trees with intertwined branches. ***See also* GREEK MYTHOLOGY; HERMES; ZEUS.**

Bellerophon

In Greek mythology, Bellerophon was a hero and warrior who accidentally killed two men, including his own brother. He sought protection from King Proteus of Tiryns, who allowed him to stay under his roof. Proteus's wife, Anteia (also called Stheneboea), tried to seduce Bellerophon, but he resisted her. Angry at being rejected, Anteia told her husband that Bellerophon had tried to rape her. Proteus was furious but did not want to kill his guest, so he sent Bellerophon to Anteia's father, King Iobates of Lycia. He also sent a note explaining what had happened and asking Iobates to kill Bellerophon.

Iobates, too, was reluctant to kill his guest, so he sent him on dangerous missions instead. First, he asked Bellerophon to kill the Chimaera, a fire-breathing monster with the head of a lion, the body of a goat, and the tail of a serpent. With the help of the gods, Bellerophon tamed the winged horse Pegasus† and then used it to fight and kill the Chimaera. Next, Iobates ordered Bellerophon to

89

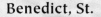

defeat two armies, including the fierce Amazons†. Bellerophon succeeded in these missions as well.

Afterward, Bellerophon told the sea god Poseidon that Iobates seemed ungrateful for his help. In response, Poseidon caused a great flood to strike Lycia. Iobates finally realized that Bellerophon must be innocent of the charges against him. When he discovered the truth, Iobates gave Bellerophon one of his daughters as a bride and made him heir to the throne of Lycia.

Proud of his success, Bellerophon tried to ride Pegasus to Mount Olympus, home of the gods. Zeus† sent a fly to bite Pegasus, who bucked and threw Bellerophon to the ground. Bellerophon survived the fall but was crippled for life. He spent the rest of his days wandering the earth as a beggar. *See also* AMAZONS; PEGASUS; PROTEUS; ZEUS.

Benedict, St.

abbot head of a monastery or abbey

patron special guardian, protector, or supporter

St. Benedict founded the Benedictine order and drew up the rules that became the basis for life in monasteries throughout Europe. Legends about him tell of his struggles with temptation and the miracles he performed.

Born into a wealthy family around A.D. 480, Benedict went to Rome to study. In time he became disgusted by the lack of morality in Rome and decided to live as a hermit in a cave some distance from the city. Benedict soon became famous in the area, and a local monastery asked him to become its **abbot.** However, the monks objected to the new abbot's strict rules of behavior and tried to poison him. Although Benedict returned to his cave, followers kept flocking to him. Eventually, he established 12 monasteries, each with 12 monks, and assumed control of all of them.

In about 525, Benedict founded the famous monastery of Monte Cassino. It was there that he wrote the Benedictine rule that set the standards for monastic life in western Europe. Because of his influence in spreading Christianity through the monastic movement, Pope Paul VI named Benedict the **patron** saint of all Europe in 1964.

Several legends tell of Benedict's struggles with the devil. In one, the devil turned into a beautiful woman to tempt him. To resist giving in to sin, Benedict threw himself into a thorn bush. In another story, the devil held down a stone to prevent it from being used to build the monastery at Monte Cassino. Workers could not move the stone, but after making the sign of the cross over it, Benedict picked up the stone himself. Other legends tell of miracles. For example, Benedict was chopping wood one day

St. Benedict is best known for establishing the Benedictine Rule, a code of monastic living that is still followed. In this Italian painting of the 1500s, St. Benedict whips a man to drive out the demon that has possessed him.

†See **Names and Places** *at the end of this volume for further information.*

when his ax broke. The head flew off the handle and landed in a lake. According to the legend, Benedict went to the water's edge and held the handle in the water. The ax head came out of the water and fitted itself back on the handle.

Beowulf

epic long poem about legendary or historical heroes, written in a grand style

pagan term used by early Christians to describe non-Christians and non-Christian beliefs

invulnerable incapable of being hurt

Beowulf is the title of the earliest existing Anglo-Saxon **epic.** It tells the story of Beowulf, a Norse† hero and warrior who fought and conquered several monsters that terrorized Denmark and Sweden. The poem combines elements of Anglo-Saxon culture with Christian moral values in an extraordinary adventure story.

Historical Background

The manuscript containing the story of Beowulf was discovered in England in the 1600s. It is written in Old English, the language of the Anglo-Saxon invaders who settled in England between A.D. 450 and 600. There is some debate about when *Beowulf* was written and who wrote it. Although the manuscript dates from around 1000, the poem was composed much earlier, sometime between 700 and 950. Certain references in the text suggest that the author was a Christian who modeled the story after **pagan** tales of Norse and German heroes of the past. The writer was probably either a monk or a poet connected to a nobleman's court in central or northern England.

 Beowulf is set in a much earlier time than the period in which it was composed, and the action takes place in Denmark and Sweden. The story reflects the warrior culture of ancient Germanic peoples, among whom wars were common and fighting was a traditional occupation. The king supplied his warriors with food, shelter, land, and weapons. In return, they were bound by oaths of loyalty and obedience to the king. The epic emphasizes values that were important to Norse warriors, such as courage, loyalty to one's king and comrades, and honor for those who fight and die bravely.

The Story of Beowulf

Beowulf is divided into two parts. The action in the first part takes place in Denmark, where Hrothgar is king. Beowulf, a mighty warrior from Sweden, comes to help the king destroy a monster. The second part, set in Sweden, provides an account of Beowulf as an old man who must rid his country of a fearsome dragon.

Hrothgar and Grendel. The story opens in Denmark. Hrothgar has built a great assembly hall called Heorot, where his warriors gather to eat, drink, and receive treasure after their victories in combat.

 Lurking in the dark swamps of Hrothgar's kingdom is a cruel and brutal monster named Grendel. Grendel lives in a cave with his mother, also a monster, and is **invulnerable** to the weapons of humans. As Grendel roams the marshes and swamps, he hears

91

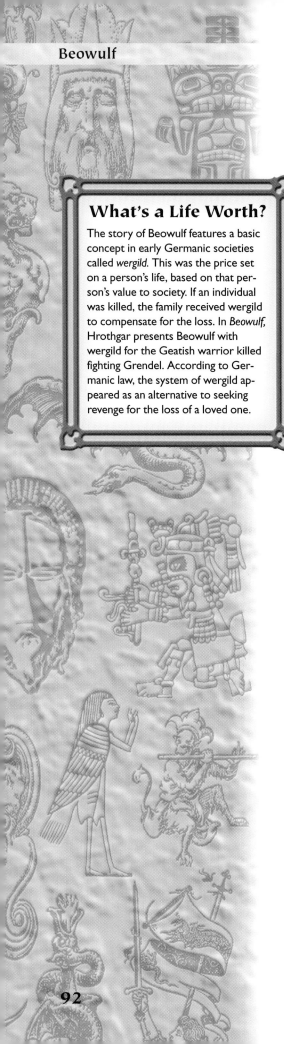

What's a Life Worth?

The story of Beowulf features a basic concept in early Germanic societies called *wergild*. This was the price set on a person's life, based on that person's value to society. If an individual was killed, the family received wergild to compensate for the loss. In *Beowulf,* Hrothgar presents Beowulf with wergild for the Geatish warrior killed fighting Grendel. According to Germanic law, the system of wergild appeared as an alternative to seeking revenge for the loss of a loved one.

the joyful sounds of song and laughter from Heorot. They fill him with envy and hatred for Hrothgar and his warriors. One night Grendel goes to Heorot and finds the warriors asleep after a great deal of drinking and celebration. He snatches up 30 sleeping men, kills them, and carries the bodies home to eat.

In the morning, Hrothgar sees the blood and the remains of Grendel's attack. Loud wails and cries replace the joyful singing of the previous night. The Danes see Grendel's footprints but do not think he will return. However, the next night Grendel comes again and kills even more warriors. The Danes gather in their temples and pray for protection from Grendel, but their prayers do not help. For 12 years Grendel terrorizes the warriors. Afraid to sleep at Heorot, they abandon the great hall.

Stories of Grendel's raids spread to the surrounding kingdoms, eventually reaching the land of the Geats in southern Sweden. Among the Geats is a mighty warrior named Beowulf, a man who has slain giants and sea monsters and is known for his strength, courage, and skill in battle. When he hears of Grendel's deeds, Beowulf decides to sail to Denmark and help Hrothgar rid his kingdom of the monster.

Beowulf prepares a ship and chooses 14 brave warriors to accompany him. They set sail for Denmark, arriving the next day. At Heorot, the Geats are welcomed by Hrothgar, who has known Beowulf since he was a child. The king throws a feast for the Geat warriors. At the feast, a Danish warrior named Unferth insults Beowulf by suggesting that he is too boastful and not a great enough warrior to kill Grendel. Beowulf responds by noting that he has heard no tales of Unferth's bravery. He says that if Unferth were as fierce as he believes himself to be that Grendel would not now be terrorizing the Danes. Pleased by Beowulf's defiant attitude, Hrothgar is confident that the Geat warrior will slay Grendel and free the kingdom from the monster's evil.

That night, the Geats stay at Heorot. Grendel soon appears and, before Beowulf can stop him, seizes and kills one of his men. Grendel then grabs Beowulf, but the mighty warrior seizes the monster's arm with his powerful grip. Beowulf and Grendel struggle until Grendel finally manages to wrench himself away, leaving his arm in Beowulf's grasp. The monster staggers back to his cave to die. The severed arm is hung in Heorot as a trophy for all to see. Hrothgar showers Beowulf with gifts and honors him with another feast. The Danes will once again be able to sleep in peace at Heorot.

Grendel's Mother. The Danes' troubles are not over, however. When Grendel's mother sees her dying son, she vows revenge. She goes to Heorot at night and surprises the Danish warriors. After killing the king's most trusted adviser, she leaves with Grendel's arm. Again the Danes call upon Beowulf for help.

Beowulf and several warriors track the monster to her lair in the swamps. The lair lies at the base of a cliff at the bottom of a pool bubbling with blood and gore. Unferth, who has by now changed his opinion of Beowulf, lends the Geat warrior his sword—named

Hrunting—to slay the beast. Brandishing the sword, Beowulf leaps into the slimy waters. Grendel's mother grabs Beowulf and pulls him into a cave where the water cannot enter. Beowulf strikes at the monster with Hrunting, but the sword does not hurt her. The two wrestle, and the monster almost kills Beowulf, but his armor saves him. Then he sees a giant sword hanging on the wall of the cave. He grabs it and, with one mighty swing, cuts off the monster's head. At the back of the cave, he sees Grendel's corpse. Using the same sword, he cuts off Grendel's head too and then returns to the surface carrying it. He also brings the remains of the sword: Its blade had melted when it cut into Grendel's flesh. Beowulf and his men return to Heorot in triumph, and Hrothgar again rewards them. Finally, the Geats go home to Sweden, and Beowulf eventually becomes their king.

Beowulf and the Dragon. As the second part of the epic begins, Beowulf has ruled for 50 years, and his kingdom has prospered. A winged dragon lives in the land, protecting an ancient treasure buried hundreds of years earlier. One day, a slave who had been punished by his master runs away and finds the cave where the treasure is buried. To earn his master's forgiveness, the slave steals a golden cup and takes it to his household. However, the dragon inspects the treasure every day and quickly notices the missing cup. To punish the Geats for stealing from him, the dragon flies over the countryside breathing fire on the villages and setting homes ablaze.

Though an old man, Beowulf decides to fight the dragon. He takes 11 warriors with him and finds the dragon's cave, but then he leaves them to watch while he fights the dragon alone. Beowulf soon discovers that his iron shield will not protect him against the dragon's fiery breath. The hero is about to be killed when a warrior named Wiglaf, Beowulf's young kinsman, rushes to his aid. With Wiglaf's help, Beowulf slays the dragon but is fatally wounded in the battle. He asks Wiglaf to bring out the treasure so that he might see it before he dies.

Beowulf's body is burned in a great fire on a cliff overlooking the sea. The treasure is sacrificed in the fire with Beowulf. A large burial mound is built over the remains of the fire to serve as a reminder of the great king and to provide a landmark for seafarers. The poem ends with a ceremony of praise for Beowulf.

The Appeal of Beowulf

Hundreds of years after it was first written, *Beowulf* is still a popular story. Why has it endured? First, it is an exciting and well-told adventure story with frightful monsters and

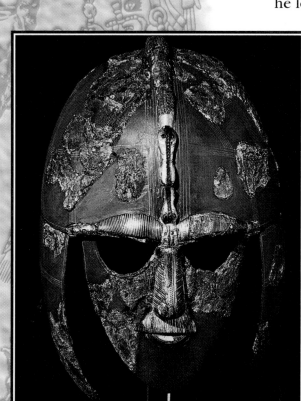

The story of Beowulf reflects the warlike society of ancient Germanic people. This warrior's helmet from the 600s was found on the Sutton Hoo estate in Woodbridge, England, in the grave of a Saxon king.

gruesome battle scenes. Second, Beowulf is a marvelous character. He is a brave warrior who shows all the heroic qualities expected of a champion. He risks his life to make the world safer for others, and he faces his fate with dignity and courage. The story also explores the psychology and feelings of other characters, such as Unferth, who was initially jealous of Beowulf, and the Geat warriors, who were cowardly when facing the dragon. These touches make the story come alive and the characters seem real.

The tale makes the reader aware of how fragile life and fame can be. Like any modern person, Beowulf must find meaning in his world while accepting the fact that he will eventually die. He meets that challenge by facing danger bravely and trusting that the story of his deeds will cause him to live on in memory. ***See also*** **DRAGONS; MONSTERS; NORSE MYTHOLOGY; WITCHES AND WIZARDS.**

Berserks

Berserks, or berserkers, were wild warriors who fought savagely in battle and worshiped Odin, king of the Norse† gods. The word *berserk* comes either from a Norse word for "bear-shirt" (meaning bearskin) or from "bare-of-shirt" (meaning without mail or armor). Either definition would be appropriate because berserks entered battle without armor and dressed in animal skins.

Some people believed that berserks could become man-wolves or man-bears. The legend of the werewolf may have grown from this tradition. It was said that berserks howled and fought with the fury of wild animals and bit their shields during battle. Their extraordinary strength enabled them to overcome their enemies. Neither iron nor fire could hurt them. Because of their fierceness and skill in battle, berserks sometimes served as bodyguards or special troops for royal households. However when not fighting, berserks often went wild, raping and robbing members of Norse communities. From such behavior, we get the phrase "going berserk." ***See also*** **NORSE MYTHOLOGY; ODIN; WEREWOLVES.**

Bhagavad Gita

epic long poem about legendary or historical heroes, written in a grand style

Written almost 2,000 years ago, the Bhagavad Gita is probably the most widely read of the Hindu scriptures, and it lays out some of the basic ideas of Hindu culture. The poem is actually part of a larger Indian **epic,** the *Mahabharata,* which tells the story of the struggle between two closely related leading families. The Bhagavad Gita begins just before the start of the great battle between the families. It is written in the form of a conversation between one of the warriors, Prince Arjuna, and his chariot driver, Krishna—actually a god in disguise.

As the poem opens, the two armies are lined up facing each other across the battlefield. Prince Arjuna questions his part in the war. He wonders whether he should follow his duty and fight, even though this would mean killing friends, relatives, and teachers in the opposing army, or whether he should throw down his arms and let himself be killed. Krishna reminds Arjuna that everyone has certain duties in society. As a member of the warrior

†*See **Names and Places** at the end of this volume for further information.*

caste division of people in Hindu society into classes based on birth

caste, Arjuna's duty is to fight and kill. Yet he should do this only after understanding that all beings have the same divine self.

Selfless devotion to duty is just one of the lessons taught in the Bhagavad Gita. Through the conversation between Arjuna and Krishna, the reader learns of the many ways to express religious belief, including meditation, worship, and work. The poem also teaches that Krishna is a loving god who is concerned about people's welfare and who appears on earth to help during times of trouble. *See also* HINDUISM AND MYTHOLOGY; KRISHNA; VISHNU.

Billy the Kid

Billy the Kid was one of the most notorious outlaws of the American West. Born William Bonney in New York City in 1859, Billy spent his childhood in Kansas, Colorado, and New Mexico. At the age of 12, he is said to have committed his first murder when he stabbed a man who had insulted his mother. In his teen years, Billy turned to a life of robbery and violence. By age 18, he had committed perhaps a dozen more killings.

In 1877 Billy became a cowhand on a ranch in New Mexico. The following year, a "war" broke out between two cattle-ranching families. Billy became a leader of one of the rival gangs and played an active role in many bloody gun battles.

In April 1878, Billy was one of a group of men who gunned down the local sheriff, James Brady, and a deputy. The governor of the territory offered Billy a pardon if he surrendered. The outlaw refused and continued with his life of violence and lawlessness. He led a gang of cattle rustlers and committed more murders.

In 1880 Patrick Floyd Garrett, a one-time friend of Billy's, became a sheriff. Determined to put an end to Billy's life of violence, Garrett tracked Billy down and captured him in 1881. Billy stood trial for the murder of Sheriff Brady. He was found guilty and sentenced to hang.

Before the hanging could take place, Billy broke out of jail, killing two guards in the process. Sheriff Garrett went after him. Three months later, Garrett caught up with Billy in Fort Sumner, New Mexico. There, in a private home, the sheriff shot and killed the outlaw.

Billy the Kid was just 21 years old when he died. Even so, he had probably killed more than 20 people. In the years after his death, tales of Billy the Kid became part of western legend. Novels and movies sometimes glamorized his life. In truth, however, Billy was nothing more than a ruthless, cold-blooded killer.

Birds in Mythology

Rising above the earth and soaring through the skies, birds have been symbols of power and freedom throughout the ages. In many myths and legends, birds link the human world to the divine or **supernatural** realms that lie beyond ordinary experience.

Birds assume a variety of roles in mythology and religion. They play a central part in some creation myths and frequently appear as messengers of the **deities.** They are often associated with the journey of the human soul after death. Birds also appear as **tricksters**

supernatural related to forces beyond the normal world; magical or miraculous

deity god or goddess

trickster mischievous figure appearing in various forms in the folktales and mythology of many different peoples

oracle priest or priestess or other creature through whom a god is believed to speak; also the location (such as a shrine) where such words are spoken

mediator go-between

primeval from the earliest times

chaos great disorder or confusion

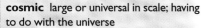

cosmic large or universal in scale; having to do with the universe

and **oracles.** Ravens and other species that feed on carrion, the flesh of the dead, may be symbols of war, death, and misfortune, as well as **mediators** between humans and the supernatural world. Other birds represent strength, love, and wisdom.

Birds and Creation

Myths from several regions associate birds with the creation of the world. One of several creation stories in ancient Egypt said that when land rose out of the **primeval** waters of **chaos,** the first deity to appear was a bird perching on that land. The Egyptians called the god the Benu bird and portrayed it as a long-legged, wading heron in the sun temple at Heliopolis. The Benu bird created the universe and then made gods and goddesses and men to live in that universe.

A number of creation myths from Southeast Asia feature birds. On the great island of Borneo dwell the Iban people, who tell of Ara and Irik, two bird spirits floating above an expanse of water at the beginning of time. Seizing two eggs from the water, Ara made the sky from one egg, while Irik made the earth from the other. As Irik squeezed the earth into its proper size, mountains and rivers appeared on its surface. Then the two creator spirits shaped bits of earth into the first people and woke them to life with bird cries.

Other creation stories begin with the laying of a **cosmic** egg from which the universe emerges. Indonesia, Polynesia, and the northern European countries of Finland and Estonia have stories of deities flying down to the primeval ocean to lay eggs that hatch into the world.

Birds appear in some myths as earth divers. An earth diver is an animal that plunged to the bottom of the primeval sea and brought up mud from which the earth was formed. Legends of the Buriat and Samoyed people of Siberia feature birds as earth divers. Water birds such as ducks or swans play this role in the creation myths of many Native American peoples, including the Mandan of North Dakota. A Navajo myth about a great flood tells that the people fled to an upper world, leaving everything behind. The bird Turkey then dived into the lower world to rescue seeds so that the people could grow food crops.

Sometimes mythological birds create more than the physical world. Cultures in northern Europe and Asia credited birds with establishing their social orders, especially kingships. A golden-winged eagle was said to have put the first Mongol† emperor on his throne. The Japanese believed that sacred birds guided their second emperor in conquering his enemies before the

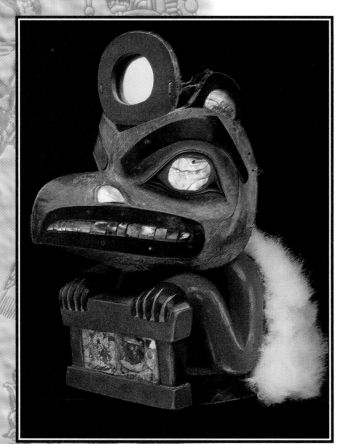

This Tlingit hat is adorned with a raven, an important mythological character for many Native Americans of Alaska. Considered both a hero and a trickster, the raven presented many gifts to humans including light, names for plants, and formations of the earth.

†See **Names and Places** at the end of this volume for further information.

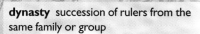

dynasty succession of rulers from the same family or group

immortal able to live forever

imperial relating to an emperor or empire

founding of his **dynasty.** The Magyar people claimed that a giant eagle, falcon, or hawk had led their first king into Hungary, where he founded their nation. The Magyars looked upon this bird as their mythical ancestor.

Life, Death, and the Soul

Many myths have linked birds to the arrival of life or death. With their power of flight, these winged creatures were seen as carriers or symbols of the human soul, or as the soul itself, flying heavenward after a person died. A bird may represent both the soul of the dead and a deity at the same time.

Bringers of Life and Death. Some cultures have associated birds with birth, claiming that a person's soul arrived on earth in bird form. A remnant of this ancient belief has survived into modern times: one traditional answer to a child's question "Where do babies come from?" is "The stork brings them."

Birds have also been linked with death. Carrion-eating birds such as vultures, crows, and ravens, for example, were connected with disaster and war. Celtic† and Irish war goddesses often appeared in the form of crows and ravens—perhaps because crows and ravens were known to gather over battlefields and to feast on the flesh of fallen warriors. It was said that if one of these goddesses appeared before an army going into battle, the army would be defeated.

The mythological bird called the phoenix combined images of birth and death to become a powerful symbol of eternal rebirth. According to Egyptian legend, the phoenix burned up every 500 years but was then miraculously reborn out of its own ashes, so it was truly **immortal.** In myths from China and Japan, the phoenix does not emerge from a fire but instead causes itself to be reborn during times of good fortune.

The Flight of the Soul. Numerous myths have linked birds to the journeys undertaken by human souls after death. Sometimes a bird acts as a guide in the afterlife. In Syria, figures of eagles on tombs represent the guides that lead souls to heaven. The soul guide in Jewish tradition is a dove.

In some cultures, it was thought that the soul, once freed from the body, took the form of a bird. The ancient Egyptians believed that the soul, the ba, could leave the dead body in the form of a bird, often a hawk. They built their graves and tombs with narrow shafts leading to the open air so that these birds could fly in and out, keeping watch on the body. The feather cloaks that Central American and Mexican priests and kings wore may have been connected to the idea of a soul journey.

Because of their great size and strength, eagles have been associated with royal or **imperial** souls. Some ancient peoples, including the Romans, would release an eagle at a ruler's funeral. As it rose into the sky, the mighty bird was seen as the ruler's spirit taking its place in the heavens.

shaman person thought to possess spiritual and healing powers
prophet one who claims to have received divine messages or insights

culture hero mythical figure who gives people the tools of civilization, such as language and fire

The Greeks and Celts thought that the dead could reappear as birds. The Sumerians of the ancient Near East believed that the dead existed as birds in the underworld. According to Islamic tradition, all dead souls remain in the form of birds until Judgment Day, while in Christian tradition, the gentle dove became a symbol of the immortal soul ascending to heaven. Birds also appear in Hindu mythology as symbols of the soul or as forms taken by the soul between earthly lives. The connection between birds and souls is sometimes reflected in language. A Turkish saying describes somebody's death as "His soul bird has flown away."

Becoming a Bird. Under certain conditions, the living could be transformed into birds. In some cultures, it was believed that **shamans,** priests, and **prophets** could change themselves into birds during trances or other mystical states. Such ideas were found in Siberia and Indonesia. In Celtic mythology, both deities and the sly supernatural beings called fairies or fays were said to have the power to transform themselves into birds.

Some legends involve birds that change into or inhabit the bodies of humans. The Central American god Quetzalcoatl, a combination of a bird and a serpent, appears as a **culture hero** or a god in human form in Toltec, Maya, and Aztec myths. Among certain peoples in northern Europe and Asia, the spirits of birds such as eagles, owls, and crows are said to enter the bodies of shamans to inspire them.

In some myths, humans and other beings acquire the ability to fly like birds. Such supernatural flight, like many mythological powers, can be either good or evil. Norse† tales told that the goddess Freya's feather cloak enabled the wearer to fly. European tradition portrayed angels with wings like those of birds, but devils often had bat wings. Japanese mythology includes a group of winged deities known as *tengu.* Part bird and part human, they live in forests and occasionally use their powers to play tricks on people.

Winged Wisdom

Birds in mythology sometimes have the ability to speak. These talking birds, often sources of wisdom, may be deities in bird form or simply messengers of the deities. Either way, their advice is generally sound, and humans ignore it at their peril. Birds warn of dangers ahead, reveal secrets, and guide heroes and travelers on their way.

Birds do not always speak in human languages; many stories tell of people who gain the power to understand the language of birds. In Greek mythology, a snake licked the ears of the prophet Cassandra, who could then understand what the birds were saying. After tasting the magical blood of a slain dragon, the German hero Siegfried knew what the forest birds were saying.

Some birds are believed to have special powers of telling the future or revealing the will of the gods. Magpies, ravens, and doves appear in myth as oracles. In Iranian mythology, birds communicate

† See **Names and Places** at the end of this volume for further information.

In Hindu mythology, Garuda was a creature with a human body and an eagle's head, wings, and talons. This Indian miniature painting portrays Garuda with the god Vishnu and his wife on his back.

Related Entries
Other entries related to birds in mythology are listed at the end of this article.

divine wisdom to people. The Hottentot people of southern Africa believe that the hammerhead, a wading bird, can see reflections of the future in pools of water. When the bird learns that someone is about to die, it flies to the person's home and gives three cries of warning.

Common Birds in Mythology

Certain birds appear over and over again in the world's myths and legends, although not always in the same roles. The crow and its close relative the raven, for example, have a number of different meanings. In some cultures, they are oracles and symbols of death. In Norse mythology, Odin† was always accompanied by two wise ravens that told him everything that happened on earth. According to Greek mythology, the feathers of crows and ravens were originally white, but the god Apollo punished the birds—either for telling secrets or for failing in their duty as guardians—by turning them black.

For some Native Americans, such as the Tsimshian people of the Pacific Northwest, Raven is both a trickster and a culture hero. Sometimes his antics shake up the gods and the established order of the universe, and sometimes they backfire and get him into trouble. Often, though, Raven's deeds benefit humankind, as in the legend

99

The Deathless Hoyl Bird

Jewish mythology includes the story of the hoyl—a bird that, like the phoenix, is devoured by divine fire only to rise from its own ashes. Legend says that after Adam and Eve ate the forbidden fruit in the Garden of Eden, Adam offered the fruit to all of the animals. The hoyl bird was the only one that refused to eat the fruit that God had said must never be eaten. As a reward, the hoyl received a kind of immortality. It never dies but only goes to sleep, after which fire destroys it. An egg remains, however, and from that egg a full-grown hoyl hatches anew.

of how Raven brought light into the world. After finding the hiding place where the Creator kept the moon, the stars, and daylight, Raven released them so that they could shine on the world.

The majestic eagle, sometimes called the king of birds, usually has divine or royal associations in myth. Images from the ancient Near East and Iran show the sun with an eagle's wings, a sign that the bird was linked to the sun god. The eagle was also a symbol of Jupiter, the supreme Roman deity, and a sign of strength and courage. By adopting the eagle as their symbol, kings from ancient to recent times have tried to suggest that they, too, had some divine or heroic qualities.

Stories of eagles fighting snakes or dragons represent the tension between light and darkness, heavenly and underworld forces. In the myths of various Native American peoples, the eagle is a culture hero, a hunter or a tornado transformed into a bird, and the spirit of war and hunting. The eagle was also the great culture hero of Siberian mythology.

In the ancient Near East and in Greece, the dove was a symbol of love and fertility, often associated with goddesses of love such as the Greek Aphrodite. In China doves represent tranquility and faithfulness in marriage, while in India they symbolize the soul.

When owls appear in mythology, their meaning is often uncertain and complex, neither all good nor all bad. Owls are symbols of wisdom, patience, and learning, yet because they hunt at night, they are associated with secrecy and darkness. In China they are seen as signs of coming misfortune. According to the Hottentot people of Africa, the hooting of an owl at night is an omen of death.

Early cultures in Mexico regarded owls as sacred to the rain god, but later the Aztecs of the same region viewed them as evil night demons. Some Native American legends portray owls as destructive and malicious; others show them as helpful beings who warn people of dangers. The stories may include a person who is transformed into an owl. In the Navajo creation myth, an owl resolves a bitter quarrel between men and women, allowing the creation of the human race.

Bats also symbolize both good and evil in mythology. Chinese legends link the bat with good fortune. A group of five bats represents five causes of happiness: wealth, health, long life, virtue, and a natural death. In various other cultures, however, bats are often connected with witches or evil spirits, and demons are pictured with bat wings.

Other birds have special meanings in myths. Swans, with their white feathers and graceful appearance, often serve as symbols of purity and feminine beauty. Both Celtic and Norse mythology included tales of women who turned into swans. Male peacocks, endowed with splendid tail feathers, can suggest either foolish vanity or divine glory. In legends from India, they often appear being ridden by one of the gods. *See also* AFTERLIFE; ANIMALS IN MYTHOLOGY; CREATION STORIES; FIREBIRD; PHOENIX; QUETZALCOATL; THUNDERBIRD.

Blackbeard

Blackbeard was the nickname of Edward Teach, a notorious English pirate of the early 1700s. He was a large, strong, fierce-looking man. According to reports, his beard stretched from his eyes to his waist and was worn in braids tied with ribbons. To make himself yet more fearsome at times of action, Blackbeard would burn fuses on his hat so that his head was surrounded by a cloud of black smoke.

The pirate and his crew operated in the Caribbean and along the coast of Virginia and the Carolinas. They captured dozens of ships, demanding money and valuables from those on board. Blackbeard was courteous to those who surrendered willingly but cruel to those who resisted. As for his crew, he once remarked, "If I did not now and then kill one of them, they would forget who I am."

In 1718 the governor of Virginia sent a British naval force to capture Blackbeard. After a bloody battle, they succeeded in killing the pirate and beheading him. They hung his head from the front of the ship and threw his body overboard. According to legend, the headless corpse swam around the ship three times before sinking. Since that time, fishermen in the area have reported seeing a headless body searching for its head. Blackbeard's treasure chest is said to lie on the ocean floor off the coast of Maryland, protected by a curse that prevents anyone from bringing it to the surface.

Bluebeard

Bluebeard is the villain in a European folktale made famous by Charles Perrault in his tale *Barbe bleue*. According to the story, Bluebeard married several women, one after the other, and murdered each of them. He threw their bodies in a special room inside his castle. He married yet again and gave his new bride the keys to the castle, telling her that she might go anywhere in the castle except for that one room. While Bluebeard was away, however, his young wife's curiosity got the better of her and she opened the door to the forbidden room. There she discovered the remains of Bluebeard's previous wives. When Bluebeard returned, he realized that his wife had found out his secret and told her that she must prepare to die.

The story has several different endings. In one version, the young wife killed Bluebeard with his own sword. In another, her brothers came to her rescue and killed him. The theme of the story of Bluebeard—the penalty for being too curious—appears in the folktales of many countries.

Book of the Dead, The

The Book of the Dead is a large collection of ancient Egyptian religious texts relating to funerals and the afterlife. The texts include spells, magic formulas, hymns, and prayers. The title is misleading. The writings do not actually make up a book but consist of many individual texts, assembled from numerous authors and sources over hundreds of years. Some of the writings are more than 4,000 years old.

The Egyptians believed that their souls had to be judged by Osiris and many other gods before they could enter the afterlife. In this illustration from the Book of the Dead, souls stand before Osiris at the moment of judgment.

The Egyptians believed that the texts in the Book of the Dead would protect and guide the deceased in the journey after death. The spells and magic words were supposed to give the dead person the power to overcome obstacles and reach the peaceful realm of the blessed.

The spells served a variety of purposes. One spell helped the deceased enter the afterworld immediately after burial. Others enabled them to revisit the earth, restored their memory, and helped them breathe and eat. The Book of the Dead also contained the magical knowledge the dead needed to pass the judgment of 42 **deities** in the hall of Osiris, god of the underworld.

Written on the walls of tombs and pyramids and on rolls of **papyrus,** the texts of the Book of the Dead were often accompanied by colorful pictures. The papyrus rolls were buried in the coffin within reach of the deceased or tucked into the wrappings of a mummy. Priests at the funeral would also recite many of the spells. *See also* AFTERLIFE; EGYPTIAN MYTHOLOGY.

deity god or goddess

papyrus writing material made by pressing together thin strips of the stem of the papyrus plant

Boone, Daniel

Daniel Boone was a legendary American pioneer who helped explore and settle Kentucky. He gained fame as a trailblazer and hero of the American West.

Born in 1734 near Reading, Pennsylvania, Boone became skilled at hunting and trapping during his childhood. Around 1767 he began making trips into Kentucky, following a trail over the Appalachian

† See **Names and Places** at the end of this volume for further information.

Mountains. In 1775 Boone and a group of men built the Wilderness Road, running from eastern Virginia to Kentucky across the Cumberland Gap, a pass in the Appalachian Mountains. That same year Boone built the settlement known as Boonesboro on the Kentucky River. He defended this fort against Cherokee attacks many times.

From his youth, Boone had earned a reputation as a brave frontiersman who explored unsettled regions and saved himself from dangerous situations. According to legend, Boone was captured by Indians one night and taken to their camp. He was able to escape by dawn and cut three notches in a tree to mark the spot. Captured by Indians on another occasion, Boone and his companions were released when the pioneer tricked them into thinking he could swallow a knife. Another story says Boone killed a she-bear with his knife just as the animal was attacking him.

Daniel Boone's fame spread across the country during his lifetime, and his legend continued to grow after his death. In 1823 the English poet Lord Byron wrote about him in his masterpiece *Don Juan.* The Society of the Sons of Daniel Boone, which later became part of the Boy Scouts of America, was founded in 1905 to teach children about the outdoors.

Boreas

deity god or goddess

In Greek mythology, Boreas was the god of the north wind and the son of Astraeus and Eos, **deities** of the stars and dawn. His brothers were Eurus the east wind, Notus the south wind, and Zephyrus the west wind. Because he was the strongest, Boreas was considered king of all the winds.

Boreas fell in love with Orithyia, daughter of an Athenian king, and carried her off to his home in Thrace. Their children, Zetes and Calais, became winged warriors who journeyed with Jason's Argonaut expedition. The Athenians regarded Boreas as a friendly relative and called for his aid during the Persian Wars.

Virgil† mentions Boreas in the *Aeneid,* as does Shakespeare in his play *Troilus and Cressida.* Boreas is often found in Renaissance art that includes references to the four seasons. Personifying winter, he is seen as an old man with long white hair, a beard, and wings. ***See also*** AENEID, THE; ARGONAUTS.

Bragi

deify to make a god or goddess

In Norse† mythology, Bragi was the god of poetry. He was the son of Odin† and the husband of Idun, the goddess of fertility. Described as an old man with a long beard, Bragi welcomed the warriors who had died in battle to Valhalla†.

Bragi had close ties to Odin. Both were gods of poetry, and both were associated with royal funeral services, when a "cup of Bragi" was used to drink to the honor of a dead king. In addition, the two gods were often referred to as "long-bearded." Some scholars think that Bragi might have been the **deified** version of Bragi Boddason, a Norwegian poet of the 800s. ***See also*** IDUN; ODIN; VALHALLA.

Brahma

cosmic large or universal in scale; having to do with the universe

In Hindu mythology, Brahma was the first god in the sacred Hindu trinity, or Trimurti. The other gods were Vishnu, the Preserver, and Shiva, the Destroyer. Brahma was the creator god, but his role was not as great as that of creator gods in other mythologies.

In the early literature of Hinduism, Brahma was one of the major gods. However, he plays little part in the modern Hindu religion. Over time, Vishnu and Shiva became more important than Brahma and are more widely worshiped today.

There are many different accounts of the origin of Brahma. According to one story, the creator made the **cosmic** waters and put a seed in them. The seed turned into a golden egg. After 1,000 years, the creator himself emerged from the egg as a younger Brahma. He then made the universe and all things in it. Another legend says that Brahma was born in a lotus flower that sprouted from Vishnu's navel. When he grew up, he had a relationship with his daughter, which led to the birth of mankind.

In works of art, Brahma is usually portrayed with four faces and four arms. The four faces symbolize the four Vedas, the ancient

This Cambodian statue of the A.D. 900s shows Brahma with four faces and arms, a typical representation of the Hindu god. The influence of Hinduism spread to lands far beyond India, possibly carried by traders from southern India.

sacred texts of Hinduism. Brahma is often shown wearing white robes and holding a scepter, an alms bowl, a bow, and other items. According to legend, Brahma's four faces came into being from his desire to gaze at his beautiful daughter from all directions. Brahma originally had five heads, but the god Shiva destroyed one of them when Brahma spoke to him disrespectfully. *See also* HINDUISM AND MYTHOLOGY; SHIVA; VISHNU.

Brendan, St.

abbot head of a monastery or abbey
patron special guardian, protector, or supporter

St. Brendan, nicknamed the Navigator, was an Irish **abbot** of the 500s who became the hero of legendary ocean voyages and the **patron** saint of seafarers. An eager traveler, Brendan journeyed to various lands bordering on the Atlantic Ocean. Some 400 years later, his travels were made famous in the *Navigatio Sancti Brendani* (Voyage of St. Brendan), a fictionalized work that became one of the most popular books of the time.

In the *Navigatio,* Brendan and a group of monks make an amazing trip in search of the "Promised Land of the Saints." According to the story, the monks wander the ocean for years, stopping at different islands and experiencing various adventures. Eventually, they reach their goal. Many of the islands described in the *Navigatio* appear to be based on real islands. Moreover, mapmakers for hundreds of years marked a St. Brendan's Island, to the west of Ireland, on their maps of the Atlantic. Many Spanish and Portuguese explorers went in search of this fictional island.

Brer Rabbit

trickster mischievous figure appearing in various forms in the folktales and mythology of many different peoples

Brer Rabbit is the main character in the Uncle Remus tales written by Joel Chandler Harris (1848–1908). As a **trickster,** Brer Rabbit outsmarts larger and stronger animals, such as Brer Fox and Brer Bear. Many stories about Brer Rabbit originated in African folklore and were brought to America by slaves.

Perhaps the most famous Brer Rabbit story is the one about Brer Rabbit and the tar baby. In this tale, Brer Fox makes a life-size figure out of sticky tar and places it on the road. Brer Rabbit greets the tar baby several times but gets no reply. Annoyed, he hits the tar baby and gets stuck in the tar. Brer Fox seizes him and wonders about a punishment. Brer Rabbit begs him to do anything he wants except throw him into the briar patch. Brer Fox, of course, does exactly that. Brer Rabbit, however, easily escapes because, as he says, "I was born and raised in the briar patch." Brer Rabbit is successful in tricking Brer Fox. *See also* AFRICAN MYTHOLOGY; ANANSI; TRICKSTERS.

Bruce, Robert

Robert Bruce, also known as Robert the Bruce, was king of Scotland from 1306 to 1329. A heroic leader, Bruce led the Scots in their fight against English rule. He suffered two major defeats and at one point was forced to flee to the remote island of Rathlin, off the Irish coast. Later he gathered his supporters once again. In 1314 he led them in the decisive battle of Bannockburn. Though

105

outnumbered by the English, the Scots achieved a decisive victory, thanks to Bruce's courage, determination, and leadership. The victory gained independence for Scotland.

Numerous Scottish legends pay tribute to Robert Bruce. One of the most often told tales involves a spider. According to the story, when Bruce fled to the island of Rathlin, he lay in hiding in a cottage. His spirits were low, and he was tempted to give up the battle for independence. Lying there he watched a spider hard at work. The spider tried again and again to attach its web to a beam in the ceiling. At last the spider succeeded. The spider's determination inspired Bruce to return to Scotland. There he led the Scots to victory and drove the English out of Scotland.

Brunhilde

epic long poem about legendary or historical heroes, written in a grand style

pyre pile of wood on which a dead body is burned in a funeral ceremony

In Icelandic and German mythology, Brunhilde was a strong and beautiful princess who was cruelly deceived by her lover. Her story is told in the *Edda* poems of Iceland and the *Nibelungenlied,* a German **epic** of the 1200s. Her name also appears as Brünhild, Brunhilda, or Brynhild.

In the Icelandic version of the legend, Brunhilde was a Valkyrie—a warrior maiden of the supreme god Odin. Because she was disobedient, Odin punished Brunhilde by causing her to fall into everlasting sleep surrounded by a wall of fire. The hero Sigurd crossed through the flames and woke the maiden with a kiss. They became engaged, but Sigurd left to continue his travels. Later, after receiving a magic potion to make him forget his love for Brunhilde, Sigurd married Gudrun (Kriemhild).

Gudrun's brother Gunnar wanted Brunhilde for himself and persuaded Sigurd to help him. Disguising himself as Gunnar, Sigurd pursued Brunhilde. Later Brunhilde realized she had been tricked and arranged to have Sigurd murdered. When she learned of his death, however, she was overcome with grief and committed suicide by throwing herself on his funeral **pyre.** In that way, she could join him in death.

In the *Nibelungenlied,* the story was slightly different. Brunhilde declared that the man she would marry must be able to outperform her in feats of strength and courage. Siegfried (Sigurd), disguised as Gunther (Gunnar), passed the test and won Brunhilde for Gunther. When she discovered the deception, she arranged for Siegfried to be killed. The German composer Richard Wagner based his opera cycle *The Ring of the Nibelung* on these legends. *See also* SIGURD; VALKYRIES.

Buddhism and Mythology

Buddhism, one of the great religions of the world, was founded in India in the 500s B.C. and then spread throughout Asia. Over time, many different Buddhist **sects** have developed, each with its own **doctrines,** gods, and legends. Although Buddhism has produced little mythology of its own, it has incorporated stories from mythologies of various groups that adopted the religion.

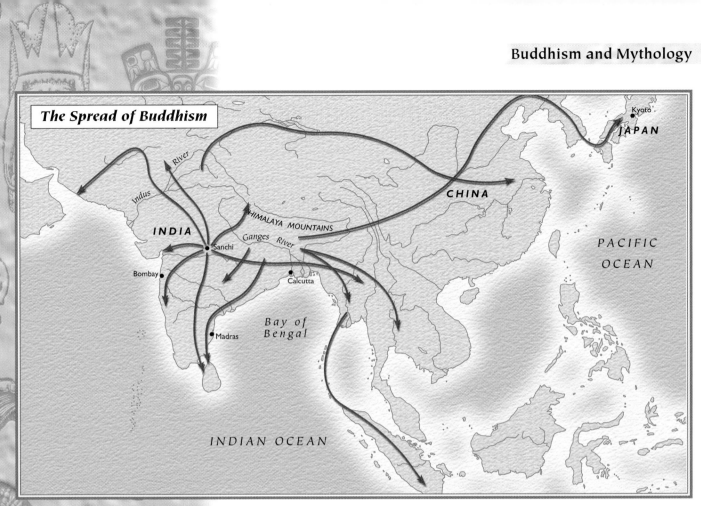

The Spread of Buddhism

sect religious group
doctrine set of principles or beliefs accepted by a group

Buddhist History and Teachings

The roots of Buddhism can be traced to one man: Siddhartha Gautama, a prince from a small state in northern India. Although he was a historical figure, many of the stories about him are based on legend. This has made it difficult to distinguish between fact and fiction. Yet the basic elements of Siddhartha Gautama's life story—whether real or invented—are well known, as are his religious teachings.

The Buddha. The son of King Suddhodana, Gautama was born around 563 B.C. According to legend, his mother, Queen Maya, had a dream in which she was expecting a child fathered by a white elephant. Local brahmins, or holy men, interpreted the dream to mean that the queen would give birth to a great man. They said that the child would become a powerful king unless he became aware of human suffering in the world. If that happened, he would become a great holy man and savior.

Some legends say that when Gautama was born the earth shook, rivers stopped flowing, flowers fell from the sky, and a lotus flower sprang from the place where he first touched the earth. Mindful of the prophecy about his son, King Suddhodana did everything possible to shield the boy from knowledge of the outside world and human suffering. He built a palace in which his son could enjoy all of life's pleasures, and he forbade any mention of death, grief, or sickness.

One day Gautama expressed a wish to see the world outside the palace. Suddhodana agreed to take his son to a nearby town, but

107

This enormous statue of the Buddha is carved into a cliff at the Yungang Caves near Datong, China.

first he had the town cleaned up and ordered that everything unpleasant be removed. During the visit, however, Gautama saw a sick man, an old man, a beggar, and a corpse. Shocked to discover that people lived in poverty, became sick, grew old, and died, the prince realized that he knew nothing about the real world. Determined to learn the truth about the world, Gautama gave up all his possessions and left his home. He became a beggar and sought truth and understanding by denying himself all pleasures.

After six years of wandering and seeking wisdom from holy men, Gautama realized that he was no nearer truth and understanding than before. He decided to look for the truth within himself and went to the town of Bodh Gaya to sit beneath the Bodhi tree and **meditate.** While he was meditating, the evil spirit Mara tried to tempt Gautama with beautiful women. When this failed, Mara threatened him with demons and finally threw a fiery disc at him. However, the disc turned into flowers that floated down on Gautama's head.

After five weeks of meditation, Gautama came to understand that the only way to avoid suffering was to free oneself from all desires. At the moment of this **revelation,** Siddhartha Gautama became the Buddha, the "enlightened one" who is free from suffering. He then began to travel and teach others how to achieve **enlightenment.** Buddha gained many followers before his death around 480 B.C.

After the death of Buddha, his followers carried Buddhist teachings throughout Asia. Within a few hundred years, Buddhism was practiced in Sri Lanka, Burma, Thailand, Cambodia, and most of Southeast Asia. By the A.D. 600s, it had spread to central Asia, China, Korea, Japan, and Tibet.

Basic Teachings. Buddhism teaches that all humans experience many lives and are constantly reincarnated—reborn after death into a different form of existence. The form each person takes in a new life depends on karma, which is the total of one's good and bad deeds in previous lives. The goal of Buddhism is to escape this cycle of death and rebirth by achieving enlightenment. When that happens, a person enters a timeless state known as nirvana and is free of all desire.

The original form of Buddhism, recorded in texts from about 100 B.C., is called Theravada Buddhism. Its followers believed that there would be only one Buddha in the world at any one time. Theravada Buddhism spread to Sri Lanka, Burma, and much of Southeast Asia. A later form of Buddhism, called Mahayana, taught that many Buddhas might exist at the same time. It attracted followers in China, Japan, Tibet, and Korea.

meditate to think
revelation communication of divine truth or divine will
enlightenment in Buddhism, a spiritual state marked by the absence of desire and suffering

deity god or goddess

Mythology Associated with Buddhism

As Buddhism spread, it divided into many different sects. Each sect developed its own traditions and mythology, often based on a combination of local beliefs and **deities** with Buddhist teaching.

India. Early Buddhism in India was influenced by Brahmanism, a form of the Hindu religion. Both religions shared the idea of the cycle of birth and reincarnation, and both included Devas, traditional Indian gods, and Asuras, powerful demons.

A principal figure in Indian Buddhism was Amitabha, who was a bodhisattva—a person who had become enlightened but postponed entering nirvana in order to help others gain enlightenment. According to legend, Amitabha was born from a lotus flower and came to the aid of Buddhists who worshiped him and pronounced his sacred name.

China. Arriving in China in about A.D. 65, Buddhism developed into one of that country's three most important religions, alongside Taoism and Confucianism. Buddhist gods came to be worshiped in Taoist temples and vice versa, and in some temples, the three religions were practiced side by side.

The Mahayana Buddhism practiced in China was an elaborate form of the religion, with more gods and myths than Theravada Buddhism. In the A.D. 600s, questions arose about certain Buddhist teachings, so a monk named Xuan Zang (also called Tripitaka) went to India to obtain copies of official scriptures. An account of his legendary trip was published in the 1500s as *Journey to the West.* In the story, the monkey god Sun Wukong and the pig god Zhu Bajie joined Xuan Zang on his journey. During the 14-year expedition, the three travelers had to endure many ordeals and tests of their sincerity, including fighting demons and monsters with the help of a magic stick.

Chinese Buddhists established a complex **hierarchy** of gods and goddesses. One of the more important deities was Shang Di, whose main assistant, Dongyue Dadi, was known as Great Emperor of the Eastern Peak. Under him were various departments where the souls of virtuous people worked to manage every aspect of human and animal life.

Some of the other important Buddhist gods were the Four Kings of Heaven, the Four Kings of Hell, and the kitchen god, the most important deity of the home. Another major deity was the bodhisattva Mi-le (known in India as Maitreya), considered to be the future Buddha. Portrayed as a fat, cheerful man, Mi-Le was sometimes called the Laughing Buddha. Worshipers prayed to join him in paradise. Each district in China had its own local deity, as did all activities and ways of making a living. Even the smallest details of life were controlled by various minor gods and goddesses.

Japan. Buddhism came to Japan in about A.D. 550 and spread quickly because of support from the Japanese royal family. Although

From God to Goddess

In Chinese Buddhism, the bodhisattva Avalokitesvara evolved from a male figure of sympathy into Kuanyin, the goddess of mercy. Tibetans gave Avalokitesvara's wife, Tara, the title Pandaravasin, meaning "dressed in white." The Chinese translation of that title is Pai-i-Kuanyin.

Chinese Buddhists apparently combined the figure of Tara with the characteristics of Avalokitesvara to create a mother goddess figure. As the one who blesses couples with children, Kuanyin appealed to the Chinese belief in ancestor worship, and she became one of the most popular and important Buddhist deities. In Japan, Avalokitesvara is worshiped in both male and female forms as the deity Kannon.

hierarchy organization of a group into higher and lower levels

109

pantheon all the gods of a particular culture

ogre hideous monster

This early Japanese painting shows Amida, who rules a paradise known as the Pure Land. Some Japanese Buddhist groups worshiped Amida as the savior of humankind.

supporters of Shinto, the native religion of Japan, at first opposed Buddhism, the two religions eventually became closely linked. Buddhist temples contained Shinto shrines, and Shinto gods (known collectively as *kami*) became Buddhist guardians. This mix of Shintoism and Buddhism continued until 1868, when the emperor declared Shinto a state religion and banned Buddhist priests and images from Shinto temples. Yet Buddhism remained popular and still has a larger following in Japan than does Shinto.

Although the various forms of Japanese Buddhism include religious ideas from India and China, they have their own mythologies and **pantheons.** One of the main deities is Amida (known in other Buddhist regions as Amitabha), ruler of a paradise called the Pure Land. He is worshiped by some Japanese sects as the savior of humankind. Kannon—a bodhisattva known elsewhere as Kuanyin and Avalokitesvara—is the protector of children, women in childbirth, and dead souls. Another popular deity, the bodhisattva Jizô, protects humans and rescues souls from hell. He is often described as a gentle monk who wanders through the land of the dead bringing light and comfort to the souls imprisoned there.

Tibet. Buddhism reached Tibet from India in the A.D. 600s and gradually absorbed native religious practices, creating a unique form of Buddhism. Tibetan Buddhists worship many groups of Buddhas, gods, and bodhisattvas. They also believe in the existence of numerous demons and evil spirits.

According to Tibetan Buddhists, the world goes through an endless cycle of creation and decay, and a new Buddha appears in each world age to teach Buddhist principles. Legend says that one of these Buddhas, Amitabha, ordered a bodhisattva named Avalokitesvara to bring Buddhism to Tibet. At the time, only animals and **ogres** lived there. Avalokitesvara thus produced a monkey and sent it to meditate in Tibet. The monkey was approached by a female ogre in the form of a beautiful woman, who offered to be his wife. The two had children, but they were covered with hair and had tails. Avalokitesvara sent the children to a forest to mate with other monkeys. He returned a year later and discovered many offspring. When Avalokitesvara gave these creatures food they turned into human beings, and he was then able to convert them to Buddhism. ***See also*** BRAHMA; CHINESE MYTHOLOGY; DEVILS AND DEMONS; FLOWERS IN MYTHOLOGY; HINDUISM AND MYTHOLOGY; JAPANESE MYTHOLOGY; REINCARNATION.

Buffalo Bill

Between the 1880s and the 1920s, Americans created a brand new national mythology based on the settling of the West. History, legends, and folktales all contributed to the mythology of the Wild West. William Frederick Cody, known around the world as Buffalo Bill, became a living symbol of the American West. Cody earned his nickname by slaughtering 4,280 buffalo in eight months.

Cody was born in the Iowa Territory in 1846. At the age of 11, he became a mounted messenger for the freight company that later organized the famous Pony Express. He went on to serve with the Union Army in the Civil War and worked as a scout on the Great Plains. An excellent rider and marksman with a thorough knowledge of Native American customs and western geography, Cody also worked as an army scout during the 1870s.

After appearing as Buffalo Bill in a number of stage plays and popular novels, Cody became one of the best-known public characters in the United States. In 1883 he organized his own traveling show, Buffalo Bill's Wild West. This dramatic four-hour entertainment included wild animals, trick riding and shooting, and stunts such as Indian war dances and stagecoach attacks. Although his show was enormously popular for a while, it went out of business in 1913. Cody toured with other Wild West shows until his death in Denver, Colorado, in 1917—an event that the newspapers called "the passing of the Great West."

Bunyan, Paul

The United States has many legends dating from the 1800s, when the country was expanding westward and people were clearing the land for farming. This folklore includes a number of "tall tales"—humorous stories about larger-than-life characters who possessed unusual strength or cleverness and performed extraordinary feats. Some of the best-known tall tales center on a backwoods lumberjack named Paul Bunyan.

Paul's Life and Adventures. Paul Bunyan, it was said, was born in Maine. His most notable feature was his immense size and the strength that accompanied it. As a baby, he destroyed acres of forest simply by rolling around in his sleep. Bunyan did everything more intensely than normal people. He slept so soundly, for example, that it once took seven hours' worth of cannon shots from the British navy to wake him.

Paul Bunyan logged throughout the upper Midwest and the Pacific Northwest, and he left his mark on many parts of the continent. He created the Grand Canyon by dragging a tool on the ground and dug the St. Lawrence River. He is also said to have driven whales out of the Great Lakes by attempting to harness them for hauling logs. Another story credits Bunyan with cutting down all the trees in North Dakota and turning the region into farmland.

A man as huge as Paul Bunyan needed grand comrades. One of his sidekicks was Johnny Inkslinger, his accountant, who used up nine barrels of ink every day recording Paul's logging feats. Slim, the camp cook, made flapjacks on a griddle so big that seven

Paul Bunyan in the Oil Fields

Although Paul Bunyan was originally created to promote the logging industry and its products, at least one other industry borrowed him. Around 1920, when oil drilling was becoming common in the United States, a few tales appeared about Bunyan as an oil worker. In these stories, he put his immense size and strength to use drilling for oil or constructing pipelines, tanks, and other equipment. Paul Bunyan also showed great skill in using the new technology of petroleum production, often inventing new tools and techniques to bring in huge quantities of oil.

A folk hero of the lumber industry, Paul Bunyan possessed many of the qualities that loggers admired. He was strong, clever, and independent. However, as his legend developed, stories focused more on his size than on his skill as a lumberjack.

youths greased it by strapping hams to their feet and skating across it. Bunyan's best-known companion was Babe, his giant blue ox. Babe measured 42 ax handles wide across the forehead and was strong enough to pull the bends out of a winding road.

Debatable Origins. According to people who study folktales, Paul Bunyan was not truly a folk hero who emerged from the fireside stories of lumberjacks. Rather he was a deliberate creation of journalists and advertisers seeking to promote the lumber industry. For this reason, some folklorists consider the Bunyan stories to be "fakelore" rather than true folklore.

Paul Bunyan first appeared in print in a 1910 article in a Detroit newspaper. The author, James McGillivray, recalled stories about the giant lumberjack that he had heard while working in logging camps. In 1914 W. B. Laughead, a former lumberjack who worked in advertising for a lumber company, used stories and cartoons about Paul Bunyan to enliven a booklet about his company's products. By 1922 the company was publishing handsome illustrated booklets about Bunyan that circulated to libraries and readers far outside the timber industry. Laughead claimed to have given Paul's blue ox the name *Babe* and to have invented Johnny Inkslinger and other characters. He also created the popular image of Paul Bunyan, complete with hat and whiskers.

By the 1940s, professional writers had produced many books, mostly for children, about Paul Bunyan. As time went on, the stories focused more on Bunyan's immense size than on the cleverness and lumbering skill that earlier versions had highlighted.

Paul Bunyan in American Culture. Some of those who wrote about Paul Bunyan were publicists for the lumber industry. Lumber and resort communities also gave Bunyan a boost by holding festivals in his honor, putting up statues of him and Babe, and claiming ties to the lumberjack and his exploits.

So quickly did the journalistic creation known as Paul Bunyan capture the American imagination that statues of him appeared at World's Fairs in New York and California in 1939, just 25 years after the first Laughead pamphlet. The legendary lumberjack has also inspired sculpture, paintings, plays, and even an opera. The enormous, unconquerable Paul Bunyan, a hero of the nation's shrinking wild country, came to be seen as a symbol of the proud American spirit.

† *See **Names and Places** at the end of this volume for further information.*

Butch Cassidy

Robert LeRoy Parker, better known as Butch Cassidy, was an outlaw of the American West whose daring exploits made him a legend. Cassidy led the Wild Bunch, the most successful and well-organized gang in the West. Even his death has the qualities of a legend, for no one knows for certain when or how he died.

Born in Beaver, Utah, in 1866, Parker learned to shoot and steal cattle from a worker on his family's ranch. He borrowed the last name *Cassidy* from this man, and he added *Butch* later while working in a Wyoming butcher shop. Cassidy started out as a cowboy and rustler stealing horses and cattle. By 1889 he was robbing banks and trains. He soon joined other outlaws to form the Wild Bunch. From remote hideouts such as Hole-in-the-Wall in Wyoming, Robbers' Roost in Utah, and Brown's Hole in Colorado, the gang raided trains and banks across the West.

Cassidy was in jail in Wyoming from 1894 until 1896. A few years later, his partner, William Ellsworth Lay, went to prison, and Cassidy teamed up with Harry Longabaugh, known as the Sundance Kid. With sheriffs and detectives on their heels and several members of the gang already arrested, Butch Cassidy and the Sundance Kid fled to South America in 1901. They ranched for a few years but then began pulling off robberies in Argentina, Chile, and Bolivia. Detectives claimed that both men died in a Bolivian shootout in 1909, although some tales put their deaths in Uruguay in 1911. Others have accepted Cassidy's sister's claim that her brother returned to the United States around 1925 and died in 1937.

Cadmus

Greek mythology was full of heroes whose lives were entangled with those of the gods. One such hero was Cadmus, legendary founder of the great city of Thebes†.

Cadmus and his brothers were sent by their father, the king of Phoenicia, to locate their sister Europa. She had been carried away by Zeus†, disguised as a bull. Unable to find Europa, Cadmus sought advice from the **oracle** at Delphi. He was told to found a city, which later became known as Thebes. He then killed a serpent (or dragon) and planted its teeth in the ground there, causing armed warriors to spring forth. The noble families of Thebes claimed descent from these Spartoi, or Sown Men.

The goddess Athena† made Cadmus king of Thebes, and Zeus allowed him to marry Harmonia, daughter of the gods Ares† and Aphrodite (Venus)†. According to myth, after living long and eventful lives, Cadmus and Harmonia were turned into snakes and carried to paradise by the gods. The Greeks credited Cadmus not only with founding a major city but also with bringing written language—in the form of the Phoenician alphabet—to Greece. ***See also* DELPHI; GREEK MYTHOLOGY.**

oracle priest or priestess or other creature through whom a god is believed to speak; also the location (such as a shrine) where such words are spoken

Caduceus

The caduceus was the staff or rod carried by the messenger of the gods, known as Hermes to the Greeks and Mercury to the Romans. The caduceus became a powerful symbol of magic. In modern times, it has been associated with medicine.

The original caduceus was a staff adorned with two ribbons. Messengers and officials carried it to identify and protect themselves during a journey. According to legend, when Hermes threw his staff at two fighting serpents, the animals stopped biting each other and became entangled. The design of the caduceus came to include two entwined snakes, and the staff became associated with peace. Wings were later added at the top to represent the god's swiftness. According to some myths, the caduceus had magical powers, including the ability to cause mortals to fall asleep or to wake from slumber.

Asclepius, the Greek god of medicine and healing, carried a similar staff with a single serpent wrapped around it. Modern physicians have adopted the caduceus as the symbol of their profession. ***See also*** A**SCLEPIUS**; H**ERMES.**

Cagn

In the mythology of the Bushmen of southwestern Africa, Cagn is the god who created the world and all the people and things in it. In some stories, he dies and then comes back to life. Cagn is also called Kaang, Kho, and Thora.

In the beginning, Cagn had a friendly relationship with human beings. After people began to show disrespect toward their creator god, however, Cagn sent death and destruction to the world. He left the earth to live somewhere far off in the sky. According to the Bushmen, only the antelopes know exactly where he is.

Cagn's power is thought to reside in one of his teeth. Sometimes he lends the tooth to someone who needs extra power. Although he can work through all natural things, he most often appears in the form of a mantis and a caterpillar. Myths about Cagn describe his triumphs over giants, **ogres,** and evil spirits. These tales inspire the Bushmen in their fight against Gauna, the evil leader of the spirits of the dead. ***See also*** A**FRICAN** M**YTHOLOGY;** G**AUNA.**

ogre hideous monster

Cain and Abel

In Jewish, Christian, and Islamic tradition, Cain and Abel were sons of Adam and Eve, the ancestors of the human race. Cain killed his brother Abel, becoming the first murderer. The story of Cain and Abel is echoed in the mythologies of many cultures and suggests several symbolic interpretations.

The First Murder. According to the book of Genesis in the Bible, Cain and Abel were the first two sons born to Adam and Eve after their banishment from the Garden of Eden. Cain, the elder, became a farmer, while Abel became a shepherd. They offered sacrifices to Yahweh, or God. Cain brought fruit and grain; Abel brought lambs. When Yahweh accepted Abel's offerings but rejected those of Cain, Cain was hurt and angry. In a jealous rage, he killed his brother.

As punishment, Yahweh ordered Cain to go forth and become "a fugitive and a vagabond in the earth." Then he placed a sign, known as the mark of Cain, on the murderer's forehead to protect

This illumination from a medieval French manuscript shows episodes from the story of Cain and Abel. The story may reflect the practice in the ancient Near East of sacrificing animals to obtain a good harvest.

anti-Semitism prejudice against Jews

him from further punishment. Tradition holds that Cain's son Enoch founded the first city and that other descendents of Cain invented music and metalworking. Cain may be a mythological representation of a Near Eastern people called the Kenites, who practiced metalworking and musicianship and who may have worn tattoos.

Medieval Christians believed that Cain had a yellowish beard, so artists and playwrights used yellow beards to identify murderers and traitors. Because Christians sometimes viewed Cain as a forerunner of the Jews who killed Jesus, yellow became associated with **anti-Semitism.** Abel, an innocent and godly victim, was often compared with Jesus.

Symbolic Interpretations. Conflicts between brothers abound in world mythology, reflecting the widespread view that conflict between good and evil is an inescapable part of human life. In Persian mythology, the rival brothers are the gods Ahriman and Ahura Mazda. Islamic tradition calls them Kabil (Cain) and Habil (Abel).

One interpretation of the Cain and Abel story is that it reflects the very ancient tension between the different values and ways of life of wandering herders, represented by Abel, and settled farmers, represented by Cain. Other views suggest that the story is about the death of innocence or that it illustrates the need for self-control and the high cost of giving in to competition and jealousy. ***See also*** ADAM AND EVE; AHRIMAN; AHURA MAZDA; EDEN, GARDEN OF.

Calliope

patron special guardian, protector, or supporter
epic long poem about legendary or historical heroes, written in a grand style

In Greek mythology, Calliope was the most honored of the nine Muses, sister goddesses who were **patrons** of the arts and sciences. Calliope, the leader of the Muses, was the patron of the **epic.** Sculptors usually portrayed her holding writing implements such as a stylus—a pointed instrument for engraving on a clay or wax tablet—and a tablet.

Calliope's name meant "fair voice," and she was said to have been the mother of Orpheus, a legendary musician of superb skill. Ironically, in the 1800s, a rather harsh-sounding musical instrument in which a keyboard operated a series of steam whistles was called a calliope. ***See also*** MUSES; ORPHEUS.

115

Callisto

chastity purity or virginity

In Greek mythology, Callisto was one of many human women who were seduced or raped by Zeus†. Daughter of the king of Arcadia, Callisto joined the followers of the goddess Artemis†. As a member of this group, Callisto swore to remain a virgin. But Zeus was tempted by Callisto—whose name meant "most beautiful"—and tricked her into lovemaking.

After her encounter with Zeus, the unfortunate Callisto was turned into a bear by Zeus, his wife (Hera), or Artemis as punishment for breaking her vow of **chastity.** Still, Callisto bore Zeus a son named Arcas, whom Zeus protected. One version of Callisto's story says that Artemis shot the bear while hunting. Another says that Callisto was shot by her own son. Feeling sorry for her, Zeus placed Callisto in the heavens, where she became the constellation known as Ursa Major, the Great Bear. *See also* ARCADIA; ARTEMIS; HERA; ZEUS.

Calypso

nymph minor goddess of nature, usually represented as young and beautiful
epic long poem about legendary or historical heroes, written in a grand style
Titan one of a family of giants who ruled the earth until overthrown by the Greek gods of Olympus

In Greek mythology, Calypso was either a goddess or an ocean **nymph,** who inhabited a mythical island called Ogygia. Calypso appeared in the *Odyssey,* the Greek **epic** that describes the wanderings of Odysseus† on his way home from the Trojan War†. Although accounts vary, Calypso was apparently the daughter of a **Titan,** possibly of Atlas.

When Odysseus was shipwrecked and washed up on the shore of Ogygia during his voyage home, Calypso fell in love with him. She kept him on the island for seven years and offered him eternal life and youth if he would remain with her forever. However, Odysseus

This Greek vase painting from the 400s B.C. illustrates an episode from the story of the Greek hero Odysseus. Returning home from the Trojan War, Odysseus was shipwrecked on an island where the nymph Calypso lived.

†See **Names and Places** at the end of this volume for further information.

yearned to return home to see his wife, from whom he had been separated for a long time. Zeus† took pity on the hero and sent Hermes† with an order for Calypso to release him. She agreed and gave Odysseus supplies for his voyage. Legend says that she bore him at least one son. *See also* ODYSSEUS; ODYSSEY, THE; TITANS.

Camelot

Holy Grail sacred cup said to have been used by Jesus Christ at the Last Supper

Camelot was the location of King Arthur's court and the site of the famous Round Table of Arthurian legend. The wedding of Arthur to his queen, Guinevere, took place in the town of Camelot, and the magician Merlin built a castle there for the couple to live in.

The castle served as headquarters for King Arthur and his knights as well. A special hall held the Round Table, where Arthur and the knights would plan their campaigns. The hall also contained lifelike statues of the 12 kings who had tried to overthrow Arthur. All had been defeated by him and were buried at Camelot. Each statue had a lighted candle. According to Merlin, the candles would stay lit until the **Holy Grail** was found and brought to Camelot. It was from Camelot that the knights rode out to perform good deeds and brave feats and to search for the Holy Grail.

Scholars have long debated the location of Camelot, just as they have debated the identity of King Arthur. In early times, it was associated with the town of Camulodunum (now called Colchester), an important site during the days of Roman rule in Britain. Other possible sites include Caerleon in Wales and the English towns of Camelford and Cadbury. In his book *Le Morte D'Arthur,* Sir Thomas Malory identified the city of Winchester as Camelot. England's King Henry VII had his first son baptized in Winchester Cathedral and named Arthur. In all likelihood, however, Camelot represents a mythical place, not a real one. *See also* ARTHUR, KING; ARTHURIAN LEGENDS; GUINEVERE; HOLY GRAIL; MERLIN; ROUND TABLE.

Casey Jones

Casey Jones, a railroad engineer, became an American legend because of a ballad about his death. Born John Luther Jones, he got the nickname *Casey* from the town of Cayce, Kentucky, where his family moved when he was a teenager. Jones was an engineer on the *Cannonball Express,* which ran between Chicago and New Orleans. On April 30, 1900, he was filling in for a sick engineer when the train's fireman warned him of trains stopped on the tracks ahead. Jones ordered the fireman to jump off the train but stayed aboard himself, holding on to the brake. After the crash, Jones's body was found in the engine with one hand still on the brake lever. Jones was the only person killed in the crash, which would have been much worse if he had not stayed aboard to apply the brakes.

Casey Jones passed into American folklore when a black railroad worker named Wallace Saunders wrote a song about the wreck. The ballad was translated into several languages and has gained popularity around the world. Later versions of the tale have portrayed Casey Jones as, among other things, a dashing ladies'

Cassandra

prophecy foretelling of what is to come; also something that is predicted

man, a World War II pilot, and an engineer who breaks a union strike and is punished by death. Robert Ardrey published a play called *Casey Jones* in 1938.

In Greek mythology, Cassandra was the daughter of Priam and Hecuba, the king and queen of Troy. Cassandra was the most beautiful of Priam's daughters, and the god Apollo† fell in love with her. Apollo promised Cassandra the gift of **prophecy** if she would agree to give herself to him. Cassandra accepted Apollo's gift but then refused his advances. Apollo was furious, but he could not take back the powers he had given her. Instead he cursed her, proclaiming that although she would be able to tell the future accurately, no one would believe her. Before announcing her prophecies, Cassandra went into a type of trance that made her family believe she was insane.

In Homer's *Iliad*†, Cassandra predicted many of the events of the Trojan War†. Priam's son Paris planned a trip to Sparta. Cassandra warned against it, but her warnings were ignored. Paris traveled to Sparta, where he kidnapped Helen, starting the war with Greece. Cassandra later predicted Troy's defeat and warned the Trojans not to accept the Greek gift of the Trojan horse. Again she was ignored, and Greek troops hidden inside the wooden horse captured the city. During the battle, a Greek soldier known as Ajax the Lesser† raped Cassandra in the temple of Athena†. Athena later punished Ajax and his men for the deed.

During the Trojan War, Cassandra, the daughter of King Priam of Troy, was attacked by Ajax the Lesser in the Temple of Athena. The scene is illustrated in this painting from a house in Italy.

† See **Names and Places** at the end of this volume for further information.

After the Greek victory, Cassandra was given to the Greek leader Agamemnon† as a prize. She bore Agamemnon two sons and later returned to Greece with him. However, she also predicted that a terrible fate awaited Agamemnon and herself. When they reached Agamemnon's home in Mycenae, they were both murdered by Agamemnon's wife, Clytemnestra, and her lover, Aegisthus. *See also* AGAMEMNON; APOLLO; ATHENA; CLYTEMNESTRA; GREEK MYTHOLOGY; HECUBA; HELEN OF TROY; HOMER; ILIAD, THE; PARIS; PRIAM.

Cassiopea

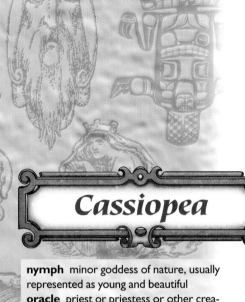

nymph minor goddess of nature, usually represented as young and beautiful

oracle priest or priestess or other creature through whom a god is believed to speak; also the location (such as a shrine) where such words are spoken

In Greek mythology, Cassiopea was the wife of Cepheus, king of Joppa (often called Ethiopia). Cassiopea once boasted that she and her daughter Andromeda were more beautiful than the sea **nymphs** known as the Nereids. The Nereids were so insulted that they asked Poseidon (Neptune), god of the sea, to punish Cassiopea. He responded by sending a flood and a sea monster to devastate the land.

An **oracle** told Cepheus that the only way he could save his kingdom was by sacrificing his daughter to the sea monster. With a heavy heart, Cepheus decided to do so. He chained Andromeda to a rock in the sea and left her there to be devoured. However, the hero Perseus† saw her and rescued her, and as a reward, Cepheus promised Andromeda to Perseus as his bride. At the wedding, though, Andromeda's uncle Phineus claimed that she had been promised to him. Perseus used the head of the monster Medusa† to turn Phineus to stone and then married Andromeda.

When Cassiopea died, Poseidon made her into a constellation in the night sky. To punish her for insulting the Nereids, however, he arranged the constellation so that at times Cassiopea appears to be hanging upside down with her feet in the air. *See also* ANDROMEDA; MEDUSA; NYMPHS; PERSEUS; POSEIDON.

Castor and Pollux

patron special guardian, protector, or supporter

In Greek and Roman mythology, Castor and Pollux (known as Polydeuces to the Greeks) were twin brothers who appeared in several prominent myths. The twins were worshiped as gods who helped shipwrecked sailors and who brought favorable winds for those who made sacrifices to them. The Romans considered Castor and Pollux the **patron** gods of horses and of the Roman social order of mounted knights, called *equites*.

Myths and Variations. There are many stories about the twins and numerous verions of those stories. According to the Greek poet Homer†, Castor and Pollux were the sons of Tyndareus and Leda, the king and queen of Sparta†. For this reason, they are sometimes called the Tyndaridae (sons of Tyndareus). Another account identifies the twins as the sons of Leda and Zeus†, from whom they received the name *Dioscuri* (sons of Zeus). Still another legend says that Castor was the son of Leda and Tyndareus—and therefore a human—while Pollux was the son of Zeus—and

119

This Roman sculpture from the 400s B.C. shows the twin deities Castor and Pollux. In Roman mythology, the twins served as patrons of horses.

immortality ability to live forever

therefore a god. This difference became significant later in their lives. All tales about the twins agree in portraying Castor as a skilled horse trainer and Pollux as an expert boxer. Inseparable, the brothers always acted together.

In one of the earliest myths about the twins, Castor and Pollux rescued their sister Helen† after she had been kidnapped by Theseus†, king of Attica. Helen would later gain fame as the person who caused the Trojan War†. The twins also accompanied Jason† and the Argonauts on their voyage in search of the Golden Fleece. During that expedition, Pollux demonstrated his boxing skills by killing the king of the Bebryces. When a storm arose on the voyage, the Argonaut Orpheus† prayed to the gods and played his harp. The storm immediately ceased, and stars appeared on the heads of the twins. It is because of this myth that Castor and Pollux came to be recognized as the patrons of sailors.

Another story concerns the death of Castor. According to one account, the twins wanted to marry their cousins Phoebe and Hilaria. However, the women were already promised to two other cousins, Idas and Lynceus. Castor and Pollux carried the women away to Sparta, pursued by their male cousins. In the fight that followed, the twins succeeded in killing both Idas and Lynceus, but Castor was fatally wounded.

In another version of this story, the four men conducted a cattle raid together. Idas and Lynceus then tried to cheat Castor and Pollux out of their share of the cattle. The twins decided to take the cattle themselves but were caught as they started to sneak away. A fight broke out in which Castor, Idas, and Lynceus were all killed.

This story also has several different endings. In one, Castor's spirit went to Hades, the place of the dead, because he was a human. Pollux, who was a god, was so devastated at being separated from his brother that he offered to share his **immortality** with Castor or to give it up so that he could join his brother in Hades. Taking pity on his son Pollux, Zeus declared that the brothers would take turns dwelling in Hades and with the gods on Mount Olympus. On one day, Castor would be with the gods and Pollux would be in Hades. The next day, the two would change places. In another ending, Castor remained in Hades, but Pollux was allowed to visit him every other day. Most versions of the myth say that Zeus placed the brothers in the heavens as part of the constellation Gemini, the twins. Today the brightest stars in the constellation Gemini are named Castor and Pollux.

†See **Names and Places** at the end of this volume for further information.

St. Elmo's Fire

St. Elmo's fire is a phenomenon that occurs during certain stormy weather conditions. It appears as a glow on the top of tall pointed objects, such as the masts of ships, and is often accompanied by a cracking noise. When stars appeared on the heads of Castor and Pollux during the voyage of the Argonauts, the twins became the special patrons of sailors. From that time, sailors believed that St. Elmo's fire was actually Castor and Pollux coming to protect them during a storm.

cult group bound together by devotion to a particular person, belief, or god

Cecilia, St.

patron special guardian, protector, or supporter

catacombs underground tunnels near Rome used as hiding and gathering places for early Christians

Celtic Mythology

The Romans developed a strong **cult** around Castor and Pollux that traditionally dates back to 484 B.C. A temple to the twins was built in the Roman Forum in 414 B.C. in thanks for their help in defeating the Latins, an old enemy, in the battle of Regillus several years earlier. The images of Castor and Pollux appear on many early Roman coins.

Literature and Music. Castor and Pollux were featured in the works of many ancient Greek and Roman writers. Besides appearing in Homer's poems, the twins have a role in the play *Helen* by the Greek playwright Euripides†. They also figure in Pindar's† *Nemean Odes* and in Ovid's *Metamorphoses*†. There is even a reference to the twins in the Bible. In the New Testament book Acts of the Apostles, St. Paul is said to sail from Malta aboard a ship bearing the sign of Castor and Pollux. The English poet Edmund Spenser included the twins in his poem *Prothalamion.* The greatest work by the French composer Jean-Phillipe Rameau, the tragic opera *Castor and Pollux,* was based on the story of the brothers. *See also* AENEID, THE; ARGONAUTS; HELEN OF TROY.

In the Christian tradition, St. Cecilia is the **patron** saint of music and musicians. According to legend, St. Cecilia was a young woman from a noble Roman family who lived during the reign of the emperor Septimus Severus (A.D. 193–211).

Raised in a Christian family, Cecilia was known for her devotion to Christ and her musical talents. It was said that the songs she wrote and sang were so beautiful that angels came down to earth to listen.

According to legend, Cecilia vowed to remain a virgin and married a young man named Valerian, who respected her vow. Valerian converted to Christianity and was baptized in the **catacombs** by St. Urban. Upon returning to Cecilia, he found her with an angel. The angel offered to grant Valerian one wish, and the young man wished that his brother Tiburtius would also convert to Christianity.

Cecilia and the two brothers traveled around helping the poor and sick, but Valerian and Tiburtius were arrested and killed for practicing their religion. Cecilia was arrested after she buried their bodies. Thrown in boiling water, she came out alive and was then stabbed in the neck and breast three times. She died three days later. Some versions of the legend say that she was beheaded, but she lived for three days after being struck by the ax.

Although some credit St. Cecilia with inventing the organ, the first organ was actually built by the ancient Greeks around 250 B.C. A feast in her honor has been celebrated on November 22 in Rome since the A.D. 300s.

Adventure, heroism, romance, and magic are a few of the elements that make Celtic mythology one of the most entrancing mythologies of Europe. Once a powerful people who dominated much of Europe, the Celts were reduced to a few small groups after the

medieval relating to the Middle Ages in Europe, a period from about A.D. 500 to 1500

The Tragedy of Deirdre

The heroine of the Ulster Cycle is the beautiful Deirdre. King Conchobhar intends to marry the young woman, but she falls in love with Naoise and flees to Scotland with him. When they return, the king has Naoise killed.

Forced to lived with Conchobhar, the grief-stricken Deirdre never smiles and makes clear to the king how much she hates him. The story ends with Deirdre taking her own life by striking her head against a rock. Deirdre's tragic tale served as inspiration for poetry, plays, and stories by later Irish writers, including William Butler Yeats and J. M. Synge.

Roman invasions. However, their mythology survived, thanks largely to the efforts of **medieval** Irish and Welsh monks who wrote down the stories.

The Celts

The Celts were a group of people who began to spread throughout Europe in the 1000s B.C. At the peak of their power, they inhabited an area extending from the British Isles in the west to what is now Turkey in the east. They conquered northern Italy and Macedonia, plundering both Rome and Delphi in the process. They had a reputation as fierce and courageous warriors and were viewed with respect by the Romans.

Celtic expansion reached its limit around 225 B.C., when the Celts suffered the first in a series of defeats by the armies of the Roman empire. Gradually, the Romans subdued the Celts, and by A.D. 84, most of Britain was under Roman rule. At the same time, Germanic peoples conquered the Celts living in central Europe.

Just a few areas, notably Ireland and northern Britain, managed to remain free and to continue and pass on the Celtic traditions. Six groups of Celts have survived to modern times: the peoples of Ireland, Scotland, the Isle of Man, Wales, Cornwall, and Brittany.

The ancient Celts were neither a race nor a nation. They were a varied people bound together by language, customs, and religion rather than by any centralized government. They lived off the land, farming and raising stock. No towns existed apart from impressive hill forts. However, by about 100 B.C., large groups of Celts had begun to gather at certain settlements to trade with one another.

Celtic society had a clearly defined structure. Highest in rank was the king, who ruled a particular tribe, or group of people. Each tribe was divided into three classes: the noble knights and warriors, the Druids (religious leaders), and the farmers and commoners. The Druids, who came from noble families, were respected and influential figures. They served not only as priests but also as judges, teachers, and advisers. In addition, it was widely believed that the Druids had magical powers.

The Myths

The ancient Celts had a vibrant mythology made up of hundreds of tales. They did not, however, record their myths in writing but passed them on orally. Our knowledge of the gods, heroes, and villains of Celtic mythology comes from other sources—mainly Roman. Yet the Romans sometimes referred to Celtic gods by Roman names, so their accounts were not always reliable. Moreover, because the Romans and Celts were battlefield enemies, Roman descriptions of Celtic beliefs were often unfavorable.

Much of what is now known about Celtic mythology is based on manuscripts that were prepared by monks in the Middle Ages. Irish collections dating from the 700s and Welsh collections from the 1300s recount many of the myths and legends of the ancient Celts.

*†See **Names and Places** at the end of this volume for further information.*

deity god or goddess

supernatural related to forces beyond the normal world; magical or miraculous
cauldron large kettle

Major Gods. The Celts worshiped a variety of gods who appeared in their tales. Most were all-powerful local **deities** rather than gods with specialized roles. Each tribe had its own god, who protected and provided for the welfare of that tribe. Some of them had similar characteristics. For example, Dagda, the god of life and death in Ireland—known as the good god—resembled Esus, the "master" god of Gaul.

Some deities had more clearly defined roles. Among these were Lug, or Lugus, a sun god associated with arts and skills, war and healing, and the horned god Cernunnos, who was god of animals and fertility. The Celts also had a large number of important female deities. These included Morrigan, the "Great Queen"—actually three war goddesses, Morrigan, Badb, and Nemain, who appeared as ravens during battle. Another important deity was Brigit, goddess of learning, healing, and metalworking. Epona, the horse goddess, was associated with fertility, water, and death.

Major Themes. Magic, magicians, and the **supernatural** played a significant role in Celtic mythology. A common theme was the magic **cauldron.** The cauldron of plenty was never empty and supplied great quantities of food. The cauldron of rebirth brought slain warriors to life again. Myrddin, a magician in the Welsh tales, later became Merlin in the Arthurian legends†.

Other important themes in the myths were voyages to mysterious and dangerous lands and larger-than-life heroes. The heroes experienced all kinds of adventures and often had to perform impossible tasks before marrying their loved one. Love, romance, and mischief also figured prominently. The gods played tricks on humans and on one another. Animals changed shape at will.

The Gundestrup cauldron is a silver vessel thought to have been made sometime around 100 B.C. A symbol of abundance and renewal, the cauldron contains many scenes and characters from Celtic mythology.

Related Entries
Other entries related to Celtic mythology are listed at the end of this article.

Celtic Deities

Deity	Role
Brigit	goddess of learning, healing, and metalworking
Dagda	god of life and death
Danu	fertility goddess and mother of the Tuatha Dé Danaan
Epona	goddess associated with fertility, water, and death
Lug	god of the sun, war, and healing
Morrigan	goddess of war and death

Many myths told of the otherworld. In this mysterious place, there was no work and no death, and the gods and spirits who lived there never got old. The Celts believed that humans could enter this enchanted place through burial mounds called *sídhe*, through caves or lakes, or after completing a perilous journey. After reaching the otherworld, they would live happily for all time.

Irish and Welsh Legends

Early Irish myths blend mythology and history by describing how Ireland was settled by different groups of Celtic deities and humans. Filled with magic and excitement, the tales tell of battles between forces of light and darkness. They describe a time when gods lived not in the heavens but on earth, using their powers to create civilization in Ireland and to bring fertility to the land.

There are four cycles, or groups, of connected stories. The Mythological Cycle focuses on the activities of the Celtic gods, describing how five races of supernatural beings battled to gain control of Ireland. The chief god was Dagda, whose magic cauldron could bring the dead back to life. The Ulster Cycle recounts the deeds of warriors and heroes, especially Cuchulain, the warrior and champion of Ireland. The Historical Cycle tells of the adventures and battles of legendary Irish kings. The Fenian Cycle deals with the heroic Finn Mac Cumhail, or Finn Mac Cool, leader of a band of bold warriors known as the Fianna. This cycle is filled with exciting adventures and tales of hand-to-hand combat.

Welsh mythology is found in the Mabinogion, a collection of 11 tales. In the Welsh myths, as in those of Ireland, the heroes often are half human and half divine and may have magical powers. Many of the stories in the Mabinogion deal with Arthurian legends, accounts of the deeds of Britain's heroic King Arthur and his knights.

In fact, the popular Arthurian tales of medieval European literature are a complex blend of ancient Celtic myths, later stories, and

† See **Names and Places** at the end of this volume for further information.

historical events. The legends are clearly rooted in Celtic mythology, however, and references to Arthur appear in a number of ancient Welsh poems. Scholars also note that there are many similarities between the Arthur stories and the tales of the Irish Finn Mac Cumhail, suggesting a shared Celtic origin.

Another famous romantic story of Celtic origin is that of Tristan and Isolde. The tragic tale, probably based on an early Cornish poem, concerns the knight Tristan who falls in love with Isolde, a princess who is fated to marry his uncle the king. In the Middle Ages, Gottfried von Strassburg wrote a poem based on the legend that is considered a literary masterpiece. *See also* ARTHURIAN LEGENDS; BADB; CUCHULAIN; DAGDA; DANU; DRUIDS; FINN; LUG; TRISTAN AND ISOLDE.

Centaurs

In Greek mythology, centaurs were creatures that were half man and half horse. They had the head, neck, chest, and arms of a man and the body and legs of a horse. Most centaurs were brutal, violent creatures known for their drunkenness and lawless behavior. They lived mainly around Mount Pelion in Thessaly, a region of northeastern Greece.

Origin of the Centaurs. According to one account, centaurs were descended from Centaurus, a son of Apollo†. A more widely accepted account of their origin, however, is that they were descendants of Ixion, the son of Ares† and king of the Lapiths, a people who lived in Thessaly.

Ixion fell in love with Hera, the wife of Zeus†. Recklessly, Ixion arranged to meet with Hera, planning to seduce her. Zeus heard of the plan and formed a cloud in the shape of Hera. Ixion embraced the cloud form, and from this union, the race of centaurs was created.

War with the Lapiths. The main myth relating to the centaurs involves their battle with the Lapiths. King Pirithous of the Lapiths, son of Ixion, invited the centaurs to his wedding. The centaurs became drunk and disorderly and pursued the Lapith women. One centaur even tried to run off with the king's bride. A fierce battle erupted. The centaurs used tree trunks and slabs of stone as weapons, but eventually the Lapiths won the fight, killing many centaurs. The centaurs were forced to leave Thessaly.

Hercules and Centaurs. A number of tales describe conflict between centaurs and the Greek hero Hercules†. In one such story, Hercules came to the cave of a centaur named Pholus. Pholus served Hercules food but did not offer him any wine, though an unopened jar of wine stood in the cave. Pholus explained that the wine was a gift and was the property of all the centaurs. Nonetheless, Hercules insisted on having some wine, and Pholus opened the jar.

The smell of the wine soon brought the other centaurs to the cave and before long a fight broke out. Hercules drove off the centaurs by shooting poisoned arrows at them. Afterward, Pholus

Chiron, a Kindly Centaur

Not all centaurs were savage brutes. One such exception was Chiron, who became a teacher of medicine, music, hunting, and archery. The son of the god Cronos (Saturn), Chiron taught gods and heroes, including Jason†, Achilles†, Hercules, and Asclepius. Chiron was accidentally wounded by one of Hercules' poisoned arrows. As the son of a god, he would live forever and suffer from the injury forever. Chiron therefore asked Zeus to let him die. Zeus granted his request and placed him in the heavens as a star in the constellation Sagittarius, the archer.

This mosaic from about A.D. 120 shows centaurs, mythical creatures that were half man and half horse, battling wild animals. Many myths about centaurs describe their unruly behavior.

was examining one of these arrows when he accidentally dropped it. It struck his foot, and the poison killed him.

In another well-known story, a centaur named Nessus tried to rape Deianira, the wife of Hercules. Hercules caught him and shot the centaur with a poisoned arrow. As he lay dying, Nessus urged Deianira to save some of the blood from his wound. He told her that if Hercules ever stopped loving her, she could regain his love by applying the blood to a garment that Hercules would wear. Deianira did as Nessus suggested and saved some of his blood.

Many years later, when Hercules had been unfaithful to her, Deianira gave him a tunic to wear, a tunic that she had smeared with the blood of Nessus. The blood was poisoned, and Hercules died. In this way, Nessus took his revenge on Hercules.

Literature and Art. Centaurs usually represented wild and bestial behavior in Greek literature and art. They appeared on many vases, and their fight with the Lapiths was depicted in sculptures in various temples. Because of their drunken behavior, centaurs were sometimes shown pulling the chariot of Dionysus (Bacchus), the god of wine and revelry. At other times, they were pictured being ridden by Eros, the god of love, because of their lustful ways. In Christian art of the Middle Ages, centaurs symbolized the animal nature of man.

The Roman poet Ovid† described the battle of the centaurs and the Lapiths in the *Metamorphoses.* This work, in turn, inspired

† *See **Names and Places** at the end of this volume for further information.*

the English poet Edmund Spenser to write about the battle in his most famous work, *The Faerie Queene.* ***See also*** HERCULES.

Cephalus and Procris

deity god or goddess

The great hunter Cephalus and his wife, Procris, appear in a Greek legend about mistrust and mistaken identity. Like many Greek myths, their story included interaction with a **deity.**

In one version, Eos (Aurora), the goddess of dawn, fell in love with Cephalus. In jealous distress, Procris ran into the forest. Cephalus searched for her but paused to rest. When Procris crept up to see if he was with Eos, Cephalus thought the rustling in the bushes was an animal and killed Procris with his spear. After accidentally killing his wife, Cephalus was sent into exile on an island. The Roman poet Ovid wrote a detailed account of Cephalus and Procris in his narrative poem the *Metamorphoses.* Ovid's version describes Cephalus's feats as a hunter and the series of crises that occur in the couple's relationship. ***See also*** OVID.

Cerberus

underworld land of the dead

In Greek mythology, Cerberus was the terrifying three-headed dog who guarded the entrance to the **underworld.** The offspring of the monsters Typhon and Echidna, Cerberus was also the brother of the serpent creature Hydra and the lion-headed beast Chimaera. He is often pictured with the tail of a snake or dragon and with snakes sprouting from his back. According to legend, his appearance was so fearsome that any living person who saw him turned to stone. The saliva that fell from his mouth produced a deadly poison.

Cerberus prevented spirits of the dead from leaving Hades and living mortals from entering. Three humans, however, managed to overcome him. Orpheus† charmed him with music. An old woman named the Sibyl of Cumae put Cerberus to sleep by giving him a cake soaked in drugged wine to give the Roman hero Aeneas access to the underworld. Hercules† used his sheer strength to take Cerberus from the land of Hades to the kingdom of Mycenae and back again, the twelfth labor of Hercules. ***See also*** GREEK MYTHOLOGY; HADES; HERCULES; HYDRA; ORPHEUS.

Ceres

See *Demeter.*

Changing Woman

Changing Woman, or Asdzáá nádleehé, is the most respected goddess of the Navajo people. All Navajo ceremonies must include at least one song dedicated to Changing Woman. She is related to goddesses found in many other Native American traditions, such as the Pawnee Moon Woman and the Apache White Painted Woman.

According to legend, Changing Woman changes continuously but never dies. She grows into an old woman in winter, but by spring, she becomes a young woman again. In this way, she represents the power of life, fertility, and changing seasons. In some stories she has a sister, White Shell Woman (Yoolgai asdzáá), who

127

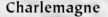

symbolizes the rain clouds. Ceremonies dedicated to Changing Woman are performed to celebrate childbirth, coming of age for girls, and weddings and to bless a new home.

Changing Woman bears the children of the Sun, Jóhonaa'éí, after he shines his rays on her. Their children are the twin heroes Monster Slayer (Naayéé' neizghání) and Child of Water (Tó bájísh chíní), who cleared the earth of the monsters that once roamed it. Changing Woman lives by herself in a house floating on the western waters, where the Sun visits her every evening. One day she became lonely and decided to make some companions for herself. From pieces of her own skin she created men and women who became the ancestors of the Navajo people. *See also* NATIVE AMERICAN MYTHOLOGY.

Charlemagne

pagan term used by early Christians to describe non-Christians and non-Christian beliefs

epic long poem about legendary or historical heroes, written in a grand style

Charlemagne, king of the Franks†, was the greatest ruler in Europe in the centuries following the fall of the Roman empire. In a long reign that lasted from A.D. 768 to 814, he conquered most of western Europe and converted many of its **pagan** peoples to Christianity. In 800 he became the "Emperor of the Romans." Under Charlemagne's rule, Europe experienced a great revival in learning and the arts, which had declined dramatically after the collapse of Rome. The legends that grew up around Charlemagne focus on his military and political skills and on his moral conduct.

Life and Achievements

Born in about 742, Charlemagne was the son of King Pepin III (known as Pepin the Short). Pepin and his brother together ruled the Franks, whose kingdom included parts of present-day France, Belgium, Germany, and the Netherlands. Upon Pepin's death in 768, Charlemagne and his brother Carloman inherited the kingdom. When Carloman died three years later, Charlemagne became the sole ruler.

Charlemagne the King. Soon after Carloman's death, Charlemagne defeated the Lombard kingdom in northern Italy and made himself king of the Lombards. He then turned his attention to the Saxons, a group of pagan tribes in central Germany. By 777 he had defeated the Saxons in several battles and converted large numbers of them to Christianity. In that same year, some Arabs from Spain asked Charlemagne to help them overthrow the Muslim ruler of Córdoba in southern Spain. Charlemagne marched against Spain in 778 but failed to defeat the Muslims. During the retreat to France, a group of mountain people known as the Basques ambushed and destroyed part of Charlemagne's army. A famous **epic** about Charlemagne called the *Song of Roland* commemorated this event.

Despite this setback from the Basques, Charlemagne greatly expanded his kingdom during the first ten years of his reign. Just as importantly, he brought together the most learned men in the kingdom

†*See **Names and Places** at the end of this volume for further information.*

This bronze sculpture from the A.D. 800s or 900s shows Charlemagne, king of the Franks, on horseback. During his lifetime, Charlemagne introduced a variety of military, economic, and social reforms in his kingdom.

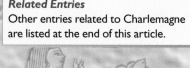

Related Entries
Other entries related to Charlemagne are listed at the end of this article.

with the goal of making his court the intellectual center of Europe. He established an extensive library and founded an academy for educating young Frankish knights. He promoted religion and morality and made strong efforts to produce an educated clergy. He also established a system of justice in which nobles and clergymen traveled about the kingdom hearing court cases and bringing the law to every town and village. These cultural, religious, and legal reforms are often called the Carolingian renaissance (after Charlemagne's Latin name, Carolus Magnus).

Charlemagne the Emperor. In the early 780s, the Saxons rose up again. Charlemagne waged a bitter war against them, executing thousands of people. It was not until 804 that he fully defeated the Saxons and made them part of his empire. During this time, he formed close ties with Pope Leo III to ensure that the church supported his rule. In 800, while Charlemagne was visiting Rome, the pope surprised him at Christmas mass by proclaiming him emperor of Rome. This announcement was not well received by the empress of the Byzantine empire, who considered herself the only

legitimate ruler of what remained of the old Roman empire. However, by 812 the new Byzantine ruler recognized Charlemagne as emperor, and from that point on, Charlemagne and his successors were given the title Holy Roman Emperor. When Charlemagne died two years later, his son Louis took over as emperor but was unable to hold the empire together.

Charlemagne left behind an impressive assortment of political, military, and social achievements. He united many different peoples into a single kingdom and led the spread of Christianity after the fall of Rome. His educational reforms laid the foundations for the educated clergy that preserved learning in Europe during the Middle Ages. Charlemagne's accomplishments were so great that many legends grew up around him to celebrate his power, wisdom, and devotion to Christianity.

Legends

The most popular legends about Charlemagne fall into two general categories. Battle stories tell of his military exploits and celebrate the adventures of his 12 most loyal warriors, called paladins. Morality stories focus on his moral strength and devotion to Christian principles. Many of the legends first appeared in a work called *History of Charles the Great and Orlando* (Orlando, or Roland, was Charlemagne's nephew). Some sources say the archbishop of Rheims, a friend of Charlemagne, was its author. It is more likely, however, that the tales were written by a monk who used the archbishop's name to lend authority to the work.

A collection of French epics called the *Chansons de Geste* (Songs of Deeds) brings together the main Charlemagne legends and characters. Dating from the 1100s to 1400s, these poems generally blend history and fiction.

Battle Legends. The most famous of the battle legends about Charlemagne and his followers appears in the epic *Song of Roland.* The tale concerns Charlemagne's defeat while retreating from Spain in 778. The rear guard of his army had fallen behind and was ambushed and wiped out. According to the *Song of Roland,* a paladin named Ganelon caused the defeat because he was jealous of Roland, the bravest and most loyal warrior.

To get Roland out of the way, Ganelon revealed to the Muslim enemy the route the army would take. He also arranged that Roland and his troops would become separated from the main army. The Muslims waited for Roland, ambushed him, and killed him and all of his men. In reality, the ambush was carried out by Basques, not Muslims, and there was no evidence of any betrayal by Ganelon. However, in the Middle Ages, the legend became a symbol of the bravery of Christian warriors and the treachery of Muslims.

Another legend says that St. James the Greater appeared to Charlemagne in a vision and told him to free Spain from the Muslims. Acting on the vision, Charlemagne led an army to Spain and attacked the city of Pamplona. His attack continued for two months

Chansons de Geste

The *Chansons de Geste* consist of more than 80 epic poems. Most tell of events during the reign of Charlemagne, and many concern the struggle between Christian France and the Muslim enemy. The earlier chansons celebrate strength and heroism and focus on battles and feuds. Later chansons are concerned more with romance and love. The chansons were popular throughout Europe and strongly influenced the literature of other countries.

† *See **Names and Places** at the end of this volume for further information.*

but did not succeed. Finally, Charlemagne prayed for God's help, and the walls of Pamplona miraculously collapsed, allowing him to capture the city. He spared the Muslims who agreed to convert to Christianity but killed those who refused. This story is clearly based on the biblical story of the fall of the walls of Jericho.

Morality Legends. One well-known legend concerns the practice of knights taking the property of others. In the story, an angel woke Charlemagne and told him to steal something. Charlemagne set out and met a strange knight who challenged him to combat. The king won, knocking the knight from his horse. The knight turned out to be a notorious thief named Elbegast. Charlemagne agreed to let him go free if he would help the king steal something. Together, they went to the castle of one of Charlemagne's advisers and hid in the bedroom. While there, they overheard the adviser telling his wife of a plan to murder Charlemagne the next day. After the couple went to sleep, Charlemagne and Elbegast took a worthless item and returned to the king's castle. The next day, Charlemagne exposed the plot but agreed to pardon the plotters if they swore loyalty to him. Elbegast was so impressed with Charlemagne's compassion and wisdom that he gave up his life of crime and entered the king's service. This story is often cited in other legends in which knights accused of unjustly taking others' property remind the king that he, too, was once a thief. ***See also*** PALADINS; ROLAND.

Cherubim

Cherubim (*cherub* in the singular) are winged creatures that appear as attendants to God in the Jewish, Christian, and Islamic traditions. Their main duties are to praise God and to support his throne, though their roles vary from culture to culture. Scholars disagree about the origin of the word *cherubim*. It may have come from *karabu,* an ancient Near Eastern word meaning "to pray" or "to bless," or perhaps from *mu-karribim,* the guardians of the shrine of the ancient Sheban moon goddess.

Whatever the origin of the name, the cherub itself can be traced to mythologies of the Babylonians, Assyrians, and other peoples of the ancient Near East. In these cultures, cherubim were usually pictured as creatures with parts of four animals: the head of a bull, the wings of an eagle, the feet of a lion, and the tail of a serpent. The four animals represented the four seasons, the four cardinal directions (north, south, east, and west), and the four ancient elements (earth, air, fire, and water). These original cherubim guarded the entrances to temples and palaces.

Cherubim were probably introduced into ancient Hebrew culture by the Canaanites†. The Hebrews expanded the role of the cherubim somewhat. For example, in the book of Genesis in the Old Testament, cherubim guard the entrance to the Garden of Eden after Adam and Eve are driven out of Paradise. Cherubim also protect the Ark of the Covenant, and God is described as riding on

the back of a cherub. In general, cherubim represent the power and glory of the Hebrew god, Yahweh.

In Christian mythology, the cherubim are the second highest of the nine orders of angels, second only to the seraphim. The cherubim excel in wisdom and continually praise God. In Islamic mythology, the cherubim (or *karibiyun*) play much the same role, dwelling in heaven and constantly praising Allah.

Cherubim are often portrayed as human figures having four wings, and they are usually painted blue, which signifies knowledge. In Jewish folklore of the Middle Ages, the cherubim were described as handsome young men. In Christian art, however, cherubim usually appear as children, most often as chubby, winged babies. *See also* ANGELS; SEMITIC MYTHOLOGY.

Chimaera

See *Bellerophon*.

Chinese Mythology

The people of China have a rich and complicated mythology that dates back nearly 4,000 years. Throughout Chinese history, myth and reality have been intertwined. Historical figures have been worshiped as gods, and ancient myths are sometimes treated as historical truths. In addition, three great religious traditions—Confucianism, Taoism, and Buddhism—have played a role in shaping the mythology. The result is a rich tapestry of characters and tales, both real and imagined, and a unique **pantheon** organized very much like ancient Chinese society.

pantheon all the gods of a particular culture

Roots of Chinese Mythology

China can trace its historical roots in a unbroken line for more than 4,000 years, and its mythological roots extend even farther back in time. From about 2000 to 1500 B.C., a people known as the Xia dominated the northern regions of China. The Xia worshiped the snake, a creature that appears in some of the oldest Chinese myths. Eventually, the snake changed into the dragon, which became one of the most enduring symbols of Chinese culture and mythology.

New Religious Ideas. From about 1500 to 1066 B.C., China was ruled by the Shang **dynasty.** The people at this time worshiped many **deities,** including natural forces and elements such as rain, clouds, rivers, mountains, the sun, the moon, and the earth. Their greatest deity, Shang Di, remains an important god in the Chinese pantheon.

When a new dynasty, the Zhou, came to power in China in 1066 B.C., significant changes took place in religion. People still worshiped the old gods, but ancestor worship became increasingly important. Confucianism and Taoism appeared near the end of the Zhou dynasty. These two religious traditions had an enormous influence on the development of the most basic and lasting principles of Chinese culture.

dynasty succession of rulers from the same family or group
deity god or goddess

Changing Old Beliefs. In 213 B.C., many of the original sources of Chinese mythology were lost when Emperor Shi Huangdi of the Qin dynasty ordered the burning of all books on subjects other than medicine, **prophecy,** and farming. This order was reversed in 191 B.C., and much of the literature was reconstructed. But works were rewritten to support ideas popular with the royal court at the time, including that of a **hierarchy** in government. These changes affected religious beliefs, producing a pantheon of deities that mirrored the political organization of the Chinese empire. Gods and spirits had different ranks and areas of responsibility, just like Chinese officials.

Shortly before A.D. 100, Buddhism arrived in China from India and added another important influence to Chinese culture and mythology. Buddhist ideas gradually came to be merged with Taoism and Confucianism in the minds of many Chinese. The three traditions often were seen as different aspects of the same religion and as having basically the same goals. Buddhists and Taoists honored each other's deities in their temples, and both incorporated principles of Confucianism, such as ancestor worship, in their beliefs.

Confucianism

Confucianism is more of a philosophy than a true religion. It does not include gods and never developed a mythology of its own. Confucianism is concerned primarily with human affairs rather than with the spirit world or the afterlife. At the same time, however, it emphasizes the importance of **ritual** and devotion to elders and ancestors.

Confucius. Confucianism sprang from the ideas of one man—Kongfuzi, or Confucius. Born in 551 B.C. to a poor family of aristocratic background, Confucius began a teaching career after working as a minor government official. For Confucius, the goal of education and learning was self-knowledge and self-improvement, which would lead one to right conduct. Although his method of education was aimed at ensuring the smooth operation of a stable and well-ordered state, his teachings became a guide to living wisely as well.

Confucius attracted many followers who spread his ideas after his death in 479 B.C. A number of legends grew up about Confucius, including one in which dragons guarded his mother when he was born. According to another story, a unicorn appeared at his birth and spit out a piece of jade with a prophecy written on it, saying that the infant would become "an uncrowned emperor." Considering the immense impact of Confucius on Chinese culture, the prophecy came true.

Confucian Principles. The basic aim of Confucianism is to live in harmony with the "Way (Tao) of Heaven" by carrying out the duties and responsibilities appropriate to one's position in society. Ancestor worship and reverence to family are fundamental elements of Confucianism. Rituals to honor ancestors are extremely

prophecy foretelling of what is to come; also something that is predicted

hierarchy organization of a group into higher and lower levels

ritual ceremony that follows a set pattern

Confucius attracted many followers during his life, and his ideas continued to spread after his death. Reverence for family and ancestors are important elements of Confucianism.

133

A scholar at the Chinese royal court, Laozi supposedly wrote the *Tao Te Ching*, the main text of the Chinese religion Taoism. Although there are many legends concerning Laozi, little factual information is available regarding his life.

important and must be performed in precise ways. By carrying them out properly, an individual can receive the aid and cooperation of deceased relatives. Misfortune, a sign of displeasure by the deceased, indicates that the proper rituals have not been followed.

Despite its spiritual elements, Confucianism is not really concerned with the spirit world. It does not teach about gods, heaven, and the afterlife. Confucius himself supposedly remarked, "I stand in awe of the spirits, but I keep them at a distance." Confucianism is basically a philosophy that focuses on the real world and provides guidelines for how people should live their lives.

Taoism

Taoism, also known as Daoism, arose about the same time as Confucianism. This religious tradition had its roots in the nature worship of the earliest Chinese people. The word *tao* means "way," and Taoist belief is based on the idea that there is a natural order or a "way of heaven" that one can come to know by living in harmony with nature. Through an understanding of natural laws, an individual can gain eternal life.

Laozi. The main Taoist work, the *Tao Te Ching,* was supposedly written by Laozi, a scholar at the Chinese royal court in the 500s B.C. Little is known about Laozi. The main sources of information, written hundreds of years after he lived, are legendary in nature. One of the most popular stories about Laozi concerns a voyage to the west, during which he wrote the *Tao Te Ching.* Other tales claim that Laozi met Confucius and that he lived more than 200 years. Although the true story of Laozi will probably never be known, he is widely respected in China. Confucianists consider him a great philosopher, while Taoists regard him as the embodiment of the tao and honor him as a saint or god.

The Tao. While Confucianists emphasize the practice of ritual and ancestor worship, Taoists seek knowledge through an understanding of the natural world. An important Taoist concept is that of yin and yang, two opposing and interacting forces of nature. Yin is a feminine principle and represents such ideas as dark, negative, cold, passive, softness, and earth. Yang, the masculine principle, represents light, positive, heat, activity, hardness, and heaven. Yin and yang exist in a delicate balance, and the harmony of the universe depends on maintaining that balance.

Originally a way of life, Taoism took on a more religious character after Buddhism arrived in China. Taoism adopted the use of temples and rituals and promoted the belief that all things have their own spirit. It also absorbed many mystical **cults** and created an elaborate pantheon as well as a new mythology.

Taoist deities include nature spirits, ancient legendary heroes, humanized planets and stars, humans who became **immortal** through Taoist practices, and animals such as dragons, tigers, and snakes. All human activities—even such things as drunkenness and robbery—are represented by deities as well. The highest deity, Yu Huang-ti (the Jade Emperor), is associated with the ancient Chinese god Shang Di. Other central figures in Taoist mythology are the Eight Immortals, humans who achieved immortality in different ways.

Buddhism

Buddhism arrived in China between 50 B.C. and A.D. 50, several hundred years after the rise of Confucianism and Taoism. One of its basic principles is that all suffering comes from earthly desire, and only by eliminating desire can one gain happiness.

The founder of Buddhism, Siddhartha Gautama, was an Indian prince who lived at about the same time as Confucius and Laozi. Gautama gave up his princely life to seek truth and wisdom. When these were revealed to him, he became the Buddha, or "enlightened one."

Buddhists believe that humans live many lives and are continually reincarnated, or reborn, to a new form of existence after death. An individual's actions in previous lives—known as karma—determine what type of existence that person has after rebirth. The goal of Buddhism is to escape the cycle of death and rebirth by achieving enlightenment and entering a timeless state known as nirvana, in which one is free of all desire.

Because Buddhism holds out the promise of a better existence in the next life, it appealed very much to Chinese peasants, who suffered great hardship and poverty. Chinese Buddhism became much more elaborate than Indian Buddhism, incorporating many Taoist and ancient Chinese gods. Among the most popular Chinese Buddhist deities are Emituofo, ruler of the Western Paradise, and Kuanyin, the goddess of mercy.

Common Themes in Chinese Mythology

Several common themes appear throughout much of Chinese mythology. Among the most significant are the creation of the world out of **chaos,** the importance of nature, and reverence for ancestors.

The main Chinese account of creation involves the god Pan Gu, the son of Yin and Yang, who came into being in the darkness of chaos. After 18,000 years, Pan Gu had grown so much that he caused the light parts of the chaos to rise and become the heavens,

---

cult group bound together by devotion to a particular person, belief, or god

immortal able to live forever

The Archer Yi and the Sun

When the world was still young, there were ten suns. Each took a turn being pulled through the sky in the chariot of their mother, goddess of the sun. One day, however, the ten suns decided to travel across the sky together. They greatly enjoyed their journey, but it brought disaster on the earth, destroying crops and drying up streams. Dijun, the father of the suns, felt sorry for humans and told his children to behave, but they would not listen. So Dijun sent Yi, a great archer, to earth with a magic bow and arrows to frighten his children into behaving. When Yi realized that neither threats nor persuasion would stop the suns, he shot his arrows into the sky and began killing them. After he finished shooting, only one sun remained—the one that travels through the sky today.

chaos great disorder or confusion

135

while the heavy parts sank and became the earth. To keep the heavens and earth separated, Pan Gu stood up and forced them apart. He grew 10 feet a day for another 18,000 years until the earth and heavens became fixed in place. Pan Gu then laid down to rest and died. Various parts of his body became parts of the universe—the sun and moon, wind and clouds, and all elements on earth. The fleas on Pan Gu's body became humans.

The importance of nature is stressed in legends such as that of the Five Sacred Mountains, which represent the main points of the compass and the axis of the world. The most sacred mountain, T'ai Shan, has Shang Di, the greatest earthly power, as its deity. Mount Kunlun, home of immortals, became the focus of various cults. Many Chinese myths deal with natural disasters, especially floods. Others deal with heavenly bodies such as the sun and moon. Animals, including dragons, pigs, and monkeys, are also important figures in Chinese mythology.

Reverence for ancestors is another common theme in Chinese mythology. Long life is viewed as a sign of the gods' favor, and for many centuries, the Chinese have sought the secret of long life and immortality. In the past, Taoists believed that magic potions could be created that bestowed eternal life on people who drank them and that beings known as *hsien* gained immortality in this way. Both Taoism and Confucianism stress the importance of paying proper respect to elders, especially parents and grandparents, and deceased ancestors are honored with various ceremonies and rituals. *See also* ANIMALS IN MYTHOLOGY; BUDDHISM AND MYTHOLOGY; CREATION STORIES; DRAGONS; PAN GU; REINCARNATION; XIAN; YELLOW EMPEROR; YIN AND YANG.

Christopher, St.

patron special guardian, protector, or supporter

St. Christopher is the **patron** saint of travelers. The Roman emperor Decius supposedly killed him around A.D. 250, but there is no historical evidence that he ever existed.

The best-known legend about St. Christopher says that he was a giant who wanted to serve the world's most powerful king. When he found out that Christ was the greatest king, he converted to Christianity. He then took up a post by a river that had no bridge and carried travelers across on his shoulders. One day he was carrying a small child who became so heavy that Christopher could barely make it across. The child turned out to be Christ himself, and Christopher had just carried the weight of the world's sins. Because the name *Christopher* means "bearer of Christ," the saint is usually shown in art carrying Christ as a child on his back.

Cid, El

El Cid was the honorary title of Rodrigo Díaz de Bivar (or Vivar), Spain's national hero and great military leader. During his lifetime, Díaz fought for and against both Christian kings and Muslim rulers in Spain. The **Moors** gave him the name *El Cid* (from an Arabic word meaning "lord") in recognition of his skills on the battlefield.

Moors Spanish Muslims descended from the Arab conquerors

Hero or Villain?

The legend of El Cid has varied widely over time. Interestingly, the hero's reputation suffers more in each retelling. In the early *Cantar,* Rodrigo is the perfect hero. The later *Mocedades* shows El Cid as rebellious and disrespectful. He is even accused of killing a foe who takes sanctuary in a holy place, a horrible offense in the Middle Ages. Works from the 1800s, based on early accounts by El Cid's Arab enemies, call him a traitor to his country and accuse him of many terrible deeds. This view of El Cid was widespread until it was disproved in the 1929 history *La España del Cid.*

tribute payment made by a smaller or weaker party to a more powerful one, often under the threat of force

dynasty succession of rulers from the same family or group

epic long poem about legendary or historical heroes, written in a grand style

He gained a reputation for defeating superior opponents against overwhelming odds, inspiring many stories, poems, and legends.

The Life of El Cid. Born around 1043, Rodrigo Díaz was the son of a minor Spanish nobleman. He spent his early years in the service of Sancho, a son of King Ferdinand I of Spain. When Ferdinand died, he divided his kingdom among his three sons. But Sancho wanted the whole kingdom and soon attacked his brothers. With El Cid commanding his troops, Sancho defeated his brothers.

On Sancho's death in 1072, his brother Alfonso took over the kingdom. Although El Cid had fought against him, Alfonso recognized the value of keeping the great warrior in his service. He gave Díaz a military position and married him to his niece to assure his loyalty.

However, two events changed the king's mind about El Cid. First, on a mission to collect **tribute** from the Moorish king of Seville, El Cid engaged in combat with an invading army led by Count García Ordóñez. Ordóñez was Alfonso's military commander and a bitter enemy of El Cid's. When El Cid won the battle and captured Ordóñez, the king faced divisions in the ranks of the army. Soon afterward, without seeking the king's permission, Díaz led an attack on a castle held by Moors in the kingdom of Toledo. Alfonso was furious and exiled Díaz from his kingdoms.

El Cid offered his services to the Moorish king of Saragossa in northeastern Spain, whom he served loyally for almost ten years. In 1082 he defeated an army led by the Moorish king of Lérida and his Christian allies. Two years later, he beat a large army led by the king of Aragon. Next the Almoravids, a Muslim **dynasty** from North Africa, invaded Spain and crushed an army commanded by Alfonso. Alfonso summoned El Cid to help fight the invasion but changed his mind again after the warrior failed to come to his aid in an important battle. This time he not only exiled Díaz but also had his family imprisoned.

In 1090 El Cid began a series of campaigns to gain control of the kingdom of Valencia in eastern Spain. After several battles and a long siege, he finally captured the city of Valencia from the Almoravids in 1094. He ruled Valencia for five years, turning its mosque—Muslim place of worship—into a Christian cathedral. During this time, many Christian settlers came to live in Valencia. Meanwhile, El Cid continued to win victories over his enemies until his death in 1099.

Tales of El Cid. After his death, Díaz was celebrated by both Christian and Muslim writers as a great warrior who never lost a battle. The most famous story is the *Cantar de Mío Cid* (Song of the Cid), written around 1140. One of the great **epics** of the Middle Ages, it combines fact and fiction to portray El Cid as the perfect Christian warrior. Some of the tales it includes contrast El Cid's honor and courage with the cowardice and brutality of the noblemen surrounding him.

One such story involves the counts of Carrion, two young nobles who married El Cid's daughters. The poem says that one day a lion owned by El Cid got loose and entered a room where his two sons-in-law were playing chess. While the two counts hid in terror,

El Cid grabbed the lion by its mane and put it back into its cage. Humiliated by their cowardly behavior, the two counts asked to leave El Cid's court with their wives. On their journey, they stopped and severely beat the women. To avenge this outrage, El Cid arranged a personal combat between the counts of Carrion and two other noblemen. The cowardly husbands were killed, and El Cid's daughters married the victorious nobles.

Other, more extravagant legends about El Cid appeared in later years. In *Las mocedades de Rodrigo* (The Youthful Exploits of Rodrigo), written about 1350, the hero defeats opponents not only in Spain but also as far away as Paris. His enemies in the story include the French, the German emperor, and even the pope. The work also contains a tale in which El Cid shelters a leper beneath his cloak. While El Cid is sleeping, the leper reveals himself in a dream to be St. Lazarus and promises the hero that God will always help him. This legend emphasizes the image of El Cid as a warrior whose military skills were combined with Christian virtues.

Another tale from the same work describes how El Cid kills the father of his fiancée, Jimena, because the man had insulted his father. Jimena begs the king to avenge her father's death, and when the king refuses, she asks that El Cid be ordered to marry her instead. This peculiar story was the basis for Pierre Corneille's 1636 tragedy *Le Cid.*

Circe

In Greek mythology, the witch Circe was the daughter of the sun god Helios and the ocean **nymph** Perse (or Perseis). According to legend, Circe lived on the island of Aeaea, where she built herself a palace and practiced spells that enabled her to turn men into animals.

nymph minor goddess of nature, usually represented as young and beautiful

This painting from the 1800s by Edward Burne-Jones shows Circe preparing potions while waiting for Odysseus. Circe first tried to cast a spell over Odysseus and his men by using enchanted food and drink to turn them into animals, but she later assisted them in their journey home.

138

The two best-known legends involving Circe concern her encounters with the fisherman Glaucus and with Odysseus†, a Greek hero of the Trojan War†.

Glaucus was changed into a sea god one day while sorting his catch. He became half man and half fish, with long strands of seaweed for hair. Glaucus fell in love with a beautiful girl named Scylla, but she was frightened of his appearance and rejected him. He went to Circe and asked for a spell to make Scylla love him. Circe offered Glaucus her love instead, but he refused to have anyone but Scylla. The jealous Circe then enchanted the water where Scylla was swimming, turning her into a horrible sea monster with six heads. Scylla fled to a cave on top of a dangerous cliff and attacked any sailors that came within her reach.

The most famous tale concerning Circe appears in Homer's *Odyssey*†. Odysseus and his crew sailed by Aeaea as they were returning from the Trojan War. Odysseus sent some men ashore, led by a warrior named Eurylochus. The group came upon Circe's palace, which was surrounded by lions, bears, and wolves that were tame and did not attack them. In fact, the beasts were men Circe had changed into animal form. Circe then appeared and invited Odysseus's men inside to dine and drink. Everyone accepted the invitation except Eurylochus, who was suspicious. After eating Circe's enchanted food, the men all turned into pigs. Eurylochus alone returned to the ship to tell Odysseus what had happened.

Odysseus decided to go to Circe himself. Along the way, he met a young man, who was actually the god Hermes† in disguise. Hermes tried to discourage Odysseus from continuing on to the palace, but Odysseus was determined to get his men back. Hermes then gave Odysseus an herb that would protect him from Circe's spells. When Odysseus reached the palace, Circe invited him in and attempted to enchant him. However, the herb protected him against her spell, and he drew his sword and threatened her. The sorceress fell to her knees and pleaded for her life. Odysseus agreed to spare her if she would return his men to their normal condition and release them safely.

Circe restored the crew to human form and offered to entertain them before they returned to sea. Odysseus and his men found life on the island so pleasurable that they remained there a full year before resuming the journey home. When they finally left, Circe sent them on their way with a favorable wind and advice about how to avoid the many dangers that lay before them.

In an Italian version of this legend, Circe and Odysseus had three children: Telegonus, Agrius, and Latinus. Telegonus traveled to Ithaca to seek his father but then killed him by accident. He brought Odysseus's body back to Aeaea, accompanied by Odysseus's widow, Penelope, and their son Telemachus. Circe made them all **immortal** and married Telemachus, and Telegonus married Penelope. Circe also played a role in the legend of the Argonauts†, cleansing Jason† and Medea† after they killed Medea's brother. Many scholars view Circe as a symbol of the luxury and

immortal able to live forever

139

unchecked desire that seduces people and causes them to ignore their duty and thus lose their dignity. ***See also*** Nymphs; Odysseus; Odyssey, The.

Clytemnestra

In Greek mythology, Clytemnestra was the daughter of Tyndareus and Leda, king and queen of Sparta†. She married Agamemnon†, king of Mycenae and leader of the Greeks in the Trojan War. In Homer's *Iliad,* Agamemnon sacrifices their daughter Iphigenia to the goddess Artemis (Diana)† in order to get a favorable wind to sail to Troy and attack the city. This act causes Clytemnestra to swear revenge against her husband. She takes his cousin Aegisthus as her lover and plots with him to kill Agamemnon when he returns. Agamemnon eventually returns with Cassandra, the daughter of King Priam of Troy, whom he has taken as a prize of war. Clytemnestra greets Agamemnon when he arrives home and prepares a bath for him. When he steps out of the bath, she snares him in a net, and Aegisthus stabs him. Clytemnestra then kills Cassandra. In some versions, Clytemnestra herself slays Agamemnon with an ax. Agamemnon's death is later avenged when his son Orestes kills both Clytemnestra and Aegisthus. ***See also*** Agamemnon; Cassandra; Iliad, The; Iphigenia; Orestes; Trojan War.

Coatlicue

Coatlicue, the earth goddess of Aztec mythology, was the mother of the sun, the moon, the stars, and all the Aztec gods and goddesses. Her name means "serpent skirt." Coatlicue was the source of all life on earth and took the dead back again into her body.

A famous statue in Mexico's National Museum of Anthropology represents the idea of Coatlicue as creator and destroyer. Her head is made up of the joined heads of two snakes, and the skirt that she wears is made of snakes woven together. Snakes are symbols of both death and fertility in many cultures. Her massive breasts show her as a nourishing mother, while her clawlike fingers and toes show her as a devouring monster. She wears a garment of human skin and a necklace of hands and hearts, with a single skull in the center, suggesting that Coatlicue consumed everything that died. ***See also*** Aztec Mythology; Serpents and Snakes.

Cockaigne, Land of

The Land of Cockaigne is an imaginary land of luxury and idleness where all physical pleasures, especially those of food and drink, are freely available. It is especially celebrated in works of the Middle Ages, when everyday life was hard and lacking in comforts. These works describe Cockaigne as having rivers of wine, streets paved with pastry, and shops that give their goods away for nothing. The name *Cockaigne* (or *cocagne* in French) is probably related to the word *cake.*

Many writers identified London as the Land of Cockaigne, which may have led to the use of the word *cockney* to refer to some inhabitants of London. An English poet of the 1200s made fun of the idea of Cockaigne in "The Land of Cockaygne," a poem about the life of monks. Other cultures have stories of similar lands, such as the German *Schlaraffenland,* or Lazy-Ape Land.

Conaire Mor

In Celtic† mythology, Conaire Mor was a high king of Ireland, the son of Mess Buachalla and the bird god Nemglan. The conditions surrounding the birth of Conaire Mor were all favorable, and it seemed that his reign would be peaceful and prosperous. In fact, Ireland did enjoy a golden age under his rule.

Like all ancient Irish kings, however, Conaire Mor was given several laws, or *geis,* that he could not break. In one situation, he was forced to choose between his love for his brothers and his royal duty not to violate the *geis.* He ended up breaking one of the rules. As a result, the good fortune of his kingdom came to an end, and Conaire Mor was killed in battle. ***See also* CELTIC MYTHOLOGY.**

Coriolanus

patrician aristocrat or member of the noble class

Roman legend tells of Gnaeus Marcius Coriolanus, a **patrician** of the 400s B.C. Although he may have been a real person, no firm evidence of his existence survives.

According to the story, Gnaeus Marcius earned the name Coriolanus by capturing the town of Corioli from the Volscian people. Proud and disdainful of the lower classes, Coriolanus opposed giving grain to the poor people of Rome in time of famine, and he sought to restore the special privileges of aristocrats. Banished from Rome, he committed treason by leading the Volscian armies against his own city. The Volscians were on the point of capturing Rome when Coriolanus, moved by the pleas of his mother and his wife, changed his mind and ordered the army to withdraw. Some accounts say that the Volscians killed him; others tell of his spending the rest of his life in miserable exile from Rome.

The legend of Coriolanus was powerful enough to make him the subject of works by the Greek writer Plutarch† and by William Shakespeare. *Coriolanus,* the last of Shakespeare's tragedies, uses strong language to portray a proud, inflexible warrior whose scorn for others brings about his downfall.

Names and Places

Achilles foremost warrior in Greek mythology; hero in the war between the Greeks and the Trojans

Aeneas Trojan hero who founded Rome; son of Aphrodite (Venus) and the Trojan Anchises

Aeneid epic by the Roman poet Virgil about the legendary hero Aeneas and the founding of Rome

Agamemnon Greek king and commander of Greek forces in the Trojan War; later killed by his wife, Clytemnestra

Ajax Greek hero of the Trojan War

Amazons female warriors in Greek mythology

Aphrodite Greek goddess of love and beauty (identified with the Roman goddess Venus)

Apollo Greek god of the sun, the arts, medicine, and herdsmen; son of Zeus and Leto and twin brother of Artemis

Ares Greek god of war; son of Zeus and Hera (identified with the Roman god Mars)

Artemis in Greek mythology, virgin goddess of the hunt; daughter of Zeus and Leto and twin sister of Apollo (identified with the Roman goddess Diana)

Arthurian legends stories about the life and court of King Arthur of Britain

Asia Minor ancient term for modern-day Turkey, the part of Asia closest to Greece

Assyria kingdom of the ancient Near East located between the Tigris and Euphrates Rivers

Athena in Greek mythology, goddess of wisdom and war; the daughter of Zeus (Roman goddess Minerva)

Atlas Titan in Greek mythology who held the world on his shoulders

Baal god of the ancient Near East associated with fertility and rain

Babylonia ancient kingdom of Mesopotamia; **Babylon** city in Babylonia; **Babylonians** (noun) people of Babylonia; **Babylonian** (adj) referring to kingdom or people

Brahma Hindu creator god

Canaan name given to Palestine and Syria in ancient times; **Canaanites** people of Canaan

Celtic referring to the **Celts,** early inhabitants of Britain whose culture survived in Ireland, Scotland, Wales, Cornwall, and Brittany

Ceres Roman goddess of vegetation and fertility; mother of Proserpina (Greek goddess Demeter)

Cronus Greek deity, king of the Titans; son of Uranus and Gaia

Cyclopes one-eyed giants in Greek mythology

Delphi town on the slopes of Mount Parnassus in Greece that was the site of Apollo's temple and the Delphic oracle

Demeter Greek goddess of vegetation; sister of Zeus and mother of Persephone (Roman goddess Ceres)

Devi Hindu goddess; wife of the god Shiva

Diana Roman goddess of hunting and childbirth (Greek goddess Artemis)

Dionysus Greek god of wine and fertility; son of Zeus by Theban princess Semele (Roman god Bacchus)

Druids priests and political leaders of an ancient Celtic religious order

Euripides (ca. 480–406 B.C.) Greek playwright who wrote many tragedies

Franks early Germanic people who invaded and eventually ruled Gaul (present-day France) between the A.D. 200s and the mid-800s

Golden Fleece hide of a magic ram that hung in a sacred grove guarded by a serpent

Hades Greek god of the underworld; brother of Zeus and husband of Persephone (Roman god Pluto)

Hector in Greek mythology, a Trojan prince and hero in the Trojan War

Helen of Troy in Greek mythology, a beautiful woman and the wife of the king of Sparta; her kidnapping by a Trojan prince led to the Trojan War

Hephaestus Greek god of fire and crafts; son of Zeus and Hera and husband of Aphrodite (Roman god Vulcan)

Hera Greek goddess, wife and sister of Zeus; queen of heaven (Roman goddess Juno)

Hercules (Heracles) Greek hero who had 12 labors to perform; Roman god of strength

Hermes in Greek mythology, the messenger of the gods; escorted the dead to the underworld (Roman god Mercury)

Hesiod (ca. 700 B.C.) Greek poet who wrote the *Theogony*

Homer (ca. 700s B.C.) Greek poet thought to be the author of the great epics the *Iliad* and the *Odyssey*

Iliad Greek epic poem about the Trojan War composed by Homer

Indo-Iranian having to do with the peoples and cultures of northern India, Pakistan, Afghanistan, and Iran

142

Isis Egyptian goddess of rebirth and resurrection; mother of Horus

Jason Greek hero and leader of the Argonauts who went on a quest for the Golden Fleece

Jupiter Roman god of the sky and ruler of the other gods (Greek god Zeus)

Mars Roman god of war (Greek god Ares)

Medusa in Greek mythology, a monster whose hair was made of snakes and whose face turned humans to stone

Mercury Roman messenger god (Greek god Hermes)

Mesopotamia area between the Tigris and Euphrates Rivers, most of present-day Iraq

Metamorphoses narrative poem by the Roman author Ovid

Mongol referring to an empire in southeastern Asia that existed from about 1200 to the 1700s

Neptune in Roman mythology, god of the sea (the Greeks called him Poseidon)

Norse referring to the people and culture of Scandinavia: Norway, Sweden, Denmark, and Iceland

Odin in Norse mythology, one-eyed deity and ruler of the gods

Odysseus Greek hero who journeyed for ten years to return home after the Trojan War

Odyssey epic by the Greek poet Homer that tells the story of the journey of the hero Odysseus

Oedipus in Greek mythology, king of Thebes

Olympus in Greek mythology, home of the gods

Orpheus Greek hero known for his musical skills; son of Apollo and Calliope

Osiris in Egyptian mythology, the chief god of death

Ovid (ca. 43 B.C.–A.D. 17) Roman poet who wrote the *Metamorphoses*

Palestine ancient land located on the site of modern Israel and part of Jordan

Pegasus in Greek mythology, a winged horse

Perseus Greek hero, son of Danaë and Zeus, who cut off the head of Medusa

Persia ancient land in southwestern Asia, including much of present-day Iran and Afghanistan

Philistines ancient people who lived along the coast of Canaan (present-day Palestine and Syria)

Phoenicia ancient maritime country located in an area that is now part of Lebanon

Phrygia ancient country located in present-day Turkey

Pindar (ca. 522–438 B.C.) Greek poet

Plutarch (ca. A.D. 46–120) Greek author who wrote biographies of important Greeks and Romans

Poseidon Greek god, ruler of the sea, and brother of Zeus (Roman god Neptune)

Prometheus in Greek mythology, Titan said to have created the human race

Pueblos Native American groups of the southwestern United States, including the Hopi, Keresan, Tewa, Tiwa, and Zuni

Quetzalcoatl Feathered Serpent god of Central America; Aztec god of learning and creation

Ra (Re) in Egyptian mythology, the sun god

Saturn Roman god of the harvest

Semitic relating to people of the ancient Near East, including Jews, Arabs, Babylonians, Assyrians, and Phoenicians

Set in Egyptian mythology, god of the sun and sky; brother of Osiris

Sophocles (ca. 496–406 B.C.) Greek playwright who wrote many tragedies

Sparta ancient Greek city-state

Sumer part of ancient Babylonia in southern Mesopotamia; **Sumerians** people of Sumer

Thebes ancient Egyptian city on the Nile River

Theogony epic written by the Greek poet Hesiod explaining the creation of the world and the birth of the gods

Theseus Greek hero who killed the Minotaur of Crete with Ariadne, the daughter of King Minos of Crete

Thor in Norse mythology, the thunder god

Titan one of a family of giants who ruled the earth until overthrown by the Greek gods of Olympus

Trojan War legendary war between the Greeks and the people of Troy that was set off by the kidnapping of Helen, wife of the king of Sparta; inspiration for Homer's epics the *Iliad* and the *Odyssey*

Troy ancient city that was the site of the Trojan War; present-day Turkey near the Dardanelles

Valhalla in Norse mythology, the home of the dead heroes

Valkyrie in Norse mythology, one of the handmaidens to the god Odin

Virgil (ca. 70–19 B.C.) Roman poet who wrote the *Aeneid* explaining the founding of Rome

Vishnu Hindu god, preserver and restorer

Vulcan Roman god of fire (Greek god Hephaestus)

Zeus in Greek mythology, king of the gods and husband of Hera (Roman god Jupiter)

Index

Italicized page numbers refer to illustrations or charts.

Index

Index

148